CLINICAL SPEECH IN THE SCHOOLS

Organization and Management

Seventh Printing

CLINICAL SPEECH IN
THE SCHOOLS

Organization and Management

Edited by

ROLLAND J. VAN HATTUM, Ph.D.
Professor and Chairman, Speech Pathology and Audiology
Exceptional Children Education Division
State University College
Buffalo, New York

CHARLES C THOMAS · PUBLISHER
Springfield · Illinois · U.S.A.

Published and Distributed Throughout the World by

CHARLES C THOMAS • PUBLISHER

BANNERSTONE HOUSE

301-327 East Lawrence Avenue, Springfield, Illinois, U.S.A.

© *1969 by* CHARLES C THOMAS • PUBLISHER

ISBN 0-398-01969-X

Library of Congress Catalog Card Number: 68-15979

First Printing, 1969
Second Printing, 1970
Third Printing, 1971
Fourth Printing, 1972
Fifth Printing, 1973
Sixth Printing, 1974
Seventh Printing, 1976

With THOMAS BOOKS *careful attention is given to all details of manufacturing and design. It is the Publisher's desire to present books that are satisfactory as to their physical qualities and artistic possibilities and appropriate for their particular use.* THOMAS BOOKS *will be true to those laws of quality that assure a good name and good will.*

Printed in the United States of America

N-1

CONTRIBUTORS

ROLLAND J. VAN HATTUM, PH.D., EDITOR, *Professor and Chairman, Speech Pathology and Audiology, Exceptional Children Education Division, State University College, Buffalo, New York. Formerly, Director of Special Education, Kent County Intermediate School District, Grand Rapids, Michigan; Consultant in Speech and Hearing, Rochester, New York, Public Schools.*

RONALD K. SOMMERS, D.ED., ASSOCIATE EDITOR, *Supervisor of Speech and Hearing, Montgomery County Schools, Norristown, Pennsylvania.*

MYFANWY E. CHAPMAN, M.S., Consultant and Lecturer, Minneapolis, Minnesota. *Formerly, Speech Clinician and, later, Coordinator of Speech Correction, Minneapolis Public Schools, Minneapolis, Minnesota.*

LEE I. FISHER, M.S., *Speech Clinician, Johnson County Schools, Iowa City, Iowa.*

GERALD G. FREEMAN, PH.D., *Director of Speech and Hearing Clinic and Consultant, Oakland Schools, Oakland County Service Center, Pontiac, Michigan.*

FREDERICK E. GARBEE, M.S., *Consultant in Education of the Speech and Hearing Handicapped, California State Department of Education, Los Angeles, California.*

CHARLES V. MANGE, PH.D., *Associate Professor and Director of Special Education, Michigan State University, East Lansing, Michigan. Formerly, Deputy Superintendent for Special Education, Kalamazoo Valley Intermediate School District, Kalamazoo County, Kalamazoo, Michigan.*

OLIVER M. NIKOLOFF, PH.D., *Professor, Department of Educational Psychology, State University of New York, Albany, New York. Formerly, School Psychologist, Board of Cooperative Educational Services, Erie County, Buffalo, New York; Secondary Teacher — Counsellor, Cincinnati Public Schools, Cincinnati, Ohio.*

PREFACE

Many fine textbooks are available in the area of therapeutic handling of speech problems. This book is not intended to duplicate the material included in these books. It does not provide information regarding the anatomy of the speech mechanism, the etiology of speech problems, the descriptions of speech problems, or the remedial techniques for speech problems. In other words, it does not seek to provide the "what" or the "why" of speech problems or the "how" of therapeutic handling. Rather, it seeks to fill a gap which has existed for some time in the professional literature in the areas of program organization and management. Persons working in supervisory capacities in schools have noted, and recent graduates entering the schools as speech clinicians have reported, a deficiency in training in these areas. In recognition of this situation, many states have added a course to their certification requirements which covers this subject area. Even in states where such a course is not required for certification, it has been added to the curricula of many training institutions. This addition has created a problem in that no textbook has existed which adequately covers the information essential for such a course. True, much of the material is available, in part, in various articles and books but not in a compiled and complete manner.

The content of this text is intended to be practical rather than theoretical. To accomplish this, persons with extensive experience in the schools have been selected as authors. In fact, every author was employed in the school environment at the inception of this book. Although the finished product contains the weaknesses of multi-authored books, in that writing styles are not consistent and some of the information is restated, the book does have the strengths of one jointly authored by persons who represent over a hundred years experience in the schools, who represent a wide variety of training and experience backgrounds, and who represent a wide area geographically.

A companion benefit of this book is the opportunity for school administrators and other professional workers in schools to better acquaint themselves with the organizational and management aspects of clinical speech programs in schools.

Special mention is due Dale Bingham for his original interest in such a text and for the contributions he has made to speech and hearing programs during his many years of association with school programs. It was Mr. Bingham who, with Dr. Rolland Van Hattum and Dr. Ronald Sommers, originally conceived this book and planned the content. Although other commitments made it impossible for Mr. Bingham to participate in the final production of the book, his contribution is acknowledged and appreciated.

Several other persons made important contributions of labor and deserve mention. These include Mrs. Joyce H. Van Hattum, Mrs. Thelma Kingsley, Mrs. Judith Janus, Miss Caroline Will, Mrs. Juanita Garner, Mrs. Ruth Smith.

In this joint endeavor an attempt has been made to combine the traditional and proven with the new and promising in an effort to carry on the relatively new but wise traditions established by the pioneers in speech and hearing services in schools, many of whom still live and many of whom are still active professionally.

It is to these pioneers, with affection and admiration, and to those speech and hearing handicapped individuals we have all chosen to serve that the authors dedicate this book.

ROLLAND VAN HATTUM

LIST OF FIGURES

ix

LIST OF TABLES

CONTENTS

UNIT I
Introduction

UNIT II
The Roles of the Speech Clinician

UNIT III
The Professional Planning of the Speech Clinician

CLINICAL SPEECH IN THE SCHOOLS

Organization and Management

UNIT I

Introduction

Chapter 1

AN OVERVIEW

ROLLAND J. VAN HATTUM

CLINICAL SPEECH IS AN exciting and challenging profession. Its demands are proportionately interesting and changing. The training is scientifically and clinically oriented, and the areas of specialization, whether a specific disorder, area of specialization, or work environment, are numerous. Speech clinicians carry on a variety of activities, namely training, service, and research, in a variety of clinical settings such as the schools, community clinics, hospital clinics, university clinics, private practice, and rehabilitations centers, and with a variety of disorders such as articulation, rhythm, and voice and speech problems accompanying specific physical disorders. The information in this book is particularly intended for those persons who function in school environments and seeks to clarify the organizational and management aspects of the clinical speech program. It attempts to avoid proposing *the* way of functioning in recognition that too many varying situations exist to be able to provide one solution. From the information provided, each individual must make his own application.

Speech is the channel through which we constantly clarify our own ideas and beliefs through communication with others and, equally importantly, with ourselves, and through which we attempt to influence one another. A disorder which interferes with communication can seriously interfere with one's social, emotional, educational, and economic adjustment. The responsibility of the speech clinician functioning in the schools is to help the pupils having speech problems to achieve better communication so that they may be able to realize the greatest success which their capabilities will permit with a maximum of satisfaction to themselves, a maximum benefit to society, and a minimum of friction and tension. There is a continued need in the speech and hearing profession for individuals who are clinically oriented, skilled in analyzing the needs of children and youth, and proficient in adapting therapy to meet these needs. In a realm that must be changing in response to changes in medical, psychological, social, and economic conditions, efforts must be directed in such a way as to increase the child's ability to cope effectively.

Gaining an overall perspective of the field of clinical speech is important though not an easy accomplishment. One needs to be aware of the historical aspects of clinical speech in the schools and developments which can be expected in the profession. This awareness may be aided by a look backward, a look at the present, and a look forward to establish a framework from which to view the profession.

A LOOK BACKWARD

Although descriptions of persons with speech problems can be found dating centuries back, and similarly, assistance for them is reported in documents preceding the Bible by some three thousand years, the speech and hearing profession as an organized, scientific group is extremely young. In fact, it is only within the last sixty years that assistance has been provided the speech and hearing handicapped by persons specifically trained for this purpose.

Just before the turn of the present century, changing educational philosophy brought about an awareness of the needs of exceptional children. This led to assistance for the speech and hearing handicapped by classroom teachers and speech arts teachers who recognized the debilitating effects of speech differences. No special training was required for these persons; although at a later time, courses were offered at training centers. Originally these persons were certified only as teachers. In educational settings, the methods tended to be curricular in nature, utilized instructional methods and materials, and were best suited for large groups of children. The techniques employed frequently included breathing exercises, poetry reading, and choral speaking. These techniques were aimed at goals of general speech improvement. Because of the backgrounds of these individuals and the settings in which they worked, it is understandable that they often became known as "speech teachers." Probably this is where the idea originated that such a person should also hold certification for classroom teaching, a requirement which still persists in some localities, reducing the amount of time available for preparation in the specialized areas.

The role of the "speech teacher" was easily misinterpreted. There was a confusion regarding the responsibilities of a person in such a position. The speech teacher had his concept; administrators and others had theirs. The frequent remark upon introduction to the speech teacher was "Oh, I'll have to watch my English!" The difference in function of the newly emerging profession from that of the curriculum-oriented personnel — teachers of general speech, drama, debate, and English and other instructional personnel — often had to be interpreted.

Since speech services were offered within the organizational framework of a school where the primary objective of the majority of staff personnel was classroom teaching largely involved with subject matter, it was difficult to understand the status of the speech clinician and the need for flexibility. Often, since he was a "speech teacher" he was expected to work in speech improvement in the classroom in addition to carrying a heavy case load. There was little understanding as to why the individual should be privileged to work with individuals and small groups, why his schedule was flexible, and why he could not become involved with certain responsibilities confronting classroom teachers.

While all this was occurring, a second type of help was being provided persons with communication disorders by specialists such as psychologists, sociologists, and physicians. Their activities tended more towards adult patients and were characterized by the application of clinical skills relating to diagnosis, prognosis, and prescription of therapeutic needs. They functioned in hospital settings, universities, and private offices, applied their ethical codes, and dealt with total habilitation based on individual need. Many of them viewed speech and hearing as an extension of their basic professional affiliation rather than a new profession. Finally, and unfortunately, many of these persons did not view the school setting as an environment capable of supporting competent professional activity.

Between these major groups existed many gradations and even other types, all providing contributions to the emerging profession. It is little wonder that from these many and diverse backgrounds came persons sharing common interests and goals for the speech and hearing handicapped persons and yet differing markedly in ideas pertaining to causation, diagnostic techniques, methods and program organization. In fact, to this day some of these differences exist. Fortunately, the differences are diminishing; the chasm is narrowing. Much of the credit for this is due to those individuals who had the foresight to create a national organization, the American Speech and Hearing Association, the courage to discuss their viewpoints in open forum, and the flexibility to alter their views and practices based on discussion, research, and clinical experience. These activities have begun to weld professional agreement which is resulting in more uniformity of role, qualifications, and function. In many respects, the speech and hearing profession has accomplished in several decades what other professions required centuries to attain.

A LOOK AT THE PRESENT

Speech and hearing specialists who function in schools have shared in the advancement made by the profession. They are better trained than ever before, they boast competent leadership personnel, they are active in national and local professional activities, and they are respected by colleagues in their own and allied professions. All these things are most fortunate since they provide more clinical services to the speech and hearing handicapped than all other areas of the profession combined.

Several problems of professional image and identification still remain generally within the entire profession but to an even greater extent with the specialist functioning in the schools because of his early beginnings and because of the way the schools and the community have viewed him as an educator rather than a clinician. Yet he *is* a clinician in an educational environment. He must understand and integrate smoothly into his environment, but he must function clinically.

In an attempt to emphasize this point, the title of the book was selected. The title will seem inappropriate to some. Yet, it was chosen with much forethought and retained after considerable reevaluation simply because it stresses the type of program the authors wish to strongly endorse. Clinical speech refers to a method of functioning rather than a setting or place. It describes a highly professional manner of conduct whereby the speech clinician, in appearance, demeanor and action, utilizes ethical conduct, enlightened judgment and skilled methods and techniques to assist those individuals to whom he provides his services towards more acceptable communication skills. This can occur in the schools as elsewhere and, hopefully, frequently does. But "frequently" must become "always." This book attempts to aid in encouraging this direction and speeding the process.

To further emphasize this point, the term "speech clinician" is utilized as the appropriate title for this specialist. The problem of the most desirable title has long plagued the profession. "Speech teacher" has already been rejected as being misleading although school children will undoubtedly continue to use it as will many educational personnel. Some persons would immediately suggest "speech therapist" since the term so well describes the activity conducted to remedy the speech problem. Also, it enjoys popular usage for other professional personnel such as occupational therapist and physical therapist. However, the speech clinician differs from these individuals. He does not function under the supervision of a medical specialist, and his functioning is not restricted to remedial measures. Rather, the competent speech clinician diagnoses, prognoses, prescribes for *and* treats speech problems. "Speech correctionist" is similarly too limiting and "speech pathologist" is descriptive but would seem too imposing for the school environment.

The problem of terminology probably will not be settled for some time. In the meantime some persons will continue to crusade for their private term, others will attempt to coin a new and clever term which describes exactly what the person is and does.

"Speech clinician" is more desirable than any available and has the advantage of suggesting a method or manner of functioning differing from the instructional and encompassing diagnosis, prognosis, prescription of treatment, and therapeutic handling. It also emphasizes the clinical nature of the functioning of the specialist working in the schools. Thus, the speech clinician performs speech therapy as *part* of his responsibilities. Some persons will still complain that this term suggests a clinical setting. Perhaps this is true, for who can say that the school is not or cannot be a clinical setting? If all our problems were only semantic!

Acceptance of the term "speech clinician" or any other title would not in itself clarify the role. The clinician must still be the interpreter of his profession. A clear understanding of the nature of his work continues to be necessary and is extremely important to a program conducive to the best results for those he seeks to help. The clinician must have an awareness that in any effective clinical work insightful liaison with other disciplines becomes an integral phase. The clinician cannot afford to be in conflict with his working environment so he must be constantly alert to the need for good public relations. He must also be cognizant of the responsibility for offering professional service which will demand the respect of the many people with whom he works — the classroom teacher, parents, administrators, nurses, psychologists, counsellors, physicians, and dental specialists.

The clinician, in any community, is the one who contributes most to the acceptance or rejection of the local clinical speech program. The school is a natural place for him to function because it is here he finds those who need not only speech help but also help in adjusting to the educational environment. The public accepts the idea that all children should be served by schools. Parents look to the schools for services of many kinds, including help for children with speech disorders. The clinician must do his utmost to see that those in his environment understand his aims, methods, and qualifications.

Since the early days of clinical speech in our schools, states have continued to raise certification requirements periodically which have consequently raised training requirements. Specific courses have been designated as a required background for the professional person. Some states indicate maximum case load.

This has assisted the clinician in making more time available for children with handicapping speech problems. Others designate the number of times an individual must be seen per week. However, the profession will never really come of age until professional decisions such as the aforementioned ones are left to the professional — the speech clinician — not to state or local rules and regulations.

Working conditions have improved and many school systems have provided working facilities specifically designed for the clinical speech program. However, the rapid growth of population still makes it necessary for clinicians to work in undesirable work space. If this is temporary, it can be tolerated. However, experience indicates that the success of the program is related to facilities, at least in part, and the clinician and school administration should work towards improved facilities.

A LOOK FORWARD

In the Profession

We live in a day when new things are coming our way to constantly challenge our thoughts and minds. Clinicians must have a zest and hunger for new things. There is new knowledge; there are new techniques; there are new professional demands. Transition is often an ordeal because it is uncertain. One must be eager for adventure.

Research will be indicating answers and approaches. Results of longitudinal studies will, no doubt, help in the better understanding of some of the problems with which clinicians are now struggling. The field of clinical speech will more and more require a variety of technical and other skills. It is of utmost importance for each person in the profession to contemplate himself carefully to see how well he is keeping the pace.

In the Book

The following chapter deals with some specifics of self-study. The remainder of the second unit deals with the roles of the speech clinician. Often overlooked are the *several* roles of the clinician. Not only must he function in his role as clinician but also as a member of the educational team, as a consultant, as a counsellor, and as a researcher. As a member of the educational team, the clinician must recognize the importance of his employment environment and the human resources available in this environment so that he can utilize them to his fullest advantage. The cooperation of school administrators, teachers, and other allied school specialists is essential to the total success of the program. The speech clinician is the "expert" in the area of speech problems. Not only is it to his advantage to enlist the cooperation of classroom teachers for carry-over of therapy techniques into the classroom, he must also serve as consultant in the interpretation of handling of speech problems, assistance with minor problems, explanation of the maturation of speech, and as advisor to classroom speech improvement programs. He must also give interpretation and advice to other professionals.

Since speech problems affect and involve not only the child but also the family unit, the clinician is often called upon to serve as a counsellor. Although he may not be fitted by training to provide psychological therapy, he cannot avoid the role of counsellor and must develop competencies in counselling. Finally, in his role as researcher, he should constantly be seeking to answer questions and to provide information either for his own enlightenment or to advance understandings of the profession.

The third unit deals with professional planning. This may be the most neglected area of information in the speech and hearing profession. The literature is sparse indeed in the areas of physical facilities, program scheduling, case finding, case selection, case load, aspects of the therapy program and records and reports. Considering the importance of these therapeutic conditions, it is difficult to understand the meager amount of available written information. Perhaps it is due to the fact that much of the organized information in these areas is relatively recent.

SUMMARY

In this first unit, a viewpoint on the history of the speech and hearing profession is presented which traces the beginnings of the profession in the educational, medical, and paramedical areas.

The merging of these groups to form the American Speech and Hearing Association and weld a professional image is discussed.

Justification for the use of the term "speech clinician" in this book is presented on the basis that the individual diagnoses, prognoses, prescribes for, and treats the person with a speech problem. Also, differentiation between clinical and educational activities is presented.

Finally, the organization of the book and a brief overview of the contents of this book are discussed.

If the coming pages can serve to impress on the readers the importance of therapeutic conditions, it will have served the speech and hearing handicapped well. Most clinicians understand speech and hearing problems, at least academically. Most clinicians have a variety of materials and techniques at their disposal. Applying these skills and knowledges effectively remains, then, as a major difference between a successful and unsuccessful program. Let's explore!

DISCUSSION TOPICS

1. What specific contributions have education and psychology — medicine made to our present methods of functioning?
2. Of what importance is the use of a single label for the professional worker?
3. Who should determine what the worker is to be called, what his function should be, and his professional conduct?
4. What specific examples are there of differences of opinion as to professional matters within the field of clinical speech?
5. What problems have been created by professionals viewing the field as extensions "of their basic professional affiliations"?
6. Will these matters eventually be minimized? Resolved entirely?
7. Is there advantage to differences of professional opinion? Explain your viewpoint.
8. Why do the authors feel a speech clinician has several roles?
9. Are there roles which were not mentioned?
10. What do you feel is meant by the statement "the speech clinician cannot avoid the role of counsellor"?

REFERENCES

1. AINSWORTH, S.: The speech clinician in public schools: participant or separatist? *ASHA, 7:*495-503, December, 1965.
2. BLACK, M.: The origins and status of speech therapy in the schools. *ASHA, 8:*419-425, November, 1966.
3. Executive Council, The American Speech and Hearing Association: The speech clinician's role in the public school. *ASHA, 6:*189-191, June, 1964.
4. HAINES, H.: Trends in public school speech therapy. *ASHA, 7:*187-190, June, 1965.
5. MOORE, P., and KESTER, D. G.: Historical notes on speech correction in the preassociation era. *J Speech Hearing Dis, 18:*48-53, February, 1953.
6. SPRIESTERSBACH, D. C.: As I see it—Clinician: a status title? *ASHA, 7:*464, November, 1965.

UNIT II

The Roles of the Speech Clinician

Chapter 2

THE SPEECH CLINICIAN — AS A PROFESSIONAL PERSON

MYFANWY E. CHAPMAN

Distinctive to nearly every profession or trade is certain equipment. The physician has his stethoscope, the surgeon his scalpel, the linotype operator his typesetting machine, the truck driver his truck. The speech clinician has primarily himself — including a good pair of ears and eyes, a good store of intellectual information and functioning sound judgment together with his personality and character. With these things at his command he examines, diagnoses, and administers remedial instruction to children, youth, and adults who have defects of speech, voice, or language. He has the exciting challenge of attempting to vary another individual's behavior, particularly in the area of communication, and this often involves changing the entire individual, not only in the way he is, but more importantly, in the way he will be. In so doing, the clinician must achieve warm relationships not only with the individuals he seeks to help but also with others in his environment. If this sounds like an awesome responsibility, it is. It cannot be taken lightly.

THE INDIVIDUAL

Understanding Oneself

Perhaps the first important factor in alertness to the problem of others is the ability to look at oneself. Unless the clinician is able to find a relatively satisfactory adjustment within himself, he will be poorly equipped for helping others. He must also be constantly making new adjustments because he has to work with and through others. He will need to explore his own reaction to frustrations, his assets, his liabilities, making the most of his assets and learning to lessen his liabilities. He must learn to relax and face up to problems. Included in this self-examination must be a

17

study of his health habits and an analysis of his ability to minimize wasted time and effort.

Since the clinicians' duties, to reiterate, are largely concerned with individuals having problems, unless he can realistically examine himself and have an understanding of his own behavior, be sensitive to the feelings of those with whom he associates, and have command of techniques for handling these feelings, confidence in him will be lacking. So long as the clinician is successful, that is, manages his adaptation to a succession of situations, he will fulfill his personal needs and those of the individuals with whom he is working.

Understanding Others

The understanding of others is equally necessary. This ability aids the clinician in working effectively with those having speech problems. Children can seldom, if ever, be deceived about one's deeper feelings towards them. Genuineness reveals itself in warmth, kindness, and frankness and leads to rapport with children as well as with co-workers. If the child knows that his clinician is interested in him personally, respects his rights, and makes fair decisions, much can be accomplished. Such understanding and interest help the clinician realize that a speech difference may lead to problems of adjustment, feelings of insecurity, inferiority, frustration, or defensiveness. He will have to make every effort to help the individual overcome not only the speech disorder but also personality and adjustment problems which may be involved. Recognition of these factors enables the clinician to guide the child in a realistic examination of his needs and abilities.

Personality and Character

Humility — Modesty

The attitude one assumes and the way he conducts himself make a world of difference in the manner what one has to offer is received. The quality of humility or modesty, defined as relative freedom from vanity, boastfulness, egotism, great pretension, or attitudes of superiority and the presence of regard for decency of behavior, in speech and dress, is an asset to any clinician. If the clinician holds himself aloof as a very special sort of person, he aids neither himself nor those he seeks to help. He should remember that no matter how brilliant and how capable he considers himself in his field of operation, no one will discover this if, by his attitude of superiority because he is in a special area, he builds a fence around himself. Once he has sold himself to his colleagues he is on the way towards free, gracious, and professional accomplishment.

The qualities of humility and modesty are lifesavers, helping the clinician modify his assumption about his professional role to fit the image expected of him and yet remain true to his convictions. Significant to this is the story which is told about Queen Victoria, who is said to have disliked Prime Minister Gladstone very much. When asked why, she replied, "When he speaks to me it's as though he were addressing a public meeting."

These aspects of character and personality are often shown in subtle ways; the friendly fraternizing with staff members during relaxation and lunch periods, as well as at staff social gatherings, helps for good relationships. Consider the difference between the clinician who becomes acquainted with staff members at such times as mentioned and the one who always seeks a place by himself during such periods with the excuse, "I don't like coffee, so I don't join the group."

Schools may have moneymaking affairs such as school carnivals. Classroom teachers are usually asked to participate in these affairs. The clinician who graciously offers to help and cooperate in whatever capacity he can is usually well received. Paper sales are frequently used as a means of raising money for equipment, books, and other school supplies. It is surprising how much co-workers in the schools appreciate the clinician's involvement in such causes.

In any school setting, it is well to abide by rules and regulations set up for other staff members — that is, as far as an itinerant schedule will permit. Usually staff members are expected to arrive at work at designated hours. The clinician will find himself less vulnerable to criticism if he observes such rules. Occasionally circumstances make it imperative for the clinician to be off schedule. At such times he should considerately explain this to persons involved. Principals appreciate knowing when exceptions to regular schedules are necessary. Each school system differs, to a degree, in what is expected of staff members, but behavior such as suggested helps the clinician's relationships in the schools which he serves.

Other aspects of modesty involve personal grooming, attire, speech, and courtesy. Just as in any profession, personal hygiene and grooming, choice of wearing apparel, manner of speaking and conducting oneself are very important to the speech clinician. Women clinicians will probably find that the selection of simple attire and avoidance of such wearing apparel as slacks or "after five" clothes for business hours will be a wise decision. The best-dressed woman is not always the one with the most clothes but the one who looks good in what she has. In high school one was likely to dress more for peer-group acceptance than for self. Always bear in mind the type of life you lead. A basic wardrobe won't be dull if you have a bright point of interest with accessories. Simple lines in many clothes are easy to dress up or down. It's not important that people remember what you wore but rather that you looked attractive. Well-selected, becoming but moderate use of makeup for daytime wear is usually in good taste. Similarly, the dress of male clinicians requires neat and professional attire.

A well-modulated voice adds to one's attractiveness. There are many correct ways of behaving in almost any situation so there is little reason for neglecting small courtesies. It is often surprising how seemingly insignificant courteous acts are observed and commented upon. One clinician was well regarded because of his careful attention to rising when guests entered his office and another was censured because he failed to remove his hat on entering the building. All the things mentioned make a noticeable difference in the acceptance or rejection of a person in a position such as the speech clinician holds.

Honesty

A necessary aspect of character and personality expected in persons to whom one turns for help is honesty. It reveals itself in many ways. A straightforward frankness tempered by tactfulness may be one way; truthfulness and trustworthiness is another. Fairness in all dealings and loyalty to those with whom one works are still further indications of this trait.

Honesty demands that the clinician examine his prejudices. Persons working in schools do not deal with select populations. The clinician working in the schools is not in a position to give service to one at the exclusion of another without defending the choice made. He should always realistically deal with what he is going to have to face. When he chooses to work in schools, he needs to be aware that here he will find children and youths who come from varying socioeconomic backgrounds, attractive as well as less attractive children, some with high intelligence as well as those with lower intelligence. He will be dealing with the needs of children of all races and creeds. Some will be multiply handicapped. Those who work in large urban areas may face a greater range of differences than those in smaller communities, and some will have to carry on work with children from less-privileged areas than others. Adjustment will have to be made to differences in parental cooperation and understanding. In some homes there is a constant state of tension, troublesome economic circumstances, dissension, and, in some cases, broken homes. It is up to the clinician to modify tension to the best of his ability. In situations where there are working parents, special arrangements to confer with these parents may have to be made outside of regular working hours.

There is need for acceptance and fairness to all as each is an individual in his own right. The effort put forth must be as great for one as for another. The clinician should realize some children have poor self-images. Some are aware of parental rejection. Clinicians who are strong, firm, and accepting create a feeling of security in children and give them increased satisfaction. Step by step they obtain reasonable satisfaction as to needs. They feel more adequate, secure and comfortable. No clinician can afford to develop strong likes and dislikes. Children are particularly sensitive to attitude. Listening is one of the important things the clinician can do. He can give support in a variety of ways. He should acknowledge people's strong feelings, and he should credit all with possessing human dignity. A child cannot be helped until the clinician has observed him. He should look for the positive things in the child and point them out. It is best to make use of spontaneous situations which arise. There is a difference between tolerating and accepting. Each child should be given reassurance. The way in which this is done is important. Honesty shows through. Providing an example of fairness, firmness, and friendliness is one of the best ways to attain this objective. Reality sets limits. The clinician is wise not to become overly attached or emotionally involved. Better clinical work can be done without excessive emotional involvement.

If the clinician deals honestly and realistically with problems, facing up to what is good for the child and what will help him get along better, he will occasionally have to admit, "I don't know the answer right now," recognizing that there are certain things he cannot do. He is a better clinician if he recognizes and honestly admits his limitations. He must realize that there are circumstances in the life of the individual with whom he works that, though he wants very much to do something to help and do it soon, make him sometimes be satisfied with slow gains and occasional failures. The important thing is that he honestly tries to find answers and does not give up because the challenge, at the moment, seems too great.

While there are no hard and fast rules regarding dropping a child from speech therapy, the clinician should give considerable thought to the reason for discontinuing the work with any given child. He must honestly weigh all aspects to determine whether personal reasons (such as inability to understand the child and cope with his behavior, a feeling of inadequacy in coping with the specific speech problem involved, or even an actual dislike for the one in question) are reasons, or whether it is truly for the welfare of the child. Consider the reaction of those concerned in the following: Tommy had caused considerable disturbance in the small speech group to which he belonged. He very much needed speech therapy, but without conference with the classroom teacher, principal, or parents, the clinician sent a note to the teacher saying, "Tommy creates too much trouble in the speech group. Don't send him anymore." One can easily imagine the results of this type of handling of a problem and no doubt agree that the element of honest evaluation by the clinician, as well as professional responsibility, was completely lacking.

This speech clinician might have asked himself these questions, What are my feelings about this child? Do I dislike this child? Is it a temporary dislike? What are my feelings about my inability to cope with this? (Cast about for what is involved.) Did I ever talk with the child, try to get acquainted when others were not present? Does my handling of this child relate to any prejudices I have? Do I object to working in this particular school district? Am I tolerating or really accepting? What did I do to encourage self-reliance and initiative in this child? Did I try to draw him out and get his ideas? Was I inclined to scold too much? How did this child behave in other situations?

Empathy

The ability to empathize with the child and get an empathic response, in other words, share the child's feelings and thinking, cannot be discounted. Some of understanding seems so commonplace that one forgets how fundamental it can be at a time when the person one seeks to help needs it most. The child who finds acceptance, encouragement, and approval in his speech performance learns to express himself verbally. It is in such an especially adjusted environment that many children for the first time experience adequacy in meeting many situations.

In working with the individual who has a speech problem it is not enough, as we have said, to give thought to the speech mechanism alone. It is necessary to consider the person who is doing the speaking and help him gain insight not only into his way of speaking but also into his manner of behaving. He must be guided in understanding the purpose of speech therapy as it applies to him. For example, the youth who has been concerned about the problem of stuttering can be helped to reevaluate situations which he has avoided and practice speaking under such circumstances. He may have had the experience of first becoming aware of severe blocking during a telephone conversation and from then on avoided answering the phone or making telephone calls. In facing up to such a problem and practicing going into situations he has previously avoided, he is likely to more adequately take control. Empathic relationship between the youth and his clinician helps him move ahead into new ventures.

The child who has been very self-conscious and lacking in self-confidence because of an articulation problem can be encouraged and led into situations where he will experience success. He can learn about speech sounds and about his particular articulatory disorder. As he understands more about these things, he becomes more enthusiastic about working on the problem and his insecurities are lessened. Here again the empathic relationship between child and clinician plays an important part.

Permissiveness

Allowing and acknowledging the presence of strong emotion in another without forcing him to lose his feeling of status is a strong supportive method in guidance and at the same time makes it unnecessary for children to exploit behavior in a futile struggle to prove their worth. This permissiveness implies friendliness without undue familiarity, listening to complaints, explaining the need for rules and restrictions, but it also includes firmness and abiding by fair decisions. There must be mutual respect between clinician and child. Relationships are better under such circumstances than when permissiveness is confused with license. The beginning clinician should be aware that it is easier to increase permissiveness than to decrease it.

Sense of Humor

The ability to see humor in a situation will not only tide one over many rough spots but certainly will be a salvation to those with whom one associates. Each day one becomes more aware of the importance and value of humor. It will aid one in appreciating many things which happen during the course of a day and will create the goodwill necessary to successful therapy. Obviously, this does not mean that the clinician should be a buffoon. A clown may be loved, but his judgment is usually not respected. Producing a smile or a laugh at appropriate times and with appropriate frequency is a sign of a well-rounded personality.

Patience

How often the clinician hears the comment, "Oh, I should think it would take so much patience to do the work you are doing." Patience is an essential quality in a clinician. Many times it takes infinite patience and calmness. The clinician is often called upon to help those whose improvement is slow and laborious, or possibly one who is multiply handicapped, or who has become frustrated because of his inability to adequately communicate. In clinical work one will experience times when he exerts every effort to help a particular individual, and yet a feeling of success eludes him. Sometimes he is dealing with an individual who cannot allow the clinician to know he is getting through to him. In such an event, the clinician needs to realize that emotional first aid and other therapy are often slow processes. He must not be easily discouraged. One never knows how much of one's self he leaves.

Imagination, Creativeness, and Originality

All these traits on the part of the clinician contribute to more effective therapy. There are many books and other resource materials available to those doing speech therapy, but the clinician must be adept in applying these to particular cases. It is also important for him to be able to draw upon his own resources, for often the material available does not meet the particular needs of the child or youth with whom he is working. The separateness and uniqueness of each human being calls upon the clinician's resourcefulness. There are no stereotyped methods which will apply. His curiosity and imagination should lead him into developing ideas and materials which will often far surpass those already available and force him to see what he can work out to meet the needs of his clients. He may feel that he does not have skill in creative work, but upon putting forth effort he will surprise himself. His interest in the needs of others will be his incentive.

Guides which present various phases of the clinical speech program, brochures which deal with it, and bulletins offering suggestions for helping the speech handicapped individual in the home and in the classroom, all appeal to the creative imagination of the clinician and become very useful tools in phases of therapy.

Resourcefulness

This is another personality trait observed in the successful clinician. It is demonstrated in his ability to hold the interest of those in therapy and maintain an atmosphere of alertness, good humor, and pleasant give-and-take conducive to harmonious, friendly, and pleasing relations. He needs to study the cause and effect relationship between procedures and results. The clinician must allow opportunities for the expression of a variety of feelings and release of the child's energy in constructive ways. He needs to become acquainted with resource materials which often provide clues for therapy. A study of learning principles, concepts, and behavior theories which have been applied to communication behavior is one source. Understanding the application of these and experimenting with various methods will help him find ways of promoting and maintaining the child's interest and drive to achieve. It is helpful to be knowledgeable about the disciplines and theories of learning. The clinician will have to decide whether individual or group therapy is indicated in planning a program for each child.

Group therapy requires considerable resourcefulness on the part of the clinician, since the desire for group approval is so prevalent under these circumstances. It takes careful handling so that competition does not discourage those with lower ability. The clinician needs to find ways for self-competition, that is, helping the child learn to compete with his own performance and record and thus gain approval. Clever handling will allow the child to have a balance of success and failure. One cannot always succeed; neither can one always fail. He must be helped to accept realities of self — his strengths and his needs. Sometimes lack of success needs to be evaluated. Apropos here might be the comment made by Edison when confronted with the statement, You have failed a thousand times. "No," he answered, "I've only found a thousand ways not to do a thing." Variation in therapy procedures, provision for new experiences, and the use of differing media to promote various aspects of treatment challenge the resourcefulness of the clinician. The clinician needs to recognize that the motivational force that exerts the greatest influence is not the same for all children, for all time, for all situations. Many times when consultants and others are asked to recommend a clinician these questions are asked, How well can he discover problems and solve them? Does he recognize them? Do his solutions represent good clinical judgment?

Dependability and Responsibility

Dependability and responsibility rank high among the assets of a good clinician. He must recognize that his first responsibility is to the child, the school, the parents, the community, and to the profession as a whole. This is shown in promptness in attending to schedules, reports, and records, by care of materials and equipment entrusted to him, by reliability in following through on suggestions, and by general thoughtfulness and cooperation. These traits are also shown in well-planned, meaningful therapy sessions which result in purposeful activity of those involved. To achieve this, a minimum of one hour a day must be spent in reviewing and evaluating the day's activities and planning the therapy session for the following day. No successful clinician functions without evaluation and planning. It should be habitual. The clinician should also experience a sense of accomplishment and satisfaction as an outgrowth of reasonable effort.

Finally, he should make certain that each member of the group understands the aims and purposes of therapeutic activities and their relation to his particular problem. If the clinician is one who uses games as a part of therapy, he needs to carefully check to see that the game actually has therapeutic value and is not just a busy-work measure. Games and other devices of this nature can serve as motivational material but should be used judiciously. Therapy time is usually at a premium and must be used in ways which can be of greatest value.

Establishing Relationships

The Administration

Organizational structure, as well as administrative policies, differs from school system to school system. In some situations the clinician is directly responsible to the school principal or school superintendent, in others one goes through the speech consultant or perhaps the director of special education. It should be part of the responsibility of the speech clinician to ascertain the existing policies and procedures. Questions which arise are many, such as to whom one reports absence or emergency, from whom one obtains permission to attend professional meetings during school hours, and other questions of a similar nature. One can improve services to speech handicapped children and youths if there is mutual understanding between the administration and the clinician.

The Classroom Teacher

The clinician should realize the importance, not only of the administration, but also of all school personnel to a successful clinical speech program in the schools. The place of the classroom teacher cannot be overemphasized. He has it within his power to aid in the promotion of such a program by a classroom atmosphere of acceptance and understanding of the speech handicapped child. By allowing this child time out of the classroom to attend speech therapy sessions without penalty, by removing pressures in the classroom, by a friendly attitude towards the program, and by helping in the carry-over work from speech therapy to the classroom and elsewhere, the classroom teacher gives positive support to speech therapy.

The classroom teacher can be brought into the picture in so many ways. Although school systems may vary in organization, in general there are marked similarities. Arrangements should be made with the principal early in the year for opportunities to present aspects of the clinical speech program at regular staff meetings. Sometimes a series of such meetings can be arranged. The clinician can encourage the teacher to visit therapy sessions.

He can participate in conferences with teachers either for the purpose of discussing individual children or just for getting better acquainted. He can arrange workshops and in-service courses which present added opportunities for discussion of various types of speech disorders and the treatment of such problems. This aids in mutual understanding. Brochures, bulletins, bibliographies, and memoranda to teachers aid in the teacher education program. Some children like to show their teachers and classmates what happens in speech therapy, so the speech therapy session can sometimes move to the regular classroom. This serves two purposes, provided, of course, the children in therapy wish to do this. It helps the child in therapy feel important because he can show others how to do something, and it serves as an educational measure for the teacher and the children not in therapy.

The Child

The child who has a speech problem should be carefully introduced to therapy. It behooves the clinician to first put him at ease and obtain a measure of rapport before he rushes into diagnostic testing and treatment. Some children become alarmed when called out of the classroom. A simple statement, perhaps to the effect that the clinician wishes to get acquainted with many of the children in the school, followed by informal chatter, serves to ease the child and readies him for the work to follow. The clinician's manner towards the child, his tone of voice, his friendliness, enthusiasm, and warmth are of utmost importance. This initial contact has much to do with relationships in the future.

The terms "child" and "children" should in this instance be inclusive of youths, for the clinician is often called upon to help those in the junior and senior high schools who have speech disorders. Many clinicians who have been accustomed to working with children in the elementary grades forget that those at secondary levels like to be treated as adults. One must remember to avoid any tendency to talk down to them.

Once the child has been enrolled for speech therapy, there are a number of important things to instill in his mind. Among these he should learn to assume the responsibility of coming to therapy sessions on time. In addition, because the atmosphere in these sessions is often less formal than in many classrooms, it is easy for the child or youth to misinterpret this and fail to understand the necessity for attention to work. The clinician must set up limitations and hold to these. Security is more likely to come about by children understanding such limitations. The habit of good listening, a very important factor in speech therapy, must be among the first accomplishments. This cannot come about if there is confusion and lack of any discipline. The clinician, from the start, must at all times be in control. This may mean that, at first, he must be a bit more positive and more firm in approach than he would like to be. It is easier to loosen the reins than to tighten them after things are out of control. As before mentioned, there is considerable difference between permissiveness and license.

The Parents

Since many school speech clinicians work in elementary schools, parents of the children who need help should be contacted and informed of the problem to see if they desire the child to have speech therapy. A telephone call to obtain the parents' permission or a note may serve such a purpose. This is not essential, and sometimes inadvisable, in junior or senior high schools as these people feel old enough to make their own decisions. However, they should be advised to consult with their parents and explain the problems as it was explained to them by the clinician. Occasionally one finds himself in a secondary school where the administrator prefers the children to get written permission from the parents before enrolling them for therapy.

Following introductory measures, it is advisable to invite the parents for a conference very early in the program. The purpose of the conference must be well in mind. It is good to remember the importance of first impressions. A cordial, friendly greeting indicating pleasure in meeting them and interest in their child helps in preparing the parents for cooperation. One must realize that most parents have within themselves the resources they need to understand and manage their feelings if given proper guidance.

Unless clinicians sense the feelings of the parents, problems which are not compatible with good mental hygiene or pleasant relationships may develop. If a stressful situation must be faced, the clinician introduces the parents to it slowly and by approaching menacing items only when the parents have acquired some feeling of ease with the clinician. It is of greater value to the therapy program to use a little more time in what appears to be superfluous bits of conversation than to strike directly at the problem if to do so is likely to entail antagonism and unfriendly feelings on the part of the parent. In acquiring information about the child which will be pertinent to therapy and since note taking may contribute to uneasiness on the part of the parents, the clinician might indicate that some memory helpers are essential for the clinician's personal use so he trusts the parents will not object to his taking a few notes. Harmonious relationships with parents are very important. When they feel comfortable with the clinician, the real work has begun.

Colleagues

The clinician's personality and character qualities are quickly noted by colleagues. Their acceptance of the clinician and the way they react to suggestions made by him are dependent upon how they regard him. If he presents ideas graciously, with self-confidence, without arrogance, they are likely to be well received and given consideration. Perhaps one of the most important facets of such self-confidence is that it is catching. The self-confident person may radiate strength and inspiration. However, there is a difference between real and affected self-confidence. Only an individual who has learned to live effectively can possess true self-confidence tempered with humility and modesty. Poise on the part of the clinician has a great influence upon others. It is not always what one says but how he says it or doesn't that matters.

The clinician who works in a large city school system frequently has more opportunity to fraternize with colleagues than one working in outlying areas. Staff meetings become a part of one's schedule. Such meetings offer excellent opportunities for an exchange of ideas. One's way of offering suggestions makes a differ-ence in their acceptance.

A clinician may accept a position where the speech program has been in effect over a period of years. In such a situation, if he wishes to make changes in procedures, the clinician should do so with assurance and tact and knowledgeable background of what he wishes to do and why. He must reeducate others, so to speak, without casting aspersions on former clinicians. Where there is no tradition to lean on, or sometimes to encumber, he will be rela-tively free to set up a program to meet the needs as he sees them. People who are engaged in clinical speech cannot be bound by tradition. They have to be experimental in their approach, but they must be able to defend their stand. A constant rule to follow is to observe the highest standards of ethical principles in all one's relationships.

Others

Many people need to be involved in a clinical speech program. This includes not only those mentioned such as administrators, classroom teachers, parents, and the children themselves but the school nurses, counselors, the office staff, and the maintenance people. If the clinician takes time to explain what he hopes to achieve with their help he will usually find that he will get excel-lent cooperation.

THE PROFESSIONAL
Responsibility

Organizations

Affiliation with certain organizations is a must for the truly professional speech clinician. He needs to lend support to organi-zations which seek to promote the welfare of the exceptional indi-vidual and keep up the standards of the speech profession. The American Speech and Hearing Association is a scientific and pro-fessional association. The purpose of this organization is stated in Article II of the by-laws and is "to encourage basic scientific study of the processes of individual human speech and hearing, promote investigation of speech and hearing disorders, and foster improvement of therapeutic procedures with such disorders; to stimulate exchange of information among persons thus engaged and to disseminate such information."* Membership in the association is highly advisable for real professional status. Applications are sent to the national office, 9030 Old Georgetown Road, Washington, D.C., 20014.

State organizations are closely allied to the national association. These also offer professional stimulation and demand the active support of the persons engaged in clinical speech. Attendance at state meetings affords one the opportunity for the exchange of ideas with those in one's more immediate environment and often the chance to hear invited speakers from other localities and other disciplines as well as to learn about research one's colleagues are doing.

With the growth of speech and hearing services many areas have local groups or organizations where opportunity is provided the clinician to meet and discuss professional matters on a community level. Such groups allow for interchange of ideas between various employment environments, i.e. the school clinician has the opportunity to meet with clinicians working in hospital or college clinics, with resultant increased understanding and rapport with professional colleagues and help in mutual problem solving. Clinicians should avail themselves of such opportunities.

Related organizations have much to offer. Many clinicians find it stimulating to align themselves with and attend meetings of associations of related disciplines such as The American Psychological Association, its state counterpart, The Council for Exceptional Children, its state counterpart, and others. Such affiliations help to broaden one's point of view and aid in intergroup communication and understanding.

Certification

Those working in the various areas of clinical speech should seek national and state certification. The American Speech and Hearing Association issues its Certificate of Clinical Competence. This certificate "is granted in speech pathology or audiology, and

---

*American Speech and Hearing Association—Directory, 1967, p. ix.

indicates that the holder thereof has demonstrated ability to conduct clinical services and train others in the arts and skills of the profession, and is a fully trained professional worker. A qualified member may be certified in both areas, speech pathology and audiology; although a joint certificate is not issued."*

State certification is usually granted by the state department of public instruction. In most states one must have certification in the state in which he is employed.

Publications

The American Speech and Hearing Association publishes the following periodicals which are invaluable to the practicing speech clinician:

Journal of Speech and Hearing Disorders
Journal of Speech and Hearing Research
ASHA
Trends
Monographs, which is issued irregularly
Directory, which includes not only the membership list but also other
 pertinent information such as by-laws and code of ethics.
 This is issued yearly.

State organizations frequently issue periodic newsletters and yearly directories containing membership lists as well as other information which should be of interest to all in the field of clinical speech.

Conventions

Association conventions are held annually at a time and place determined by the executive council. These are planned to stimulate exchange of information, report research, and conduct the business of the association. Short courses in various areas are offered at such times.

Many state organizations also hold annual conventions and offer similar opportunities for professional stimulation.

One of the greatest dangers is that one will miss the experience of participating in meaningful decisions concerning one's own

*American Speech and Hearing Association—Directory, 1967, p. vii.

work if he does not affiliate with the professional organization and participate in the business sessions of his associations. To actually be a part of any organization one must be aware of the inner functioning and there is no better way of achieving understanding than by attendance at business meetings and reading published reports of such meetings.

Membership

In conversation with clinicians one is often asked, What do these associations do for me, that is, what have I to gain by investing my money in such organizations? The answer might well be in the form of a question, What is an association? To quote a dictionary definition, "An association is an organization of people having a common purpose and having a formal structure."*

This brings to mind the old adage, "A chain is only as strong as its weakest link." So one needs, in order to answer the original question, to ask still further questions. How much are you willing to give of yourself to this job of making the association program a really vital force for the exceptional child, youth, or adult as well as for the professional worker in the field? What can be your greatest contribution? Are you going to sit on the sidelines and find fault? Are you the person who says, "Oh, let Pete do it. He likes the limelight?"

One of course knows that there are those who have a natural talent for leadership, but it must be remembered that a leader has to have cooperation and if you are the person who feels more comfortable in other capacities, don't forget workers, other than leaders, are also very necessary parts of the organization to which you belong. But be sure you are not hiding your talent. Decide where you can be of assistance. As one writer puts it, "The mature person does not overestimate himself, nor does he underestimate himself. It is in the area of our voluntary group organizations that the great battle between maturity and immaturity goes on. In this area the individual finds his best chance to join his own feeble strengths with the greater combined strengths of those who

---

*Random House, *The American College Dictionary*, p. 76.

care about the fulfillment of life."* Here one joins with the researcher who is constantly seeking answers, and with the clinician
who seeks clues from research for the improvement of therapy,
and with the professors who seek to impart this knowledge. To
reiterate, the national, state, and local associations offer opportunities for sharing and lend status to the profession. Everyone
is needed to make them really functioning organizations.

One must remember that there is no magic wand that such
organizations can wave to solve all problems which confront each
individual member. One cannot expect to pay dues and immediately have a package of answers to all problems delivered to him.
One cannot be an inert component of the group. He must remember that he obligates himself to activity and participation, if he
is to gain by membership. Too often the clinician expects the
organization to solve problems which may be his own responsibility and perhaps highly individual or local and can only be
solved by one's own persistent good work.

Honors

Association honors are given for achievement. These are perhaps best explained by the by-laws of the American Speech and
Hearing Association, Article XII, Section 1: "The Honors of the
Association may be presented to an individual by the Executive
Council upon recommendation of the Committee on Honors.
This award recognizes distinguished contribution to the field of
speech and hearing and is the highest honor the Association can
give." Section 2: "Fellowship, an award recognizing professional
or scientific achievement, may be given to a Member on recommendation by the Committee on Honors and approval by the
three-fourths vote of the Executive Council. The status of Fellow
shall be retained by the individual to whom it is awarded as long
as he remains a Member in good standing of the Association."†

Self-improvement

Self-improvement has much to do with the attitude one assumes towards himself and his work. The difference between

---

*Overstreet, H. A.: *The Mature Mind*. New York, Norton, 1949, p. 281.
†*American Speech and Hearing Association—Directory*, 1967, pp. xiv-xv.

merely fulfilling attendance requirements and the demands of the moment and moving toward a goal of self-improvement must be recognized by every clinician. There are many ways of looking at this and many goals one may set for oneself.

The clinician may be located where classes for professional- and self-improvement are available, such as college and university centers. This of course is not always true, but it would be difficult to imagine a situation where it would not be possible to gain knowledge through reading. Many people have contributed to the literature articles and books which will prove helpful in promoting professional and personal maturity. Summer session courses are often especially designed for professional growth. In large urban areas one has the advantage of being with others who are in the same or related fields. Each can be of mutual assistance. In-service courses can be arranged and visits to those doing speech therapy in clinics such as hospital, university, and rehabilitation centers can be arranged. The work which is required of clinicians in such centers is very closely related to public school speech therapy.

Broadening one's point of view through association with those in related disciplines and in other vocations is important. In addition, one must not forget that travel does a great deal in expanding horizons and enhancing one's understanding of people. As previously mentioned, attendance at professional conferences is an excellent help in self-improvement.

The clinician must remember that good clinical work doesn't just happen. Wide knowledge and, above all, an acquisitive obsession beyond the call of duty are great attributes. Since assessment is a continuous process, one must be constantly on the alert. This is an increasingly scientific age. It is an age of intense competition, bringing with it strains upon human relations and demanding higher social and professional skills. It is an age which will tolerate less and less of anything that hinders smooth and efficient relations. It is imperative that one work for self-improvement not only professionally but in understanding and improvement in one's own personality and character.

The Community

Agencies

Opportunities for the child or youth to identify with groups which help in a program for social and physical adjustment, when this is an indicated need as part of therapy, are provided by groups such as Scouts, Little League, and Camp Fire. Sometimes Big Brother, Big Sister, Family Welfare, public school organizations, and crippled children's associations can offer help in a program for the child. It is necessary for the speech clinician to accept the responsibility of interpreting the clinical program to such groups. This can be done through talks at their staff meetings and by furnishing such groups with literature pertaining to the treatment of children having speech problems.

The school clinician sometimes feels that further examination than he is equipped to give is advisable in some cases. Referral to clinics such as hospital clinics for such additional information is occasionally indicated. The clinician should acquaint himself with such services and with the proper method of referral, and he must not forget that parental cooperation is necessary in the event such services are advisable.

Clubs

Mothers' clubs, parent-teacher groups, service clubs, and church groups are frequently seeking speakers. These groups offer excellent opportunities to the clinician for helping to increase understanding of the profession of speech pathology and the needs of children having speech disorders.

Staff Meetings

Such meetings, to reiterate, should be scheduled early in the year and periodically during the remainder of the year to explain the aims and needs of clinical speech. At these meetings the clinician can enlighten the staff members regarding the various types of speech disorders. Arrangements for meetings of this nature are made through the principals of the schools which the clinician serves. They serve as an excellent means of increased understanding and enhance the value of the clinical speech program in the schools.

Parent Groups

Parent meetings serve as another educational measure. Some clinicians have great success with group gatherings for parents. They invite parents whose children have similar speech problems; for example, parents of those having such problems as severe articulation disorders might be included in one group; those having language or delayed speech in another; and those who have nonfluencies in still another. It is often consoling to parents to find that their child is not the only one having a problem. Following such group meetings individual conferences are arranged. Usually the clinician has a conference day scheduled in his weekly itinerary. In working out a program for clinical speech, it is important to allow time for such conferences.

Radio and Television

These are now a much used means of communication. Many schools now have radio and television facilities and some have audiovisual departments making it possible to arrange for the speech clinician to use equipment of this nature to conduct demonstration work, participate in broadcasting panel discussions, and prepare video tapes to help enlighten those in the community regarding clinical speech. If children are being used in such programs, written permission should first be obtained from parents in advance.

Political Action

Some states have compulsory laws for furnishing help to handicapped children. Sometimes special legislation needs to be considered. The clinician can help lay the groundwork for such legislation and do much to promote what is needed in the area of clinical speech. Legislation may be concerned with state or federal aid, certification of clinicians, provisions for therapy for speech handicapped individuals, or other areas related to speech pathology such as mental health, psychology, child welfare, and physical health measures. It is important to keep track of those measures which are directly or indirectly the concern of the persons in one's field.

ETHICAL PRACTICES

Code of Ethics

The preamble to the code of ethics of the American Speech and Hearing Association states, "The preservation of the highest standards of integrity and ethical principles is vital to the successful discharge of the responsibilities of all members."* It is imperative for all clinicians to carefully study the code of ethics of the association. Copies are available by addressing the office of the American Speech and Hearing Association. Stressed here are some of the essentials.

Confidentiality

Respecting privileged communication is of outstanding importance. The clinician has, by the very nature of his work, available to him information about individuals which consists of various records, test scores, reports of interviews with parents, clients, doctors, nurses, psychologists, research workers, and observations of teachers. All of these must be treated in a confidential way. Such material cannot be used for general information or as food for gossip. In counselling either clients or parents, the clinician may often receive direct or indirect evidence of conflict or conditions with which the individual has to contend. It is of utmost importance for the clinician to realize that most of this information was obtained by virtue of his having established rapport with the person with whom he was conferring and because this individual viewed the clinician as a professional person who could be entrusted with personal information. What he learns at such times must not be divulged except as it can be used for the good of those involved. There must be fairness and a professional attitude toward all, and no client should be embarrassed or exploited. Public meeting places, including school cafeterias, are no place to discuss confidential information. Neither should any child or parent be the brunt of humor or scorn. Professionalism and con-

*American Speech and Hearing Association—Directory, 1967, p. xix.

fidentiality are almost synonymous. Confidential exchange can be prearranged with agencies so that one may have the benefit of information which will be of value in helping those with whom the clinician is working.

Parental Permission

The importance of having parents sign releases for medical diagnosis must be considered. In a similar way, if tape recordings or movies have been made of those in speech therapy, and the clinician has legitimate purpose for which he wishes to use these outside of therapy time, it is important to get permission from

---

Tuesday, November 16,

Everybody's Column
READERS' OPINIONS

Teachers' Talk Resented By ██████████ Parent

Those who attended Parents Night at ██████████ Senior High School Nov. 8 certainly must be interested in their children's education and improvement. Otherwise they would not have attended this event.

The principals, teachers and student attendants were more than polite.

This letter does not pertain to this part of the evening, but to a later incident when some of our teachers came to an establishment where we had stopped for something to eat and drink

It was a conversation even a deaf person could have heard. The teachers referred to the meeting which took place before the class sessions.

One teacher laughed and said he was watching the faces of the parents and remarked that the whole thing was above their heads and he could actually see the ignorance in the faces of these people.

They laughed and insulted the people they interviewed. They remarked about one parent who had a below average child in school. Instead of trying to help a child like this, they hash it over with a few beers and do nothing.

Where do these people think their wages are coming from if not from school taxes paid by the ignorant parents?

Next year, instead of Parents Night, they should call it Educate the Educator Night and let the parents teach them something they forgot, respect.

IRATE PARENT.

FIGURE 1. Violations of professional conduct can injure public relations. Courtesy of "Everybody's Column," the *Buffalo Evening News*.

parents and clients for their use, explaining the purpose for which one wishes to use them. The same is true if children are to participate in demonstration work or to be pictured on slides or in photographs.

Guarantees

A guarantee of a "cure" must not be made or implied. There are too many unpredictable and unknown factors in each case. To again quote from the code of ethics of the American Speech and Hearing Association, "A reasonable statement of prognosis may be made; any warranty is deceptive and unethical."*

Treatment by Correspondence or Telephone

The clinician may be consulted by parents or others about problems which extend beyond the immediate school situation. He can often be very helpful in advising parents when regular clinical speech services are not available. He must, however, be sure not to give advice without first seeing the individual concerning whose problem he is advising. The code of ethics states that "he must not diagnose or treat individual speech or hearing disorder by correspondence. This does not preclude follow-up by correspondence of individuals previously seen, nor does it preclude providing the persons served professionally with general information of an educational nature."*

Ethical Relationships

Parents

Occasionally, probably because good rapport with the clinician has been established, parents ask for advice regarding matters not related to the speech problem or to areas in which the clinician is not qualified. The clinician may be flattered by this but must guard against offering such advice. Pertaining to this may be a request for suggestion on what doctor or other professional person to consult. The clinician should refrain from suggesting a specific name. It is general professional practice to suggest three alternatives.

---

*American Speech and Hearing Association—Directory, 1967, p. xix.
*American Speech and Hearing Association—Directory, 1967, p. xix.

Some parents are prone to bestow gifts upon the clinician. This is often done in the spirit of appreciation. It is much safer to remain on a professional basis and not accept such gestures. This eliminates any danger of undue influence. Some school systems have set policies about accepting gifts.

Occasionally the clinician may encounter parents or others who come with fixed ideas or complaints about various things. Sometimes such complaints may be about school personnel. It is advisable not to argue with such people and certainly important not to discuss colleagues with them. The art of listening to complaints and handling such situations judiciously, calmly, avoiding controversy, is one to cultivate. It is a professional asset to be able to differ without becoming angry, sarcastic, or discourteous.

Children

Relationship to those in therapy must follow acceptable patterns of behavior. Clinical distance on the part of the clinician is important, especially on the part of the inexperienced clinician. A person who can achieve this is more assured of the respect of his clients than one who thinks and acts too much the age of the children or youths. This does not imply a rigid person, but does imply a slight difference in status. The clinician is saying, in effect, not "I am superior to you," but, "in my field of specialty I possess knowledge and skills which are superior to yours." Avoiding physical contact or fondling is one means of helping achieve such status. Treating all on an equal basis is very essential. Firm but friendly management pays dividends.

In selection of individuals for treatment, as before mentioned, one must give careful thought to the *why* of selection and also to the *why* of dismissal, always acting in a way that is best for the individual who needs therapy.

Co-workers

Professional attitude towards co-workers should be observed as part of the ethical code of the speech clinician. Most school clinicians operate on an itinerant basis and are therefore in a position where they meet many administrators, teachers, and other professional workers. For example, on the average in an urban area, the clinician probably visits four schools during the week. Administrators differ in the policies they set up for their schools and staff. So as the clinician travels about, he must be an adjusting individual; but, in addition, he must be a good listener and a very poor reporter. By this we mean he does not relate from one school to another what he hears and sees. He remains an impartial observer, at least as far as verbalizing. If he is to maintain good working relationships, he must avoid personal controversy, seek professional discussion, and project the clinical techniques he has at his command in learning to understand the adults with whom he associates, seeking to recognize and appreciate their good qualities and skillfully finding many opportunities to foster mutual respect and cooperation.

The relationship between the clinician and other school personnel — superintendents, principals, nurses, visiting teachers, and others — should be one friendly give-and-take. Though these relationships will be discussed in detail in further chapters, we mention them here because it is an important function of the clinician to see that the speech program in the schools is well articulated with other areas.

Other Professions

The need for mutual understanding between various medical specialists, orthodontists, dental specialists, audiologists, psychologists, social workers, and speech clinicians is readily seen when one considers such disorders as cleft palate and lip, some voice problems, language dysfunctions, some cases of delayed speech, cerebral palsy, paralytic disorders, speech problems related to hearing disorders, orthodontic conditions, and the like. Many clinicians in the past have recognized this need and have laid foundations for such interdisciplinary understanding and mutual acquaintance with services rendered. And yet, there is pretty general agreement among these specialists that interdisciplinary communication is relatively poor, both with these individuals and ancillary services such as health departments and nursing services, and that each knows too little about what the others have to offer. This is unfortunate because many times the problems with which each is concerned are interrelated. It becomes more and more important, then, to set up better communication between these specialized areas so as to be of mutual assistance in diagnosis and treatment. In some communities, meetings have been arranged between groups representing the various specialists. Panel discussions have been conducted to create better understanding and to arrive at ideas for better communication. It is not the function of the speech clinician to make medical diagnosis or one which involves aspects which his training has not warranted. In turn, he may expect those in other professions not to advise in areas in which they are not qualified.

In order to gain and hold the respect of people in other disciplines, the clinician must be well informed. He must be aware of the need for referral, when indicated, to other specialists, but not make medical or dental diagnoses such as "infected tonsils" or similar diagnoses, and must be prepared to listen to others when their knowledge in a particular area has something of value to teach him. He must know the type of information he desires from other specialists but not accept a subservient role.

Supplementing One's Income

Private Practice

Rules regarding private practice in clinical speech should be carefully investigated before one undertakes such a venture. Clinical certification requirements of the American Speech and Hearing Association should be met if one is undertaking such work unless under the supervision of a person who is properly qualified. In such practice one works, as a rule, with those referred by professional workers, clinicians, physicians, psychologists, and others. It is well to refer to the code of ethics of the association before making plans to undertake such a venture. In addition to this, the clinician working in the schools needs to check to see if further rules are in effect. School systems differ in this respect, but in some communities the school clinician may not act as a paid private clinician for a child or youth enrolled in speech therapy or on a waiting list. It is also thought advisable not to enroll a child in a school speech clinic if that child is being seen by a private practitioner, the premise being that there may be a difference in therapy which may tend to confuse more than help the child.

Other Means

Rules regarding outside work are among those to which all school employees are expected to conform. An example might be that all employees shall devote their entire time during regular hours of employment designated for them for the duties to which they have been assigned. Such a rule does not apply to commitments after school hours. Clinicians sometimes supplement their income with outside employment of varying kinds. In many places this is permissible. However, since clinical speech is an energy-demanding profession, one must guard against work which is too time consuming and too strenuous or one contrary to professional image. Some school clinicians carry on private practice on the side. This appears to be acceptable if it conforms with the code of ethics of the American Speech and Hearing Association. However, one's first obligation is to the individual in the schools which employ the clinician.

As a specialist, the speech clinician needs his convictions, but he also needs to temper his approach to meet special situations and adjust to certain conditions. In addition, he needs to be constantly alert to ways in which he can improve therapy. He should be aware of ways in which he can contribute to research as well as to articles for the professional journals. He must constantly take stock of his assets and work to lessen his liabilities.

Self Rating

An experiment in self-analysis is often helpful. It is suggested that the readers follow the outline presented here, using the measures "Extremely Adequate," "Very Adequate," "Adequate," "Inadequate," or "Very Inadequate" as they check in the proper column their self-evaluation.

$\longrightarrow$

Qualities	Extremely Adequate	Very Adequate	Adequate	Inadequate	Very Inadequate
1. *Appearance* Makes a good impression Healthy Well groomed					
2. *Honesty* Truthful Trustworthy Professional integrity					
3. *Humility and Modesty* Respect for the opinion and rights of others Regard for rules and regulations Fraternizes with staff members Avoids attitude of superiority					
4. *Personality* Establishes rapport easily and quickly with adults and children Friendly Makes a good impression Happy and cheerful Tactful Courteous Patient Enthusiastic Tolerant Cooperative Businesslike					
5. *Dependability* Promptness: Keeps to schedules Records submitted on time Keeps appointments Follows through on suggestions					

QUALITIES	EXTREMELY ADEQUATE	VERY ADEQUATE	ADEQUATE	INADEQUATE	VERY INADEQUATE
5 (Continued) Starts tasks with a minimum waste of time Senses responsibility toward: The client The school The profession Self					
6. *Speech, voice, language, and hearing* Voice well modulated Good articulation Expresses ideas well Good command of English Discriminative hearing					
7. *Interests* Breadth of interests: Recreational Cultural Intellectual					
8. *Professional attitudes* Toward information: Refrains from gossip Toward other staff members General helpfulness and cooperation Refrains from overfamiliarity Self-improvement Ability to recognize areas of weakness Ability to work out remedies for weaknesses Affiliation with professional					

Qualities	Extremely Adequate	Very Adequate	Adequate	Inadequate	Very Inadequate

8 (Continued)
  organizations:
    A.S.H.A.
    State S.H.A.
    Others
  Certification in
    A.S.H.A.
  Attendance at
    workshops
  Attendance at
    conventions
  Keeping up
    therapeutic
    competence
  Ability to
    relate well to
    those in other
    disciplines:
    medical, dental,
    etc.					

9. *Organization of*
  program
  Selection of cases:
    Surveys
    Testing
    Diagnosis
  Scheduling of
    classes:
    Well thought
      out in relation
      to all con-
      cerned
    Obtaining
      suitable
      working
      facilities—
      making needs
      understood
    Making the most
      of available
      facilities,
      effort to
      improve
      appearance of
      the room and
      make it as
      attractive as
      possible
    Learning names
      of those in
      therapy					

10. *Clinical planning*
  Creativeness and
    originality shown
    in planning
    therapy					

QUALITIES	EXTREMELY ADEQUATE	VERY ADEQUATE	ADEQUATE	INADEQUATE	VERY INADEQUATE
10 (Continued) Well-thought-out plans and assignments Ability to motivate and stimulate participation and hold the attention and interest of those in therapy Ability to shift procedures if things planned work out poorly Ability to handle interruptions and take care of emergencies Ability to understand and help children having behavior problems					
11. *Objectivity* Willingness and ability to look at one's self and evaluate one's own assets and liabilities					

SUMMARY

Responsibilities

This chapter considers specifically the responsibilities of the clinician working or planning to do clinical speech work in the schools. Three main areas of responsibility have been discussed: the *individual* and his understanding of self and others, his personality and character, and his relationship to others; the *professional* and his responsibility to organizations, certification, self-improvement, community, and political interests, and *ethical* responsibilities.

A school clinician must be cognizant of the need for understanding self and others and will realize that this requires hard work, enduring patience, certain character and personality traits. In addition he must be aware of the need for a close alliance between speech and hearing services, educational staff, administrators, curriculum consultants, and guidance personnel if a sound therapy program is to materialize. Teacher education is most vital. Parents of children and youths having speech problems need guidance, and this takes careful handling. Speech therapy extends beyond the therapy room and school into the community. There should be a close relationship with other specialists — doctors, dentists, audiologists, psychologists, and personnel in social agencies. Through trustworthy leadership and careful attention to ethical practices the clinician will win confidence and set up a system of communication feedback from himself to the lay and professional community and back to him. He will be aware that all these responsibilities demand a program for constant self-improvement. To quote Eleanor Roosevelt, "Don't dry by inaction — but go out and do things; learn things and see new things with your own eyes. Don't believe what somebody tells you, but know things yourself by your own contacts with life."

Satisfactions

Implied throughout this chapter are the satisfactions derived of working with those who need one's help. Successful clinicians will guarantee that satisfactions are many and tend to outweigh the discouragements. To see individuals who have been unable to verbally communicate adequately become participating members of their community is rewarding in itself for the effort put forth. In addition, in any job well done the ego is exploited, giving a sense of achievement, but more important the honesty and sincerity demanded of the clinician and the involvement in something greater than one's own selfish interests are the things that give true meaning to the profession of speech pathology.

DISCUSSION TOPICS

1. Discuss some of the essential characteristics and personal qualities of a successful clinician.
2. How can the clinician give an image of the truly professional person?

3. How can a clinician coming into a school system change any unfavorable impressions which may possibly have been created previous to his coming?
4. There is an old adage, "When in Rome do as the Romans." How can this apply to the clinician working in the schools?
5. How can prejudice affect the quality of work which the clinician is able to do?
6. The American Speech and Hearing Association is the official organization in the field of speech and hearing. Assume that you have been asked to influence a clinician to affiliate with this organization and its state counterpart. Present the issue.
7. It has been suggested that other disciplines may be involved in the speech correction program. Enumerate some and indicate the relationships.
8. What dangers do you see in not maintaining clinical distance?
9. Why would it be wise not to use the term "cure" in relation to a speech disorder?
10. Summarize the essential ethical practices for a school clinician.
11. What are some of the essential qualities of good speech therapy?
12. Why is the clinician advised not to start formal therapy on first meeting with the child?
13. When do you especially need to take a look at yourself?
14. What satisfactions do you predict for a job well done?
15. Enumerate reasons for fraternizing with other staff members in the schools in which one works.

REFERENCES

1. AINSWORTH, S., Ed.: Speech and hearing problems in the secondary school. *Bull Nat Ass Secondary School Principals, 34,* November, 1950.
2. ALLEN, E. Y., *et al.*: Case selection in the public schools. *J Speech Hearing Dis, 31:*157-161, May, 1966.
3. BARNHART, C. L., Ed.: *The American College Dictionary.* New York, Random House, 1956 .
4. BLACK, M.: *Speech Correction in the Schools.* Englewood Cliffs, New Jersey, Prentice-Hall, 1964.
5. BRYNGELSON, B.: *Personality Development through Speech.* Minneapolis, Denison, 1964.

6. *Career Information Booklet on Speech Pathology and Audiology. ASHA, 6:*168, May, 1964.
7. *Directory. ASHA,* Washington, D.C., 1967.
8. Executive Council, ASHA: The speech clinician's role in the public school. *ASHA, 6:*189-191, June, 1964.
9. JOHNSON, W., and SPRIESTERSBACH, D. C.: *Diagnostic Methods in Speech Pathology.* New York, Harper, 1963.
10. KELLER, S.: *Learning Reinforcement Theory.* New York, Random, 1954.
11. LIDDLE, G. L.: Pupil personnel services as seen by the speech specialist. *ASHA, 9:*43-44, November, 1967.
12. LILLYWHITE, H. S., and SLEETOR, R. L.: Some problems of relationship between speech and hearing specialists and those in the medical profession. *ASHA, 1,* December, 1959.
13. McDONALD, E. T.: *Understand Those Feelings.* Pittsburgh, Stanwix House, 1962.
14. Minneapolis Public Schools: *Speech Correction in Practice.* Minneapolis, Board of Education, 1961.
15. National Society for the Study of Education: *Theories of Learning and Instruction,* 63rd Yearbook. 1964.
16. OVERSTREET, H. A.: *The Mature Mind.* New York, Norton, 1949.
17. PERKINS, W. H.: Our profession: What is it? *ASHA, 4:*339-344, October, 1962.
18. POWERS, M. H.: What makes an effective public school speech therapist? *J Speech Hearing Dis, 21:*463-467, December, 1956.
19. SHEEHAN, J.; BADLEY, R., and WHITE, G.: The speech pathologist: his interests, activities, and attitudes. *J Speech Hearing Dis, 25:*317-322, 1960.
20. STEER, M. (Project Director), and DARLEY, F., Ed.: Public school speech and hearing services. *J Speech Hearing Dis, Monogr Suppl 8,* June, 1961.
21. VAN HATTUM, R.: The defensive speech clinician in the schools. *J Speech Hearing Dis, 31:*234-240, August, 1966.
22. VAN RIPER, C.: *Speech Correction Principles and Methods.* Englewood Cliffs, N. J., Prentice-Hall, 1963.
23. WEBSTER, E. J., *et al.*: Case selection in the schools. *J Speech Hearing Dis, 31:*352-358, November, 1966.

Chapter 3

THE SPEECH CLINICIAN — AS A MEMBER OF THE EDUCATIONAL TEAM

FREDERICK E. GARBEE

T HE SPEECH CLINICIAN is an essential member of the school's professional staff. In today's enlightened school environment he is recognized as a significant contributor to the total welfare and educational achievement of the child with a communication disorder. The clinician plays a vital role in assisting the school in accomplishing its commitment to education.

COMMITMENT TO EDUCATION IN OUR SOCIETY

The school's commitment to education embraces an ideal of the best education possible for every citizen including children with communication disorders. This commitment includes an interest in the quantity and quality of education at all levels. It encompasses achieving competence in skills, e.g. reading and arithmetic, as well as general competence such as ability to work cooperatively towards group goals, development of problem-solving skills, flexibility in behavior and thought, and creativity.

In order to fulfill this commitment to education, schools are assigned the systematic development of intellectual, social, and vocational competence of the individual child. Also, the effective school is always concerned with the promotion of physical and mental health as well as satisfying human relationships in a setting of moral and ethical values. Its teaching must be based upon the best that is known about human development and the understanding and application of learning concepts.

An important study by the Educational Policies Commission of the National Education Association stated these basic areas as essential to a good educational program.

1. The objectives of self-realization.
2. The objectives of human relationship.

3. The objectives of economic efficiency.

4. The objectives of civic responsibility.*

An even more specific statement of the role of the public school is found in the conference statement of the 1956 White House Conference on Education which encompasses the following points:

1. The fundamental skills of communication — reading, writing, spelling — as well as other elements of effective oral and written expression; the arithmetical skills, including problem solving. While schools are doing the best job in their history in teaching these skills, continuous improvement is desirable and necessary.
2. Appreciation for our democratic heritage.
3. Civic rights and responsibilities and knowledge of American institutions.
4. Respect for and appreciation of human values and for the beliefs of others.
5. Ability to think and evaluate constructively and creatively.
6. Effective work habits and self-discipline.
7. Social competency as a contributing member of his family and community.
8. Ethical behavior based on a sense of moral and spiritual values.
9. Intellectual curiosity and eagerness for lifelong learning.
10. Esthetic appreciation and self-expression in the arts.
11. Physical and mental health.
12. Wise use of time, including constructive leisure pursuits.
13. Understanding of the physical world and man's relation to it as represented through basic knowledge of the sciences.
14. An awareness of our relationships with the world community.*

The object of the educative process in our schools is to assist the child by increasing his power to communicate, to understand, and to live effectively and meaningfully with his fellows, to emphasize what is possessed in common and what makes a community possible.

While the common characteristics of people make a community possible, it is their uncommon qualities that make it better. Leadership, variety, innovation, and progress, to a great extent, come only from individuality. As a part of our commitment to the

---

*Educational Policies Commission. *The Purposes of Education in American Democracy*. Washington, D. C., NEA, 1938.

*The Committee for *The White House Conference on Education*. Washington, D.C., Government Printing Office, 1965, pp. 91-92.

educative process of children our educational purpose must be understood in the broad framework of our convictions concerning the worth of the individual and the importance of individual fulfillment.

SCHOOL SYSTEMS AND THEIR ROLES IN EDUCATION

Just what is a school system like? What is this employment environment in which the competent speech clinician is to work?

Actually, the citizens in each state in the United States hold the key to the potentialities of education. They elect the legislators who, representing the citizens, determine the enactment of laws pertaining to education. In most local communities the citizens select the members of the board of education. In many communities citizens' committees have been organized to assist the local school board and the staff with studies and problems.

The board of education in the local community represents the people of the school district on matters pertaining to the schools, yet it does not administer school affairs. The chief functions of the board are to select a well-qualified administrator and assign him the responsibility of operating the educational program and to determine policies in developing and carrying out the school system's program.

A good board of education distinguishes between its responsibilities as a policy-making body and the superintendent's (administrator's) responsibility as its executive officer. The board should guarantee freedom for expression of local ideas and freedom for tailoring school programs to fit local needs. The board also does not limit itself to business and financial affairs alone, but also considers educational problems and policies brought to it by the superintendent. The board establishes personnel policies wherein the superintendent represents the board in negotiating with the staff of the schools. The superintendent makes all personnel recommendations for the board's consideration, including employment, promotion, and dismissal.

The administrator or superintendent of schools is usually the secretary and executive officer of the board. He executes the policies formulated and adopted by the board. Ideally, he is the educational leader in the community. He should provide leadership in facing and solving problems in building an effective school system. The administrator must be efficient in making decisions, organizing, planning, communicating, influencing, coordinating, and evaluating the many aspects of the educational process.

The staff of a school system may include professional members such as teachers, principals, supervisors, psychologists, speech clinicians, social workers, and counselors. It may also include custodians, bus drivers, clerical and secretarial staff. In effective school systems the staff cooperates with the superintendent and the board, and through a cooperative endeavor promotes developing policies and planning in carrying out a good program. In planning and providing for good schools this teamwork and coordination is so very important.

The organization and the administration of education in this country vary greatly from state to state and often among communities within the same state. The similarities appear to outweigh the differences, however.

The State

The major responsibility for education is found in the states rather than in the federal government. The people of each state make the basic policies and framework for education through their constitutional provisions and laws enacted by their legislatures. State boards of education have been established by most states to determine state-wide policies and rules and regulations relating to the operation of the schools. A chief state school officer (state superintendent of schools or director of instruction) has been provided by all states. He usually serves as executive officer of the state board. A state department of education, i.e. state educational agency, is responsible to the chief state school officer, and through him to the state board in providing leadership, developing policies and regulations, and carrying out research and studies relating to the educational program.

Even though a consultant of a state educational agency or state department of education is not ordinarily a member of the educational team providing direct services to children, he has an important role in providing professionally sound programs for communication impaired children. Most state departments of education employ consultants in speech and hearing. Consultants in speech and hearing in state departments of education or state educational agencies have the following duties:

1. Providing statewide consultative services to all counties and school districts needing assistance.
2. Cooperating and participating in district, county, regional, and state conferences and in projects pertaining to meeting the needs of children with speech and hearing handicaps.
3. Promoting an understanding of sound professional criteria and the procedures used in establishing and maintaining public school programs for the speech handicapped and hard of hearing.
4. Identifying needs and areas for development and improvement in the state's programs for the speech and hearing handicapped as an outgrowth of objective study, research, and observation.
5. Promoting and assisting in establishing and organizing programs in locales where programs are nonexistent or in need of expansion.
6. Explaining state department of education policies, standards, and regulations.
7. Evaluating objectively speech and hearing services throughout the state.
8. Working closely with college and university personnel responsible for the preparation of speech clinicians and placing primary importance on keeping the colleges informed of public school needs, objectives, and unique characteristics.
9. Encouraging sound professional standards and practices for all speech clinicians.
10. Working closely with professional organizations promoting the enhancement of research and services to children with speech and hearing handicaps.
11. Representing within the department of education the interests of speech and hearing handicapped children.
12. Preparing information for dissemination which will assist those responsible for helping children with speech and hearing disorders.
13. Coordinating information on professional needs, with supporting evidence for meeting these needs, and channeling this information to the state department of education for consideration and possible action.

The Local School District or School System

Local school districts or school systems have been provided by all states. Some states have fewer than one hundred; others have over five thousand districts. The small school districts established in the early days of the country are definitely on the decline. They

SIMPLIFIED ORGANIZATION CHART

LOS ANGELES CITY SCHOOLS

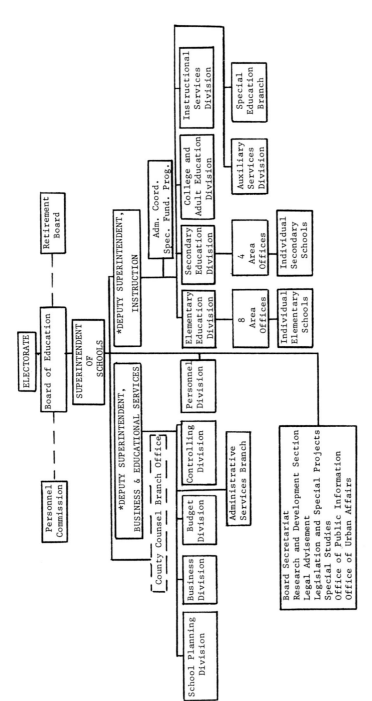

*In the absence of the Superintendent, a designated Deputy Superintendent assumes full responsibility for all divisions.

FIGURE 2. A large school system, Los Angeles.

are being replaced in many parts of the country by more efficient and satisfactory larger (unified) districts.

The local system is responsible for the organization and implementation of school programs within its area. Within the boundaries of state legal provisions, the people in each local school system determine directly or indirectly the essence of the educational program. The people of the area usually elect a lay board of education to determine policies. The board selects a superintendent of schools who is the administrator. On his recommendations the needed staff is appointed to operate the schools.

The individual school in the local school system is organized to carry out an instructional program for students. A principal is

LOCAL SCHOOL ORGANIZATION

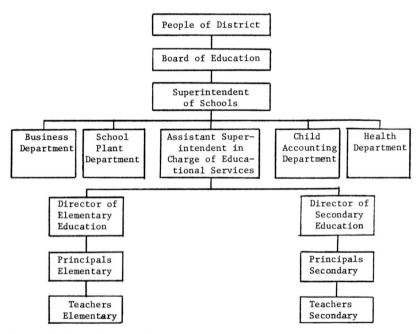

FIGURE 3. Simplified sketch of line-and-staff plan of organization of local school personnel. By permission from *Local Public School Administration,* by Benjamin F. Pittenger, p. 47. Copyright, 1951, McGraw-Hill Book Company, Inc.

usually the local school administrator. Sometimes in small districts the superintendent serves as the principal of the school. The principal is the main spokesman for the school in the local community. It is very important for the speech clinician and the school principal to understand one another's roles and functions. They can be of great assistance to one another in helping the child with a communication disorder.

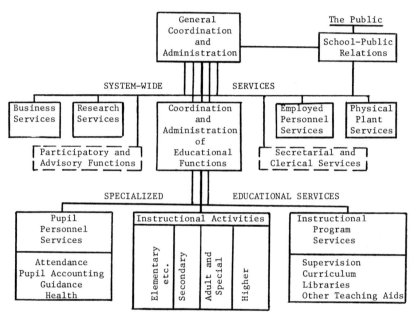

FIGURE 4. Function of local public school personnel. By permission from *Local Public School Administration,* by Benjamin F. Pittenger, p. 65. Copyright, 1951, McGraw-Hill Book Company, Inc.

The better school programs are always making energetic efforts to know thoroughly the wide variation in interests, needs, and abilities existing among pupils. They are constantly redefining and reappraising their goals in terms of the changing needs of society. The effective school is also evaluating the outcomes of its program in terms of the development of individual pupils and the successes of its graduates. It is striving to improve its methods for encouraging the development and success of individual pupils. In providing a staff, materials of instruction, and physical facilities, it insures, along with good service, the maximum progress of each pupil towards his specific educational goals.

No two schools are exactly alike. This is also true of all school systems. The speech clinician should be realistic in his conceptualization of the public schools and be aware of the many idiosyncracies in organization from one program or system to another. Figures 2, 3, 4, and 5 show only four examples among an infinite variety of school system organizations.

In many parts of the nation the trend seems to be to have the speech clinician work directly under the supervision of a director of special services or special education. In other school systems he

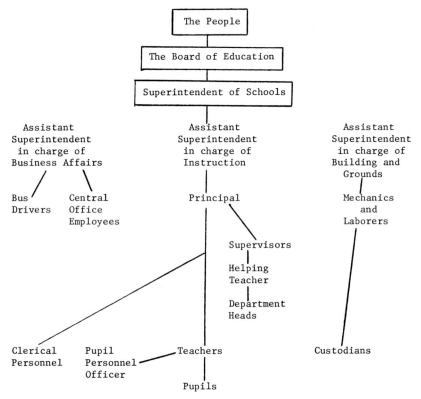

FIGURE 5. An example of an administrative staff's organization in a large school district.

may be supervised under the director of pupil personnel services. The speech clinician should be alert to policies in a school system which give him the prerogatives and flexibilities necessary to carry out a good clinical program of thorough assessment as well as speech, hearing, or language therapy for the pupil with a communication disorder.

The Intermediate Unit

In many states the intermediate unit for schools, oftentimes known as the county schools office, performs a valuable coordinating function. It usually provides leadership and services to certain or all districts in the area. It also compiles and transmits important information on the schools' programs. These intermediate units may cross county lines. Many of the large counties employ county speech and hearing consultants or coordinators. Their responsibilities may include the following:

1. Planning professional meetings to better coordinate efforts and upgrade services to children with speech, hearing, and language disorders. Each year specific meetings may be coordinated for all concerned with the speech and hearing programs, i.e. a county-wide orientation meeting for all new personnel and administrators, an all-day study conference, monthly area institutes for district clinicians, meetings with personnel from the state department of education, other county offices, and those who work in community centers. Additional professional and working committee meetings are held as needed and requested.

2. Working closely with the state department of education and clarifying state policies, standards, and regulations for school districts.

3. Working with school district personnel, upon request, in a joint evaluation of their speech and hearing program for the purpose of improvement of service and better integration with the total school program.

4. Giving consultative service to those concerned with speech and hearing programs in areas such as legal aspects, scheduling and organization of programs, assessment of children, parent conferences, therapy, and coordinative responsibilities.

5. Assisting school districts in planning and establishing new speech and hearing programs, and in expanding programs already in existence.

6. Coordinating the publication of a county speech and hearing communication exchange, guidebooks, films and filmstrips, and other speech and hearing projects and materials requested by the profession.

7. Coordinating joint research projects involving school districts,

colleges and universities, the state department of education, other county school offices, and professional organizations.

8. Helping small school districts in identifying and evaluating children with speech, hearing, and language disorders; holding conferences with administrators, parents, and teachers, and, when indicated, making referrals to community facilities.

9. Planning with local colleges and universities for the education and orientation of students who plan to work in school speech and hearing programs.

10. Working closely with professional organizations.

The Federal Government

In the United States the Federal Government has no direct control over the organization and administration of education. The Federal Government has established within the Department of Health, Education, and Welfare an Office of Education to provide leadership and information; it administers funds that have been provided by Congress for certain areas of education, and it carries out certain coordinating functions. Recently the Federal Government has assumed its appropriate role in assuring adequate educational opportunity for all American children. Educational needs in an increasingly complex society are national in scope; state and local financial resources are now being complemented and supplemented by significant federal support. The United States Office of Education has consulting and coordinating personnel in the area of speech and hearing to augment and improve services and research in the fields of speech pathology and audiology as they relate to school programs.

The Role of the School Administrator

Leadership and cooperation from school administrators and supervisors are extremely crucial to the success and effectiveness of the speech and hearing program. Ideally, school administrators will do the following to ensure that pupils with speech and hearing handicaps be given the help they need:

1. Encourage communication among their staff members, including the speech clinician. Through bulletins, memoranda, and other established media of communication within the school system, e.g. discussion at staff meetings, elucidation of the speech clinician's services including the nature, scope, and availability of his services may encourage a better flow of information among staff members concerning

individual students with whom the clinician is extending his services. The support and endorsement of the clinician's speech program and services may be of immeasurable assistance, particularly to the beginning clinician.

2. Keep informed regarding the roles of the speech clinician. The well-informed administrator keeps himself up to date on the philosophy and nature of speech pathology as it relates to the service of the speech clinician in his school system. By conferring with the clinician, maintaining mutual professional respect, and sharing ideas, he keeps informed of this complementary service to individuals with communication impairments in his school or school system.

3. Support development and expansion of the speech and hearing program. The effective administrator acknowledges the importance of special programs as well as programs for the majority of the pupils in his school. His support manifests itself in his pursuing all avenues possible in obtaining financial support for programs, upholding the best recommended professional standards, and encouraging improvement and enhancement of programs when needs exist.

4. Urge and assist speech clinicians to attend local, state, and national professional conferences to increase their professional growth and effectiveness. In-service training and professional development contribute to upgrading and perfecting needed services to the communication-impaired pupils with whom the clinician works. The administrator may be of valuable assistance to the program by being sympathetic to in-service activities, representing the speech clinician in getting board approval for participation in conferences, and recommending financial support for such endeavors.

5. Encourage classroom teachers to participate in the speech and hearing program. Ask the classroom teachers to cooperate with the speech clinician when children need to be scheduled for therapy or need special assessment by the clinician or other specialists. Let the teacher know she is a valuable member of the professional team in understanding and alleviating the child's communication disorder. Encourage the teacher to take the initiative in contacting the speech clinician when a need exists for a better understanding of any individual child. Suggest to teachers that they air freely their needs in meeting the special needs of the communication impaired child.

6. Seek support for adequate local financing of the program. The effective administrator studies the financial adequacies and inadequacies of his speech and hearing program. He recommends augmentation of the support of the program, if needed, and furnishes specific evidence for that which is needed. He never permits financial inadequacies to defeat his program until all avenues of local, state, and federal support have been exhausted.

7. Help secure and maintain community understanding and acceptance of the program. Furnishing the board of education with information about the nature and scope of the speech and hearing porgram and sending press releases to local papers are helpful in keeping the

community informed. Encouraging the speech clinician to meet with parent and teacher groups is desirable. Upholding the highest standards in speech therapy services to students needing the help is probably the most effective way to maintain acceptance of the program.
8. Support study and research on a school district and county level. Research delving into the merits of various practices and procedures in surveying, assessment, and therapy may call attention to areas needing improvement in the program. Studies showing specific results of therapy or the extent of needs in the school system may contribute information needed in supporting and perpetuating the speech habilitation and rehabilitation program. An ongoing alertness to study, research, and evaluation of the program is vital in a progressive program.

The initial success of the speech and hearing program depends, to a great extent, on the superintendent's support. It is important that he show interest in this program as he does in any other phase of educational programs offered by the school system. He needs to interpret the program accurately to the board of education and seek its support. Understanding and support are equally important in informing the community, classroom teachers, supervisors, other administrators, and specialists throughout the school system.

The continued success of the speech and hearing program depends considerably on the cooperation of the school principal. He can aid the program in these ways:

1. Provide quiet facilities in the school where diagnosis and therapy can be done with few interruptions.
2. Visit therapeutic sessions and confer with the clinician as frequently as he does with teachers and other school personnel.
3. Cooperate with the speech clinician in scheduling children for therapy and in seeing that the schedule is maintained.
4. Provide the opportunities for the clinicians to meet with parent and teacher groups to explain the purposes and goals of the speech and hearing program.
5. Make it apparent to everyone concerned that the speech clinician is an essential member of the school staff.
6. Keep well informed about the speech and hearing program so that he can accurately and realistically discuss it with members of the community.

The principal is sometimes the immediate supervisor of the speech clinician. He is very often the most direct liaison with the classroom teacher. Most often he is the real spokesman in the community of closest proximity for all of his school's functioning. It is therefore so very essential for the speech clinician and principal to understand, appreciate, and support one another's role and function.

Other administrative personnel in the public schools, including directors of special education, supervisors of speech and hearing, and elementary and secondary supervisors in charge of all special programs, play vital roles in ensuring that the speech and hearing services in their schools are effective. The people in these positions should work closely with the speech clinician. Whenever a speech clinician is employed in a specific school system he should familiarize himself with the availability of these professional staff members. District policies vary in assignments of these individuals but in almost every instance a close working relationship between them and the speech clinician is necessary and advantageous. In working with the speech clinician their duties usually include:

1. Carrying out policies concerning speech and hearing services as they relate to the total school program; these policies should clearly reflect the professional objectives and standards of the field of speech and language pathology.
2. Serve as liaison between the clinician and other school administrators when appropriate.
3. Coordinate and use the services of all personnel available in the school system with the services of the speech and hearing clinician as feasible.
4. Assist the speech clinician in obtaining adequate materials, equipment, and working facilities.
5. Provide secretarial assistance for the speech clinician.

The supervisor of speech and hearing services contributes to the efficiency of the school's program in the following ways:

1. Provides specialized staff assistance to speech clinicians and to other personnel concerned in the development, coordination, and maintenance of the speech and hearing program.
2. Acts as administrator for speech clinicians.
3. Serves as a consultant to line and staff officials in the regular school program.
4. Furnishes specialized technical assistance in the evaluation, selection, and effective use of specific instructional and clinical materials, equipment, and supplies.
5. Assists in conducting research to improve the program.
6. Participates in the preparation of resource materials.

7. Participates in the promotion of in-service professional growth, teacher training, and personnel activities such as employment and evaluation of speech clinicians.
8. Carries out policies established by the local school system and the state department of education.
9. Functions as liaison representative of his administrative office in committees, conferences, and meetings related to speech and hearing (for lay and professional groups).

When personnel and services of different school systems are shared, all administrators concerned should understand their roles and make maximum use of the services and personnel. Conferences to clarify procedures should be held during the beginning stages of the program, whenever policy changes occur, and whenever new personnel are added to the program.

The Role of the Classroom Teacher

The classroom teacher, of course, greatly influences the development of a child with a speech and hearing handicap. Motivating the child to improve his speech and language and incorporating well-planned objectives for speech and language development in classroom curricula are vital goals the classroom teacher should seek.

To qualify as an effective classroom teacher for the speech or hearing handicapped child, the teacher should do the following:

1. Accept the child and help his classmates accept him.
2. Make sure that the classroom invites communication.
3. Foster good relationships among the children.
4. Be cooperative.
5. Take the necessary steps to make his own speech and voice worthy of imitation.
6. Hear accurately the speech errors his children make.
7. Have accurate knowledge of how the sounds of our speech are produced.
8. Create a good speech environment for speech and language improvement.
9. Be cognizant of the values of speech and hearing services.
10. Be able to identify students in his class who need the speech clinician's service.
11. Understand normal speech and language development and concepts.
12. Be well informed on how to incorporate the objectives of the speech and language program with the objectives of the regular classroom curricula.

Appropriate times for scheduling children in the therapy sessions should be arranged as a cooperative endeavor between the classroom teacher and the speech clinician. If possible, children should be scheduled for speech therapy sessions so that they can continue to participate in the major school activities. Denying the children opportunity to participate in these activities may make them feel resentful, isolated, different, or penalized because of their speech and hearing handicap. Still, if the child has a severe handicap, speech therapy may be more valuable to him than any other school subject or activity scheduled at a conflicting time.

The classroom teacher and the speech clinician have separate but joint roles in the development of good speech for all children. The teacher and clinician work closely together in sharing the responsibility of distinguishing which children need speech improvement and which children need clinical speech services. The clinician makes the final decision concerning which children will be placed in his case load for therapeutic services. The effective speech and hearing clinician profits from valuable information furnished by the classroom teacher. In turn, the teacher may integrate suggestions given by the speech and hearing clinician into the child's daily experiences.

THE CLINICAL SPEECH PROGRAM AND THE SCHOOLS

The child's ability to preserve and utilize his individuality is enhanced by his effectivenes in communicating.

Through communication a child both conveys and interprets feelings and thoughts as he interacts with other individuals. In the process of communication, language becomes the all-encompassing construct of symbols used to represent experiences, thoughts, and feelings, and a child needs language if he is to comprehend the speech of others and express his ideas through the medium of speech. Teaching accurate speech to the child, therefore, is a vital aspect of a good language program and important to meeting the child's total communication needs.

In order to understand and help the child with a communication disorder, his maturation, intelligence, physical condition, hearing, motivation, psychosexual development, environment, social behavior, and emotional development must be understood. All perceptual and cognitive aspects of the individual need to be carefully considered. Achieving this goal in the educational setting of the school demands coordination and unity of an educational team. The speech clinician must receive from and extend cooperation to parents, teachers, psychologists, nurses, school administrators, and other school personnel if his services for the child are to be effective.

The primary purpose of clinical speech programs in the schools is to provide a thorough assessment, diagnosis, and evaluation of each child's speech, language and/or hearing disorder and to provide a therapeutic program to meet the individual's needs. In meeting these individual needs, coordination of services and cooperation of school personnel are essential and extremely important.

In discussing "the speech clinician—as a member of the educational team," focus in this chapter is on an overall understanding of the school, its place in the community, and the speech clinician's position as related to the public school as his employment context. No written information or explanation of the educative process or the schools or the educational team is a good substitute for the real primary experiences an individual speech clinician may receive from observing and functioning in the schools themselves. All encompassing college and/or university curricula are developed and available on the many aspects of public education, e.g. school organization and administration. No attempt is being made in this chapter to make a comprehensive coverage of the many aspects of public school education including a detailed explanation of public school systems. Instead, emphasis is placed here on calling the speech clinician's attention to the realization that his speech program must be planned and carried out in a manner consistent with the primary goals and functions of the schools. This means the clinician must possess and demonstrate sufficient knowledge of the goals and processes of public education to coordinate and integrate the speech program with the total educational program of the school.

As stated by the Council for Exceptional Children the following competencies must be assured in the speech clinician:

1. Knowledge of goals, general organization and procedures for achieving these goals, and the basic issues in public education.
2. Knowledge of the school's responsibilities and of the way the responsibilities of the speech and hearing specialist relate to this broader framework.
3. Awareness of the precise contributions that the speech and hearing program makes to the total educational program.
4. Preparation for participation in activities usually associated with speech and hearing programs in the schools; for example, conferring with parents and teachers, conducting speech and hearing surveys, and preparing reports.*

These competencies should complement the competencies specified in meeting the certification requirements established by the American Speech and Hearing Association.

The role of the speech and hearing clinician in the public schools is a vital one. All of the clinicians are obligated to uphold the best professional standards, a responsibility which involves their assisting the school systems in which they are working to establish policies and procedures which will provide for speech and hearing programs that effectively meet the needs of the children being served.

Among responsibilities of the clinician is knowing how to make the special speech and hearing program objectives further those of the regular school program. This means cooperating with other teachers and administrators in scheduling speech therapy sessions, always notifying school officials of changes in schedules, and attending faculty meetings to keep well informed regarding school policies.

Another important responsibility of the clinician is making proper referrals to other professional personnel within the school program or in the community. Many children with speech and hearing handicaps also have physical, educational, psychological, and social problems which require the services of a physician, psy-

---

Professional Standards for Personnel in the Education of Exceptional Children (Professional Standards Project Report). Washington, D.C., The Council for Exceptional Children, 1966.

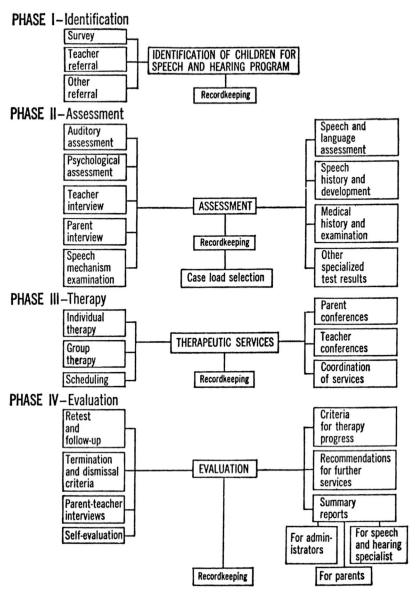

FIGURE 6. A comprehensive program for speech and hearing handicapped children. The California Program. Prepared by Frederick E. Garbee, *California State Department of Education Bulletin, Vol. XXXIII (4):12, 1964.*

chologist or psychiatrist, social worker, counsellor, nurse, or audiometrist, to name a few. If medical help is needed, this should be given before any therapeutic goals are established. All phases of a speech and hearing program as shown in Figure 6 should be given careful attention and recognition.

In all four phases of a comprehensive program for speech impaired children, a team approach is so essential. In identifying children in Phase 1, for example, without the cooperation of teachers, principals, and clinicians the task could not be accomplished. Scheduling the appropriate time for surveying, locating a site for the clinician to work, obtaining basic information on each child, contacting the parent about the survey results, all demand a team approach.

In Phase 2, 3, and 4, the role of the parent on the educational team is indeed evident. The parent's role should never be overlooked in an effective speech and hearing program in the school. Not only does the parent supply the professional team with information but he or she also contributes insight into the interpersonal (parent, peer, sibling) relationships and an infinite number of variables in understanding the many facets of the child's development.

Hoffman and Hoffman (1966), in their *Review of Child Development Research,* synthesize findings which clearly point out not only the influences of parents on children and their development but also the dynamics of parental participation in the child's maturational processes. In other words, evidence is available to show that the clinician must always include the parent in the team in habilitating, rehabilitating, and educating the communicatively handicapped child.

Parents may become part of the team by the following ways:

1. Contributing information to the clinician and other school personnel about the child.
2. Solving psychological problems which may contribute to the child's disorder.
3. Assisting the clinician in carrying out therapeutic goals for the child when appropriate.
4. Helping the child "carry over" the accomplishments of his therapy.
5. Contributing to the child's self-concept, identity and maturation.
6. Cooperating with school personnel in the educative process.

Parents may function on the educational team by writing communications, telephoning, and attending conferences. Conferences may be with the clinician and 1) parent (s) , 2) parent and child, 3) parent, child, and teacher, 4) parent and teacher, 5) counsellor, parent and child, 6) parent and administrator, or any other combination deemed necessary.

The role of the speech clinician on the educational team is not an easy one. He must continually make his unique objectives and capabilities known. He is a specialist with skills geared to appraising and assessing the child with a communicative handicap. One of his major goals is to utilize his assessment findings to guide him in eradicating the child's communicative disorder in a therapeutic setting. In accomplishing this goal the clinician, along with his professional colleagues and parents, must complement the other educational processes in the child's total development.

SUMMARY

The speech clinician plays a vital role in assisting the school in meeting its responsibilities of providing the best possible education for each citizen.

The clinician must understand the nature of the school system in which he functions. The board of education represents the people of the school district, yet it does not administer school affairs. This responsibility is delegated to the administrative staff headed by the superintendent.

Although the organization and administration of school programs may vary from one school district to another, certain similarities exist. For example, it is the state's major responsibility to provide education for its citizens rather than the federal government's. From a speech standpoint, it is the state consultant in speech and hearing who represents the clinicians in the state department of education and who works cooperatively with colleagues throughout the state in schools and in training centers.

It is the local school district which has the most direct responsibility for the school program. The local board of education employs a superintendent and school principals. The principal is usually the local school administrator and is most directly responsible for the clinical speech program. The speech clinician should work closely with the school principal and be well informed in the area of local policies.

Whether the clinician works for a local district or intermediate district, it is becoming increasingly likely that he will be under a supervisor of speech and hearing. This person can provide many important functions to assist the clinician in functioning more effectively.

The importance of the classroom teacher cannot be overstated. The classroom teacher and the speech clinician have separate but joint roles in the development of good speech for all children.

Finally, in addition to school administrators and teachers, other specialists function as important members of the educational team. In addition to psychologists, nurses, and social workers, parents play a vital role.

It is the wise speech clinician who not only understands his role as a member of the educational team but who, in addition, understands, respects, and utilizes to the fullest advantage other members of the team in order to assist each child toward his potential.

DISCUSSION TOPICS

1. What are the relative responsibilities of the state and Federal governments in education?
2. In what ways has this appeared to change in recent years?
3. What is the relationship of the state department of education to local districts?
4. What are the advantages and disadvantages of the federal-state-intermediate district-local district hierarchy?
5. Why should the speech clinician be familiar with local board policies?
6. How can the relationship between the speech clinician and school principal affect the clinical speech program?
7. What advantages are there for the clinician to work in a district where adequate supervision exists?
8. What is adequate supervision and who should provide it?
9. What barriers exist to the adequate functioning of an "educational team"?

10. Who comprises the team and what is the role of each member?

REFERENCES

1. AINSWORTH, S.: The speech clinician in public schools: Participant or separatist? *ASHA, 7:*495-503, December, 1965.
2. AINSWORTH, S.: *Speech Correction Methods, A Manual of Speech Therapy and Public School Procedures.* Englewood Cliffs, New Jersey, Prentice-Hall, 1948.
3. AMERICAN SPEECH AND HEARING ASSOCIATION, STEER, M. (Project Director), and DARLEY, F., Ed.: Public school speech and hearing services. *J Speech Hearing Dis, Monogr Suppl 8,* June, 1961.
4. BLACK, M. E.: *Speech Correction in the Schools.* Englewood Cliffs, New Jersey, Prentice-Hall, 1964.
5. BRICKMAN, W. W.: *Educational Systems in the United States.* New York, Center for Applied Research in Education, 1964.
6. BRUNER, J. S.: *The Process of Education.* Cambridge, Harvard, 1960.
7. BURR, J. B.; COFFIELD, W.; JENSON, T. J., and NEAGLEY, R. L.: *Elementary School Administration.* Boston, Allyn & Bacon, 1963.
8. CAMPBELL, B.: *Sixty-three Tested Practices in School-Community Relations.* New York, Bureau of Publications, Columbia University, 1954.
9. DEAN, S. E.: *Elementary School Organization and Administration.* Washington, D.C., U.S. Dept. HEW, Bulletin 11, 1960.
10. Educational Policies Commission: *Education for All American Children.* Washington, D.C., N.E.A., 1948.
11. EISENSON, J., and OGILVIE, M.: *Speech Correction in the Schools,* 2nd ed. New York, Macmillan, 1963.
12. Elementary school organization, purposes, patterns, perspectives. *The National Elementary School Principal, 61,* December, 1961.
13. GARBEE, F. E.: *The California Program for Speech and Hearing Handicapped School Children.* Bulletin 33. California State Department of Education, Sacramento, December, 1964 (revised 1967).
14. HANSEN, K. H.: *Philosophy for American Education.* Englewood Cliffs, N. J., Prentice-Hall, 1960.
15. HOFFMAN, M. L., and HOFFMAN, L. W.: *Review of Child Development Research.* New York, Russell Sage, vol. 1, 1964; vol. 2, 1966.
16. JAMES, T. H., *et al.*: *Excellence in Administration: The Dynamics of Leadership.* Stanford, California, Stanford, 1963.
17. JOHNSTON, H.: *A Philosophy of Education.* New York, McGraw, 1963.
18. MILISEN, R.: The incidence of speech disorders. In *Handbook of Speech Pathology,* L. Travis, Ed. New York, Appleton, 1957.
19. MILISEN, R.: The public schools as a site for speech and hearing. *The Speech Teacher, 12:* January, 1963.
20. MORPHET, E. L.; JOHNS, R. L., and RELLER, T. L.: *Educational Adminis-*

tration—Concepts, Practices, and Issues. Englewood Cliffs, N. J., Prentice-Hall, 1959.
21. POWERS, M. H.: What makes an effective public school speech therapist? *J Speech Hearing Dis, 21:*463-467, December, 1956.
22. Services and functions of speech and hearing specialists in public schools. *ASHA, 4:*99-100, April, 1962.
23. SMITH, E. W.; KROUSE, W. S., JR., and ATKINSON, M. M.: *The Educator's Encyclopedia.* Englewood Cliffs, N. J., Prentice-Hall, 1961.
24. The speech clinician's role in the public school. *ASHA, 6:*189-191, June, 1964.
25. VAN HATTUM, R. J.: Elementary school therapy. *Exceptional Children, 25:*411-415, May, 1959.
26. WILLEY, N. R.: An examination of public school speech and hearing therapy facilities. *Exceptional Children, 28:*723-727, November, 1961.
27. WILLIAMS, S. W.: *Educational Administration in Secondary Schools.* New York, Holt, 1964.

Chapter 4

THE SPEECH CLINICIAN — AS
A CONSULTANT

GERALD G. FREEMAN

A RECENT DEFINITION OF THE responsibilities of public school speech clinicians (Ainsworth, *et al.*, 1964) includes the provision of consultation along with special services through diagnostic and remedial methods. Although these are basic professional functions which are adaptable to any work environment, frequently it has been difficult for speech clinicians in the public schools to provide effective consultative services. It is the purpose of this chapter, therefore, to explore opportunities for school speech clinicians to serve in a consultative capacity. While consultation is an interactive process, the emphasis of this discussion will be on the responsibilities and contributions of the speech clinician rather than on those of other professional personnel.

THE NATURE OF CONSULTATION

The primary purpose of professional consultation is to seek the opinion of a person with particular knowledge, information, and skills. The public school speech clinician, no less than any other, should be prepared to fulfill this purpose. Periodically, he is called upon to consult with various diagnostic and treatment teams; he continuously is required to contribute to the educational team.

The key to effective consultation is proficient clinical practice and the projection of a competent clinical attitude. The public schools by nature of purpose and organization are not a clinical facility in the usual sense of the term. However, it is possible for speech clinicians working in schools to create conditions favorable to clinical practices and thereby provide an environment and develop interpersonal relationships which facilitate consultative services.

78

The diminished self-confidence experienced by school speech clinicians in their efforts to achieve such ends often is related to a lack of firm convictions in at least one of the following areas: commitment to the profession, definition of the relationship between verbal communication problems and the educational process, and appropriate utilization of school resources. A brief discussion of each of these areas follows.

Requisites of Consultation

Commitment to the Profession

From a historical standpoint many school speech clinicians have received basic or advanced training in general education, speech arts, or related areas. In addition, most states require that speech clinicians earn teaching credentials to qualify for public school positions. These circumstances have led to confusion as to the professional status of school speech clinicians.

A basic tenet always has been that a speech clinician should have an understanding of any setting in which he works in order to integrate his services into the broader framework. In the case of public schools, many training institutions and state departments of education have regarded background and experience in general education as requisite to such an understanding. Whether or not this belief is true, and among professional workers it is still a moot point, it hardly seems possible for a school speech clinician to exercise effective consultative practices unless he is a specialist in the area of speech and language development and its disorders.

Some school speech clinicians have been sensitive about the semantic overtones of the word "specialist." They feel that it implies a degree of superiority to other school personnel. Obviously, there is no intent to equate the terms "special" and "superior." The speech clinician in the school may or may not be a superior person. However, he is a professional specialist in the same manner that he would be were he working in a community agency or hospital. As Garbee (1964) reports, the specific responsibilities, skills, and basic identity of the school speech clinician should remain that of the speech and hearing specialist within the total group of his colleagues who work in other settings.

The school speech clinician who wishes to engage in effective consultation must earn the confidence of others through demonstration of specific competencies in the area of speech and language disorders. He is committed to the speech and hearing profession and to the belief that the demands of his profession rewardingly can be fulfilled in the public schools.

Speech Problems and the Educational Process

The philosophy that public education should provide opportunities for each individual to develop to his fullest potential long has served as the foundation for clinical speech in the schools. Black (1964) also suggests that the schools provide a logical means of reaching children in a natural setting where service readily is accepted. In addition, recent trends in the speech and hearing profession as well as in public education have broadened the practical foundations of school programs while increasing the consultative responsibilities of speech clinicians.

From the standpoint of the profession, the emphases of school programs have changed or are changing as the functions of speech clinicians become more clearly defined. In all geographical areas speech clinicians are attempting to develop programs which provide competent clinical services to those children who demonstrate significant verbal communication problems. Case load requirements are deemphasizing arbitrarily determined numbers of children; the number of case contacts per week is being determined by the specific needs of each child.

Concurrently, the variety and number of public school facilities for exceptional populations of children are expanding rapidly. As they do so, the speech clinician more frequently than not is faced with a group of children whose verbal communication disorders are one aspect and an integral part of broader educational problems. Such children include those who are physically, mentally, visually, acoustically, perceptually, emotionally, or otherwise handicapped and for whom special education classes have been and will continue to be established.

Under these circumstances the speech clinician in the schools has unparalleled opportunity to be a vital resource consultant whose knowledge and experience is as applicable to education as it is to rehabilitation. His educationally oriented responsibilities include the identification and exploration of potentials which may be used to teach linguistic and other skills as well as diagnosis and remediation of circumscribed speech behavior. He must determine the relationship between verbal communication disorders and overall learning disabilities and interpret these relationships to others in terms of the educational process and plan for each child. He need not be a teacher because he works in the schools; although his consultative efforts may contribute substantially to the education of children.

Utilization of School Resources

Knight *et al.,* (1961) report that school speech and hearing personnel consider the team approach highly desirable. They find opportunities to engage in team efforts discouragingly limited because of a lack of such people as clinical psychologists, social workers, and physical therapists. In all probability this suggestion indicates an inability on the part of speech clinicians to adapt consultative functions to the schools. There seems to be a marked tendency for them to limit the concept of consultation to diagnostic procedures.

To be sure, the availability of clinical personnel varies from school district to school district although an increasing number of schools employ psychologists, social workers, nurses, physicians, and others. The school speech clinician should be aware of allied resource personnel in the schools and consult with them in behalf of a given child. In the absence of one, several, or all resource services, referrals to outside agencies and specialists long have been deemed appropriate.

The school speech clinician definitely should seek the professional challenge and stimulation of consultative involvement with diagnostic teams in and outside of the schools. However, he also should recognize that the lack of a diagnostic team in a school district does not preclude the lack of any team. He should reflect juxtaposition of a fact-finding clinical attitude and the realities of available or possible courses of action. Even if comprehensive diagnosis of a child with a speech problem is necessary for appropriate management of his education, the primary function of the schools, and one in which speech clinicians can play a key consultative role, is the facilitation of programs based on diagnostic findings.

The most meaningful interdisciplinary consultations in schools involve the utilization of diagnostic findings and impressions for implementation of practical, workable programs for children. Interdisciplinary diagnosis is impossible in some schools; interdisciplinary planning and programming always can become a reality — every school has administrators and teachers; some have special education teachers, and some run the professional gamut. The effective school speech clinician contributes as a consultant to the diagnostic team. His concept of interdisciplinary consultation extends beyond this point, however, as his work environment permits the freedom for and challenge of continuous consultation with the educational team.

CONSULTATION IN THE SCHOOLS

One of the most essential elements to the success of the school speech clinician's program is that members of the community have a clear understanding of his work — his professional reason for being. Yet, a national survey (Knight *et al.,* 1961) revealed that even school administrators and teachers often have a meager conception of the speech clinician's background and role. In order to promote understanding the authors suggest a variety of measures of a consultative nature including in-service training programs, speaking before other professional groups, and better management of more referrals.

The fact that such activities are not regarded by a community, including school staffs, as routine consultative responsibilities of school speech clinicians is symptomatic of a lack of sufficient development and projection of a clinical attitude through the schools. The speech clinician earns the role of professional consultant through exemplary clinical behavior. When he fails to do so, he contributes to misunderstandings and the formulation and perpetuation of erroneous notions. For example, classroom teachers too often view the speech clinician's itinerant job as one of comparative ease and diversion — driving from school to school and working with small groups of children. Or, time and again children report that they love speech class since all they do is "play games" — while classroom teachers and administrators feel increased parental pressures to promote academic subjects.

The establishment of clinical practices in schools is not easy. However, it is possible and essential to consultative activities. One chief difficulty seems to be that for years school speech clinicians have sought "the clinical approach in schools" as if it were an evasive panacea. Actually, the concept is relatively simple; the clinical approach is active rather than nominal. It is a function of the clinical person in much the same way that cutting is the function of a knife. Nobody doubts that a sharp knife cuts; nobody doubts that a "sharp" clinician functions clinically.

Schools, by nature of their purpose and organization, present the types of problems which most easily are resolved by dilution of clinical methods. For example, it is true that many school districts require case loads which are too large, and speech clinicians often have too little time for intensive individual work. On the other hand, there are speech clinicians who capably strive to attain more ideal selection and enrollment procedures but, in the meantime, actively demonstrate a clinical approach. Insofar as possible, such speech clinicians apply their discipline. They are concerned with children and their behavior disorders, specifically disorders in verbal communication as they relate to the educational process. They engage each child in diagnostic therapy. They resist the use of superfluous time-saving activities and develop adaptations of clinical methods to meet the needs of individual children within small groups. They are aware of the distinctive features of their professional competencies as well as features which overlap with those of other professional workers. In a word, through clinical practice they establish themselves as well-defined professional workers to whom others automatically turn for appropriate consultation.

Types of Activities

Most of the consultations in which school speech clinicians engage focus in one of three areas: 1) those which deal with specific children and their verbal communication disorders, 2) those concerned with interpretation of the profession as it relates to the local school program, and 3) conferences regarding specialized resource materials and techniques and their applications to school and home.

The nature and purpose of a given contact with administrators, teachers, parents, civic or professional organizations, or other professional workers necessarily determine the degree to which any one area may be emphasized.

The speech clinician called upon to discuss a particular child, for example, inevitably becomes involved in interpreting the program in which the child is enrolled, as well as recommendations by which others can cope more successfully with the speech behavior. Similarly, a session with teachers concerning the logistics of a program hardly can avoid some attention to delineation of professional roles and responsibilities.

The ensuing discussion provides suggestions which relate to the core of emphasis in a variety of actual consultative situations. The discussions will be specific for the sake of clarity; in practice, effective consultation is broad.

CONSULTING WITH SCHOOL SPECIALISTS
Administration
The Superintendent

The school speech clinician's success in gaining administrative support is largely dependent on his ability to interpret to the superintendent the relationships between clinical speech practices and educational objectives. The speech clinician should identify the commonalities of his own concerns and those of other school personnel; he should clarify these commonalities for the superintendent. Although the speech clinician should establish himself as a professional worker, he must define his functions in terms which indicate their integral and necessary relationships to the accomplishment of broader school objectives. There is a distinct difference between the professional identification of speech clinicians with school personnel and the identification of common concerns to both. The speech clinician who is able to make these distinctions and project them into consultations with his superintendent will foster understanding, respect, and support.

Boards of Education

The well-informed superintendent generally will represent the speech clinician's viewpoint to his own board. Periodically, however, speech clinicians may be called upon to present a summary of their programs to a board. As elected officials, one of the chief concerns of boards of education is the appropriate expenditure of funds earmarked for education. Again, it behooves speech clinicians to consult with board members regarding the educational significance of clinical speech practices and the relationships between speech development and academic achievement.

Directors of Special Education

Many speech clinicians are directly responsible to directors of special education. If this is the case, the director of special education should be consulted regarding all aspects of the speech clinician's program. With regard to consultation specifically, the director of special education should be acquainted with those functions which deal primarily with role definition, as described above, as well as with the nature and purpose of various consultative contacts which will be described later.

Aside from this general administrative type of consultation, the speech clinician may often be called upon to assist a director of special education with a specific case. The director of special education usually is responsible for the educational screening, planning, and placement of exceptional children in his school district. He views reports of findings and impressions as means to an end; the desired goal is transformation of such material into educational practices which best meet the needs of children. A speech clinician in any environment may engage in diagnostic practices and acquire information about a child. The school speech clinician, however, most effectively assists the director of special education when he is able to interpret his information so that it readily can be applied to the speech program, the classroom, or any school service. He must be prepared to answer the question, So what?, which the special education director frequently will ask following a careful case presentation.

Principals

In an outline of criteria for evaluation of effective public school speech clinicians, Powers (1956) suggests two items which capture the essential elements of primary consultative responsibilities to school principals. These criteria are 1) skill in presenting the objectives and policies of the program and 2) the degree to which the principal is kept informed of the program through conferences or written reports.

Although most principals are eager to provide speech and hearing services to children in their schools, the depth of understanding which they possess regarding the objectives and needs of speech clinicians varies considerably. Subsequently, their degree of appreciation of management problems connected with the provision of such services also varies, among school districts as well as within them.

Past experiences indicate that early clarification of policies and objectives with each principal promotes administrative support and prevents the development of perturbing procedural difficulties. It is impossible in this regard to project an exhaustive list of areas in which speech clinicians appropriately might serve as consultants to principals, although basic considerations are inherent in each program.

First, there is a broad framework within which speech clinicians function. It is composed chiefly of local administrative policy, state department rules and regulations governing practices in the schools, and the code of ethics of the American Speech and Hearing Association. It seems self-evident that the school principal who possesses information regarding these overall policies can be more realistic in his daily expectations and demands and more appreciative of idealistic professional strivings. For instance, he more readily can understand the basis for the amount of time allotted to his school as well as the quantitative and qualitative bases of case selection.

Second, speech clinicians should find it beneficial to consult with principals regarding specific case selection procedures. Such discussions involve consideration of screening procedures, channels through which teachers and other school personnel may make referrals to the speech clinician, and criteria for inclusion of children in the program.

Third, school principals should be apprised of considerations and procedures which relate to scheduling. Factors such as optimum class size, grouping techniques, appropriate times to take certain children from classroom activities, and adequate physical facilities should be clarified.

Fourth, it is essential to define consultative functions that the speech clinician may provide to other school personnel, parents, and the community, particularly with reference to time allotments for fulfillment of such functions.

In such consultative contact the speech clinician must differentiate clearly those policies which should be professionally determined from those which rightly and justly are determinations of the school administration. It is the speech clinician's consultative function to enable school administrators to gain appreciation of professional policies to the extent that administrative policy formulations support rather than restrict the program.

A well-informed principal can design administrative policies which promote an environment in which a program can be carried out effectively. To this end, the speech clinician consistently must provide information, opinions, and judgments in a capable, tactful, intuitive manner.

In most instances the principal is the chief administrator in his school. He is charged with the full responsibility for members of his staff and is entrusted with the educational management of each child enrolled in his school. Although most school speech clinicians conduct itinerant programs, they are considered bona fide staff members of schools in which they practice. As such, they are responsible directly to their several principals. Their professional practices and management of children with speech and language disorders are under his jurisdiction. They are expected to appreciate each principal's concern for the educational needs of every child as well as the programs designed to meet these needs. The speech clinician's program reflects on the principal and he is answerable for it, as he is for all activities carried on in his school.

The amount of interest and involvement shown by principals varies considerably as does the extent and types of demands which they make of speech clinicians. Nonetheless, the speech clinician has a professional consultative obligation to provide each principal with information regarding the program and the children it serves. It is the principal's prerogative, thereafter, to involve himself to a lesser or greater degree.

As a consultant, the speech clinician should supply the principal with a list of children enrolled in the case load and those who are on the waiting list. These lists should be kept current. If they are well organized, a principal can learn at a glance the number and distribution of children involved as well as which children are being served.

When children present special problems, the speech clinician should consult with the principal regarding the nature of the problems and procedures which might be followed to investigate them. In such cases the need for referrals to other specialists often is indicated. The speech clinician, in general, should consult with the principal as a first step in initiating a referral.

The process of referral is a professional function which clearly falls within the realm of clinical speech activities. However, in schools as elsewhere, referrals can be expedited more efficiently when appropriate channels have been established. If such channels do not exist, the speech clinician should serve as a consultant in the development of a referral system. Sometimes a school speech clinician is the only staff member with a clinical orientation. If so, effective consultation regarding referrals — reasons and methods — facilitates opportunities for involvement of the principal in a clinical approach.

The principal usually serves as a referral clearing house within the school to avoid duplication of services and to prevent several staff members from simultaneously sending a child and his parents in two directions. He must cope with the parents for whose child staff members have requested psychiatric, psychological, physical, or other evaluations. His staff members, including speech clinicians, serve as consultants to him by indicating the needs for referrals and providing him with pertinent information in writing and during discussions.

Some principals serve as coordinators of a team in their schools; others relegate such responsibilities. In any event, principals should be informed of measures which are being followed to promote the educational welfare of children with problems.

The speech clinician frequently interviews parents with whom the principal has had little or no contact. Or, in the case of parents well-known to the principal, the information gleaned by the speech clinician may have value for other school personnel. For example, parents may discuss factors pertinent to the physical, social, and emotional development of a child which relate to speech and language problems and also have broader educational implications. The speech clinician serves as a consultant to the principal by sharing vital information with him.

Finally, many principals appreciate an annual written summary report of the speech clinician's program. School administrators most clearly can demonstrate the relationships between the scope of current services and projected program needs in terms of longitudinal statistical reports. The speech clinician who supplies and discusses such reports with principals is assured of accurate representation at administrative board meetings.

Virtually all administrators wish to provide the best possible clinical speech services to children in their schools. It is paramount that the speech clinician exercise a consultative function in the accomplishment of this goal. The task is not easy, since the differences in characteristics of schools prevent application of a single formula to do so. On the one hand, it may involve basic ground work in a school which never has employed a speech clinician. On the other, it may involve the slight alteration of a scheduling procedure where the program is established and well organized. The need for improvement always is probable; the well-informed administrator makes it possible.

Classroom Teachers

An important part of the speech clinician's professional challenge is the establishment of positive working relationships with classroom teachers. Such relations should be based on mutual respect for the skills and talents that each can bring to bear in behalf of the child with a speech impairment. Classroom teachers are as individually different as are speech clinicians. Yet, in time, if each develops insight into the professional assets and limitations of the other, meaningful consultations will result.

It is the responsibility of speech clinicians to evaluate children, diagnose their speech problems, and formulate and direct plans which facilitate improvement of their verbal communication skills. In schools, classroom teachers are an integral part of these functions.

Powers (1957) states that the examination and the diagnosis of any speech case are designed to determine the kind of person who has the speech disorder, the nature of the disorder, and the reasons for it. It is evident that a classroom teacher's knowledge about a child and his family is essential to such an evaluative process. In addition, the skilled speech clinician recognizes that dialogue with classroom teachers about etiologic factors and diagnoses is a basis for future contacts regarding formulation and implementation of plans. Attention to diagnostic concerns provides an interdisciplinary foundation; sound consultative services to classroom teachers provide a framework for effective practice.

Most often the focus of consultation with classroom teachers relates to management of a child with a speech disorder and includes special emphasis in such areas as interpreting the speech problem and defining the role of the teacher in its remediation. If the classroom teacher understands the speech clinician's program, the discussions concerning these areas will result in an integrated viewpoint regarding a given child. Such consultations lead to the transformation of ideas into practical plans.

Interpreting the Speech Problem

Most classroom teachers are concerned about the nature of a child's speech problem, how it affects his adjustment, attitudes, and learning, and what they can do to help him overcome it. Time and again teachers raise the questions, Should I call on him? Should I correct him? Should I protect him?

In responding to these and other concerns, the speech clinician should be sensitive to the fact that valuable interpretation fosters insight and action. Interpretations to classroom teachers should promote intellectual appreciation of the problem as well as its pedagogical implications.

The Nature of the Problem

To date, the vernacular of the speech and hearing profession is an enigma even to those in the field. It cannot be employed consistently in an intradisciplinary manner; it should not be used blatantly in an interdisciplinary setting.

When a poorly defined diagnostic term is used to interpret the nature of a speech problem, the emphasis in consultation shifts from the behavioral disorder to an academic discussion of nomenclature. Such discussions may have secondary benefits for the classroom teacher as well as the speech clinician, providing each has sufficient time and interest. However, in light of a specific child and his speech disorder, more expedient means of communication generally are in order.

One of the most effective ways to interpret speech disorders to classroom teachers is through description rather than classification. An analysis of what the child actually does is more meaningful than a categorical pronouncement about him. In other words, in the perspective of school life, what the child *does* has more significance than what he *is*.

Several advantages are inherent in this orientation. First, it promotes a child-centered conference rather than a speech defect-centered discussion. The description of speech deviations in a behavioral sense serves as a central body of commonly understood information to which specific causal factors may be related dynamically. Similarly, it clarifies the relationships between the speech deviations and factors in the classroom which precipitate and perpetuate them.

The descriptive analyses provided by speech clinicians generally are not startling findings to astute classroom teachers. In fact, they usually corroborate many of the teacher's impressions. If so, a comfortable communication environment has been established in which a child's acquisition of speech skills can be related to other aspects of his behavior and school adjustment. His reactions to learning situations, the extent to which the speech deviations seem to be effecting such reactions, and the relation of other behavioral tendencies to the total learning process can be discussed in a comprehensible way.

A behavioristic context readily enables the teacher to gain insight into the speech problem and at the same time helps to define a planning structure similar to that with which most educators are familiar. The goal of improved speech and the approaches utilized to enable a child to learn appropriate speech patterns in many ways resemble teachers' daily goals with respect to other skills. The individual characteristics of the child, on the one hand, and the application of principles and theories of learning in his behalf, on the other, are common concerns of speech clinicians and classroom teachers.

The establishment of this overall commonality of endeavor highlights the interrelationships between the educational process and the speech therapy program. Further, a broad interpretation of the nature of a speech disorder enables the teacher to view circumscribed speech behavior in its complex relationships to other behavioral modes. It lays the groundwork for interpretation of functions of classroom teachers and speech clinicians in the accomplishment of general and specific goals.

The Child with a Speech Problem

Pendergast (1963) states that much confusion has existed in school speech programs because of a lack of clear delineation between speech improvement and speech therapy. She suggests that speech improvement is concerned with deviations within the normal range and is the responsibility of classroom teachers; deviations outside the range of normalcy are the responsibility of speech clinicians.

There is no question that speech clinicians determine which children should be enrolled in speech therapy. The speech clinician who capably has performed consultative functions also has established the concept that classroom teachers continue to share some of the responsibility for these children.

Although school speech clinicians frequently feel little professional obligation to the speech improvement program, in practice they often are called upon to provide advice and direction in the establishment and continuation of such programs. The consultative role of the speech clinician in each of these situations is worthy of consideration.

Speech Therapy

Aside from the fact that the classroom teacher can be a primary source of current information about a child and his problems, the teacher long has been regarded as a key to carry-over. School speech clinicians have valued the opportunity to promote carryover in the classroom as a logical sequential step to a child's total integration of a new verbal pattern. They are eager to enlist the teacher's aid in this vital effort.

In this regard, past experiences have indicated that speech clinicians at times have been unrealistic in their expectations of classroom teachers. The result is that teachers feel that their responsibilities for carry-over exceed their level of training and are too demanding for the available time. For these and other reasons, consultation regarding carry-over should include well-defined specific goals which can be accomplished in the framework of daily classroom activities.

The speech clinician usually engages a child in a skill-by-skill program. That is to say, the plan for most children includes reasonable mastery of one sound or technique before another is stressed. Similarly, the carry-over demands, if logically structured, should provide for skill-by-skill reinforcement.

The speech clinician who supplies a classroom teacher with a portfolio of sounds and words which should be reinforced for each child encourages defeat. In the face of other pressures the classroom teacher has little inclination to study or remember the contents of such a document despite her concern for children. However, a well-phrased succinct statement concerning a newly acquired skill may leave an indelible impression.

Speech clinicians in their earnest zeal often provide teachers with elaborate schemes for promoting carry-over in the classroom. At the same time, classroom teachers rightfully may resist involvement in too many extracurricular functions. Again, these factors may be reconciled through consultation which emphasizes utilization of regular classroom procedures for purposes of specific speech-goal achievement.

Much has been said and written about the value of coordinating the vocabulary of speech therapy activities with that of classroom activities. During reading or spelling, for instance, the classroom teacher is requested to provide a positive comment when a child spontaneously demonstrates a newly acquired speech skill. At times these methods have proven unsatisfactory. If the child fails to use a corrected response, the opportunity for carry-over is lost, since the teacher's chief concern is subject matter rather than improved verbal communication. Moreover, certain children use new skills only in speech class and rarely demonstrate them spontaneously in other situations without some encouragement.

In practice, improved carry-over techniques in the classroom should include opportunities for encouragement as well as reward. The teacher's responsibilities should be well defined and as effortless as possible.

One effective method of coping with this problem has been coordination of vocabulary used in speech therapy with that applicable to classroom procedures rather than curricular activities. The teacher is requested to structure a specific procedure in behalf of a given child so that he may use and practice a meaningful language response which he has mastered.

For example, if a given child uses the k sound appropriately in such phrases as "come up" or "take one" during speech therapy, the speech clinician may advise the classroom teacher accordingly. Although a kind word of acknowledgment is in order whenever the child uses his new pattern in these or other phrases, the classroom teacher also should capitalize upon the more direct, yet natural, opportunities which exist to strengthen and reinforce the pattern. How many times are papers or materials distributed to class members? If chosen to distribute these items, a given child could practice "take one" a number of times and receive the praise and acknowledgment of his teacher and peers. Or, during dismissal, which often is a table-by-table or row-by-row procedure, the child in question could be asked to assist — "Come up row two."

Regardless of the specific speech skill, the opportunities for structured classroom carry-over are boundless and seem to be a logical intermediate step between speech therapy and spontaneous usage. Through their utilization, the classroom teacher actively may become involved in the speech therapy process without feeling the stress of additional responsibility, the need for more time, or concern about lesson interference. The speech clinician, as a consultant, has demonstrated understanding of the teacher's responsibilities and has adapted techniques to capitalize on significant elements in the school environment.

Speech Improvement

The American Speech and Hearing Association (Ainsworth *et al.,* 1964) suggests that the speech clinician's role in speech improvement should be one of consultative help in the development of procedures directed towards supplementing the efforts of teaching personnel. Van Riper and Butler (1955) point out that speech clinicians may recognize the need for assisting children with minor speech deviations, but large case loads and a shortage of time prevent anything but stopgap measures. They also conclude that the basic responsibility for speech improvement is with the classroom teacher.

One of the practical problems faced by school speech clinicians is that administrators and classroom teachers often are not in full accord with this philosophy. On the one hand, they view oral communication as one aspect of the language arts curriculum; on the other, they place little curricular emphasis on the development of verbal skills. They regard children with maturational and minor speech deviations as candidates for the speech clinician's program.

The consultative efforts of speech clinicians concerning these conditions should be directed to two major points. First, it should be established that speech is a form of language that deserves the attention of classroom teachers in much the same way that attention is paid to reading and writing. The objectives of a language arts program include a sequential development of communicative skills. Consequently, one aspect of the curriculum should be aimed towards a sequential development of speech skills.

Second, the principal obligation of speech clinicians is to children whose disorders require clinical attention. Although some clinical practices are adaptable to the classroom and the speech clinician is a logical resource person, speech improvement is a responsibility of curriculum planners and classroom teachers.

Speech clinicians have several alternatives as consultants to classroom-centered speech improvement programs. In some situations they may provide assistance to teachers in the organization of a curriculum. If this course is followed, it should be remembered that many classroom teachers engage in a good deal of incidental speech improvement without recognizing it as such. Efforts should be made to integrate all appropriate existing practices into the speech improvement curriculum so that it loses its overtones of specialization.

Other speech clinicians may find it desirable to arrange periodic demonstration lessons with entire classes. For example, they may teach the first in a series of speech improvement lessons and rely on the teacher to proceed during the interim between visits.

Both of these schemes demand more time than usually is available if they are to be carried out in a thorough, effective manner. Past experiences have indicated that in-service training programs regarding speech improvement can be equally effective. They also more readily reach larger numbers of teachers and provide opportunities for exploration and interpretation of the relationships between the speech clinician's role and program and the speech improvement program.

Interpreting the Program

It is essential that classroom teachers understand the speech clinician's program if it is to be integrated into the educational framework. Although case conferences with teachers about given children or problems provide numerous opportunities to interpret specific aspects of the program, the need for establishing a broader foundation too often is overlooked.

Time and again teachers make such remarks as "The speech

clinician spent five minutes with a child whom I can't hear — she hardly opens her mouth when she talks. He told me there was no speech problem. What do children have to do to get help around here?" This type of question, if unanswered, leads to suspicion and confusion and interferes with communication and coordination. The main reason that teachers become perplexed by such situations is their lack of information regarding the nature of speech disorders. Without such information they cannot understand case selection and teacher referral procedures even if they participate in them in a mechanical way.

Elementary classroom teachers in particular should have background in the development of speech and its disorders. Their roles in speech improvement, referring children with suspected speech disorders, participating in carry-over, and teaching children with developmental learning disorders require information in this area. It is impossible for teachers to understand the design and implementation of the speech clinician's program without knowledge of the factors that determine who, why, and how certain children are provided service.

For these reasons, speech clinicians should seek ways of providing teachers with basic information concerning speech disorders. In the past, in-service training programs, sessions at workshops and conferences, lecture series, and short courses all have proven effective means of doing so.

Once teachers are informed, they appreciate the reasons for providing clinical speech services to given children at specific times. They can answer many of their own questions concerning why some of their students with severe problems are in speech class while others are not. They can formulate criteria for referrals and assume increased responsibility for the speech of those children who do not qualify for the speech clinician's program.

The speech clinician should consult with teachers about his program and should involve them in it. The degree to which teachers are willing to become involved is reflected in their basic understanding of children with speech disorders. Speech clinicians must provide such understanding.

Special Education Teachers

During the past decade special facilities for various populations of educationally handicapped children have expanded rapidly. Through support of government funds, such facilities will continue to increase in type and number. Since speech and language
problems frequently are one aspect of educational handicaps, it
stands to reason that the speech clinician's consultative role to
special education teachers will increase.

A difficulty in the management of speech and language disorders among educationally handicapped children is that their
verbal communication problems are integrally related to their
total academic needs. The acquisition of social competencies, including verbal skills, is a major educational goal for many of
them. The speech clinician's responsibilities to the accomplishment of this goal have been questionable since the needs of the
children should be met by classroom curricula rather than clinical
speech procedures.

The experience of recent years has demonstrated that speech
clinicians should not work intensively with all mentally, perceptually, acoustically, emotionally, or otherwise handicapped children
who demonstrate speech and/or language problems. Rather, they
should participate with teachers of these children in the formulation of a coordinated interdisciplinary speech and language program. The plan should define which aspects of verbal communication disorders are managed best in the classroom and which
demand the particular skills of the speech clinician.

Freeman and Lukens (1962) outline a speech and language
program for educable mentally handicapped children which also
has proved useful with other populations. In essence, it defines
a consultative role for speech clinicians. The plan states that it is
the responsibility of speech clinicians to examine each child, diagnose his speech problem, and formulate and direct a program for
improving his verbal communication skills. In many instances the
speech and language problem will be judged fairly typical in view
of the educational handicap; in others, it is not totally attribut-
able to the overall condition. Speech and language must be taught

as part of the regular classroom curriculum to meet the needs of those children whose difficulty in these areas is one aspect of total developmental delay. The speech clinician, however, must treat specifically those children who demonstrate deficiencies in oral communication which are atypical of their generalized disorder.

It is the responsibility of classroom teachers to cooperate in the formulation and execution of a curriculum designed to improve verbal skills. This curriculum should provide opportunities for the development of verbal language, meet the needs of children with delayed articulation development, and provide carry-over situations for children enrolled in the speech clinician's program.

The nature of speech and language disorders among handicapped children requires that speech clinicians become involved in planning educational procedures. They should establish themselves as resource consultants to all special education programs. At the same time, they must maintain their clinical responsibilities to those children who require diagnostic therapy. The speech and language needs of all handicapped children then can be met at appropriate levels.

Other School Personnel

The school speech clinician has the opportunity to contribute significantly to the educational management of children with verbal communication disorders. As a member of the school staff he need not feel that educationally oriented recommendations are outside his sphere of influence or responsibility. Rather, he should be able to interpret his findings in a developmental and educational sense, integrate them with those of others, and play a prominent role in the formulation of educational plans.

It is common for administrators to organize an educational planning committee to consider long-range programs for children with learning difficulties. The speech clinician logically should participate in this decision-making process when it involves children with communication disorders. Too often, however, he is viewed as being concerned only with speech, and it falls to others to relate speech behavior to educational goals.

These circumstances can be averted through consultation with members of the educational planning committee — psychologists, social workers, remedial or helping teachers, directors of special education, or similar personnel.

Seeking Information

One of the most effective means of integrating clinical findings and viewpoints with those of others is through the process of seeking information about a case. Speech clinicians are aware of the need for a broad clinical base of information in the diagnosis and treatment of children with speech disorders. However, it is important to realize that the type of information which is requested from a social worker, psychologist, or other school staff member also reflects the speech clinician's functions and concerns. Aside from the value of receiving information, requests should inform others about communication disorders, increase their sensitivity to specific informational needs and provide the means for coordinating school services.

For example, the speech clinician who submits a request for psychological test findings wishes to use this information to gain increased insight about a child and his problems. At the same time this request provides a practical opportunity for consultation with the psychologist. It is practical and stimulating to relate the test findings to such factors as the speech diagnosis, the child's progress or lack of progress in speech class and the behavioral management problems which the child presents. It is equally important to discuss the ways in which a child's habitual speech behavior may have interfered with or altered test results.

This type of dialogue provides the speech clinician with opportunities to inform the psychologist about children with speech disorders while indicating the need for specific types of psychological information. It enables both parties to direct their attention to interrelated concerns for children with speech and educational problems.

A similar model is applicable when seeking information from other specialized school personnel. Social workers can provide speech clinicians with detailed case histories; they can provide information more pertinent to speech disorders if they have been made aware of the relationships between speech development and family and environmental factors. Remedial reading specialists may be aware of children with verbal problems; they may be able to teach these children more effectively if oriented to the relationships between verbal and written symbolic disturbances.

The speech clinician should be able to identify his significant contribution and relate it to the contributions of other staff members. If he has consulted meaningfully with them, they will provide the types of information which he requires.

Other Speech Clinicians

There are numerous opportunities for school speech clinicians to serve as consultants to each other. Aside from participating in local, state, and national meetings, they should establish regular means for case studies and interchanges of ideas. Unfortunately, even in school districts which employ several speech clinicians, each tends to become preoccupied with the conduction of his own affairs with minimum involvement of co-workers.

Clinical Activity

The large number of variables involved in most speech problems contributes to the complexities of attempting to resolve them. The speech clinician who works in a clinical unit usually has the advantage of having several colleagues readily available with whom to discuss, verify, or dispute findings. Although it is not always an easy task, the school speech clinician should create the same opportunities.

In some instances a supervisor of speech personnel is available to coordinate departmental functions, some of which are consultative in nature. Even if such a resource person is not available, however, speech clinicians should seek to utilize the talents of others.

Case Observations

One of the most valuable experiences in working with a difficult case is to observe another speech clinician in action with him. This activity provides the regular speech clinician with new perspectives. It serves to stimulate discussions of diverse observations and opinions. The speech clinicians benefit from the exchange of information and viewpoints; the cases benefit from ensuing procedural modifications based on the development of increased objectivity and new insights.

Staff Meetings

Another method of utilizing the skills and knowledge of other speech clinicians is through regular staff meetings. These may be arranged on a regional basis for districts which employ only one or two speech clinicians. Such meetings should provide opportunities to discuss clinical problems, innovations in practices, and academic considerations. They also may be used for case presentations and demonstrations followed by group interaction and case planning. They result in practical in-service training.

CONSULTANT TO THE COMMUNITY

The school speech clinician can provide a variety of consultative services to members of the community. These include participating in programs designed to educate and inform parents and other interested adults, serving as a liaison between the schools and community agencies, and consulting with members of related professions.

Educating the Public

Most communities have a number of child-centered organizations whose members are concerned about speech. Some of these are closely allied with the schools and provide speech clinicians with logical means for informing parents about speech disorders and the school program. The groups include parent-teacher associations and various organizations of parents whose children have learning disabilities — parents of retarded children, deaf children, and so on. In addition, speech clinicians should provide continual consultative services to child study groups and parents of children in nursery schools. These groups often demonstrate interest in the promotion of good speech habits among preschool children. The speech clinician should work closely with them and encourage them to practice measures which prevent speech problems.

Community service clubs also should receive the attention of school speech clinicians. These groups frequently offer financial assistance, transportation, or other services to children with special needs. The speech clinician should provide these clubs with background information about speech disorders and concomitant problems. A well-informed group readily appreciates the needs for its services and is willing to participate when asked to do so.

Agency Contacts

In given cases it is necessary for speech clinicians to work closely with child guidance clinics, family service agencies, and other social service organizations. The speech clinician is in an optimum position to serve as a liaison between these agencies and the schools. His background and training coupled with his work environment and experiences enable him to interpret the clinical viewpoint to educators and the educational viewpoint to agency workers.

Through consultation the speech clinician may use this position to promote greater understanding between schools and community agencies, in behalf of specific cases as well as with general reference to programs, services, and facilities. When this type of consultation is successful, the recommendations of agencies to schools become more practical, the referrals from schools to agencies become more appropriate, and the mutual expectations of schools and agencies become more realistic.

Related Professions

School speech clinicians often are confronted with the need to coordinate diagnostic and treatment plans with professional members of the community — physicians, occupational and physical therapists, dentists, and others. Although it has been pointed out that a team approach can be accomplished within school staffs, it is necessary at times to extend this approach to others in the community. A community resources team, unlike a school team, may never meet face to face to examine and discuss a case. However, it is possible to establish communication channels among team members in order to coordinate efforts.

Most consultations with allied professional workers involve exchanges of case material. These usually are instigated by speech clinicians in the form of referrals. Again, the types of information requested and the methods used to seek information can serve consultative ends. They also reflect on the speech clinician's professional capacity and competency.

The chief difficulties which speech clinicians encounter in their associations with professional workers in the community stem from poor referral practices. Such difficulties occur when parents or professional specialists deem that the speech clinician's referral was inappropriate. It is essential for school speech clinicians to engage parents in prereferral consultations which relate the needs for referral to educational ramifications. Similarly, referral contacts with specialists should ask specific questions and clearly state the relevance of answers to future school-management practices. The content of every referral should have secondary consultative value. If it does, it will yield cooperative results.

Whenever possible, speech clinicians should take advantage of opportunities to address specific professional groups. On the one hand, these presentations should attempt to clarify professional roles; on the other, they should interrelate them. In all instances speech clinicians should stand firmly on definitions of the scope and limitations of their professional responsibilities. They should indicate their appreciation of the contributions and limitations of others, and elicit the same treatment in return.

SUMMARY

The schools present many opportunities for speech clinicians to engage in consultations of the highest professional order. As in the case of all clinical functions, the success of consultative services depends on the practitioner's ability to adapt to the needs of his work environment. When school speech clinicians orient their specialized roles to the broader educational framework, their consultative responsibilities increase in number, scope, and depth. On the one hand, consultation is the means through which all professional functions may be integrated into school programs; on the other, it is an intrinsic aspect of daily clinical speech procedures which can be practiced successfully in schools.

DISCUSSION TOPICS

1. How is the speech clinician prepared to function as a consultant?
2. What limits are there for the consultation he provides?
3. How can consultation be an economy measure in his valuable time?
4. What is the "clinical approach in the schools"?
5. How are the "clinical approach" and consultation related?
6. On what matters should the principal be particularly consulted?
7. In what areas should the speech clinician consult with the classroom teacher?
8. What are several ways in which consultation with the classroom teacher can fail?
9. What is the speech clinician's role in speech improvement?
10. How does the consultant role of the speech clinician differ from regular class teacher to special class teacher?

REFERENCES

1. AINSWORTH, S., *et al.*: The speech clinician's role in the public school. *ASHA, 6:*189-191, June, 1964.
2. BLACK, M.: *Speech Correction in the Schools.* Englewood Cliffs, N. J., Prentice-Hall, 1964.
3. FREEMAN, G. G., and LUKENS, J.: A speech and language program for educable mentally handicapped children. *J Speech Hearing Dis, 27:* 285-287, August, 1962.
4. GARBEE, F. E.: The California program for speech and hearing handicapped school children. *Bulletin California State Department of Education, 23,* 1964.
5. KNIGHT, H.; HAHN, E., *et al.*: The public school clinician, V professional definition and relationships. *J Speech Hearing Dis, Monogr Suppl 8:* 10-21, June, 1961.
6. PENDERGAST, K.: Speech improvement and speech therapy in the elementary school. *ASHA, 5:*548-549, 1963.
7. POWERS, M. H.: Clinical and educational procedures in functional dis-

orders or articulation. In *Handbook of Speech Pathology,* L. Travis, Ed. New York, Appleton, 1957.

8. Powers, M. H.: What makes an effective public school speech therapist. *J Speech Hearing Dis, 21:*461-467, December, 1956.

9. Van Riper, C., and Butler, K. G.: *Speech in the Elementary Classroom.* New York, Harper, 1955.

Chapter 5

THE SPEECH CLINICIAN – AS A COUNSELLOR

CHARLES V. MANGE

"Don't say no more words to me." This statement, made by an elementary school child after an especially frustrating experience in dealing with words, represents a very real expression of the emotional impact of speech. For children with communication disabilities, speech directed towards them may have a most unappetizing flavor. There may be words of reproof, words of coercion, or words reminding them of problems over which they have little control. More importantly, words directed towards a child usually require speech in reply. When that reply is in some way different or defective, the child is forced to display his disability publicly. For the child with a speech disability, to speak is to bare one's defect, thereby exposing it to public view and chancing ridicule or other negative reactions.

For parents and teachers of the speech handicapped, the child's words represent a persistent and sometimes embarrasing problem. They may elicit feelings of guilt or inadequacy, or they may precipitate concern for a perceived social stigma. The teacher may interpret the presence of a speech problem as indicative of other learning problems, especially those relating to reading and language arts. The presence of these problems also makes it more difficult for the teacher to work with her class as rapidly and efficiently as she may desire. Reactions to the disability by these most important people in the child's life are recognized and subtly reflected in the behavior of the child with a speech problem. Words and speech quickly become associated with some of the less pleasant aspects of living. It is unusual, then, to find children who look forward to the prospect of speech therapy without certain reservations, or who have no apprehension about the course of such therapy. Consequently, the speech clinician often finds it necessary to deal with words not only as phonemes and syllables to be corrected but also as representations of meanings, attitudes, and experiences.

To assist the child in better understanding himself and his environment, to aid him in clarifying his problems and possible solutions, to work toward the alteration of unhealthy attitudes, to guide him in cancelling failure experiences and, importantly, to serve as a source of strength for the child in his search for improved communication and adjustment, these are the needs and essences of counselling for the speech handicapped child. In addition, since the child is a product of a family unit, counselling other members of the family regarding the speech problem, may be indicated. Finally, members of the school staff may need similar assistance. This counselling is appropriate and necessary. It is within the province of the speech clinician as long as its primary focus is the speech problem.

COUNSELLING AS A FUNCTION OF THE SPEECH CLINICIAN

There are some who question whether there are areas of counselling specific to work with the speech handicapped child which could not better be handled by a child psychologist or psychiatrist. There are those who seriously question the advisability of counselling as a legitimate function of the speech clinician, and there are those who express concern that the clinician may not recognize when psychological or psychiatric treatment is indicated. There are those clinicians who feel they are not equipped to handle such an activity. Such concerns have been expressed many times and have been debated at length. Yet, counselling has many dimensions. In its broadest sense it includes a talk before the Parent-Teacher Association on the nature of speech defects, or a discussion with a parent group on the development of speech. It is also counselling when the clinician suggests to a parent that some pressure be taken off the child.

In actuality, counselling exists along a continuum. At one end of the continuum is group information giving. A step away is the giving of specific advice to a parent. The next step is discussions regarding a child. Further along is counselling a parent regarding a child. The other end of the continuum is actually providing counselling to the child or a parent. The question is not whether the clinician should provide counselling. He does, in some form. It is the clinician's responsibility to continually improve his skills in counselling and to recognize his limitations along the continuum.

Most of the real controversy regarding the clinician's ability to provide counselling relates to the area of emotional adjustment counselling. Many of the adjustment problems of children with speech disabilities are strongly associated with reactions resulting from the disability. The clinician is uniquely qualified by training and experience to assess the influence of emotional, organic, perceptual, and habit patterns and to detect the elements of commonality in the behavioral responses which are present. Reluctance to speak, use of very short verbal responses requiring few words, verbal hostility and aggressiveness, circumlocutions, and a host of other patterns of substitution, avoidance, and procrastination are often present. Such self-defeating patterns of behavior are useful as focal points for counselling approach.

Those who feel that counselling should only be attempted by persons specifically trained in these techniques argue that potential harm to the client is an ever-present threat. There is some merit to the argument, and the speech clinician must never extend beyond his competency. Further he should seek professional counsel should the slightest doubt arise in his mind. It must be pointed out however, that human beings, especially children, are gregarious and social beings who seek out those contacts which provide satisfying relationships. Indeed, the development of a stable personality and an adequate self-concept requires the repeated contact and experience of extensive verbal relationships with others. Those which are most satisfying are with warm and responsive friends who provide stimulation and personal acceptance.

More counselling is done by the layman than by all professionals combined. It is done because people seek close personal relationships with others. It is the normal and necessary result of these relationships. To be a friend; to converse, suggest, discuss, and explore ideas, problems, and solutions; to do these things with a group or with one other person is the essence of counselling. When the effect is a change of feeling and attitude, a change of behavior or an adjustment for a more effective life, the goals of counselling are achieved. The speech clinician who spends many hours with the child, in individual and small group settings, cannot deny the counselling relationship. Instead, it should be developed as an efficient tool in the improvement of the child's speech and emotional adjustment.

The Public School Setting

The training regimen of most speech clinicians in a university clinical setting deviates in at least one important way from the setting of the public school speech clinician. In the training program one or both parents frequently accompany the child and are included in discussions of the progress of therapy as well as analysis of the interactions of parent and child. These opportunities are generally quite extensive and are required for every child accepted in the therapy program. The university setting also includes opportunities for gathering rather complete case histories, observation of parent-child interaction, medical evaluation, and psychological diagnosis including both intellectual and emotional aspects. These necessitate close contact with professionals in other fields. Fortunately, these relationships are particularly productive because of the mutual understandings developed by continuing association as a team, working towards solutions to mutual questions and problems.

The public school setting is seldom so permissive as to time, case load, and resources. Consequently the approach taught in its totality in the training program is seldom possible of complete achievement, in the public school setting, for every child included in the program. Selection of those to be included in the counselling program, and subjective judgments of the relative worth of certain information must be made. The responsibility for these decisions rests upon the clinician almost entirely. There are, however, occasions when the observations of other teachers and of school special service personnel and community agencies can provide many helpful insights. In some instances, pupil personnel files may contain other significant and useful information pertinent to an understanding of the child, his speech, and his behavior. Each of these sources should be explored. All too often, however, the clinician must rely on his own analysis and judgments because few school systems possess the psychological and diagnostic resources necessary for objective decisions.

The school counselling setting also carries with it the attitudes built up by children and parents which relate to all parts of the school function. When counselling opportunities are provided to parents, the clinician may develop a closer relationship with the home than any of the other school personnel. Frequently questions such as these are asked, Will Johnny be promoted? Why doesn't his teacher like him? How can I get him to bring home his arithmetic work? and a host of others of similar nature. Most of these are not within the province or responsibility of the speech clinician. They are, however, vehicles for better understanding and counselling relating to behavior, school achievement, and speech therapy. Certain other aspects of the school setting with an important bearing on the counselling program will be discussed in following sections.

The Speech Clinician in Counselling

Three important and distinguishable areas are included within the counselling function of the speech clinician: emotional-adjustment counselling of the child, parent counselling, and educational counselling. Although the clinician must work with a variety of different persons and in somewhat different settings for the areas mentioned, the techniques and approaches of counselling should be directed toward stimulation of independent constructive behavior, toward alteration of noxious environmental factors, toward an improved self-concept, toward improved social relationships and increased efficiency of the total school learning experience.

Counselling of the Child with a Speech Problem

The clinician frequently meets and recognizes adjustment problems which are secondary to the speech disorder, i.e. they result from listener and self-reactions to the deviant speech pattern. Certain listener reactions and attempts to correct the defective pattern are easily sensed by the child and quickly internalized. Although corrective attempts by adults, including the speech clinician, may be tolerated with little overt reaction, they hold great potential for inadequate development of the self-concept.

Avoidance

Many children resort to avoidance learning in which any speech attempts likely to elicit negative reactions are inhibited. The clinician most frequently deals with avoidance behavior which tends towards denial or superficial acknowledgment of the problem, towards withdrawal from situations likely to require speech and towards expressions of hostility and aggressiveness.

An alert third grade teacher reported the development of avoidance behavior in Tim, a boy whose articulation errors were very noticeable to his classmates.

> Several times Tim told me he had a cold and no voice when he was supposed to give a report. At first I excused him, but then I arranged for Tim to see the nurse. She found nothing unusual and told him so. I was quite sure his reports were done so I talked with him about his feelings when talking to the group. He seemed somewhat relieved that I knew his desire to keep silent, but soon after he began to be absent whenever he was due to report. Each time he sent his written report to me with an older brother. We finally began to make progress only when we arranged it so he could use pictures and exhibits or write on the blackboard at the same time he was talking. He seems to get along better when attention is directed towards the materials he uses rather than towards himself. His reports are always very brief, he almost never looks at the children, and he seems to do everything possible to direct attention away from himself — but at least he is now talking a little more.

Secondary Symptoms

There are also many children with both general and specific types of avoidance resulting from other deviations associated with cleft lip, protruding teeth, and cerebral palsy. Varying forms of this behavior in the speech handicapped child are so frequent that the term "secondary," as used to explain the symptom patterns of stuttering, can be extended to include associated behavior patterns in articulation, voice, and other speech disorders. Secondary symptoms are learned behavior which, although not a part of the symptomatology of the basic problem, result from it and add to the severity.

It is the clinician's task to stimulate development of constructive behavior which permits the intrinsic rewards of speech to be experienced more frequently, while the self-destructive avoidance behavior is reduced.

TECHNIQUES AND APPROACHES TO COUNSELLING

Withdrawal and Hostility

There is a tendency for the layman to suggest that the symptoms of withdrawal and hostility be explained verbally and that the child should be told that others really do accept him despite the speech deviation. Advice, admonition, and exhortation to participate and to feel more positively towards others is then advised. The clinician, however, recognizes that the child's behavior is a result and an expression of attitudes and feelings and that the cause-and-effect relationship seen by others is almost never applied to one's own behavior through such a direct approach. "Bootstrap psychology," with its "get hold of yourself and act differently" approach, has not proven effective in counselling. The child may understand all the logical reasons for behaving in a different fashion and yet he experiences negative emotional reactions and responds with behavior symptomatic of them. He understands that it is wrong to steal, that it is immature to cry, and that fighting with others is inappropriate—yet he does these things, not because of his understanding, but because of his feelings.

Children and adults typically react to stimuli on the basis of their emotional impact first rather than to the actual content of the stimulus. To point out that one has made an error, that one is lazy, that one is acting "like a baby," or that one may have forgotten something he should have remembered, is likely to elicit an emotional reaction which may be defensive or hostile. Positive learning is not enhanced under these conditions.

Bobby, a third grade boy with a persistent lateral lisp, was a case in point. Although his mental abilities were considerably above his group, Bobby experienced continuing correction by his parents in every aspect of his behavior. When things went well and he performed as desired, little was said and few verbal rewards were offered, but when he experienced some difficulty his parents were overly quick to correct. Bobby generalized these corrective attempts to his elementary teacher and particularly to the speech therapy situation. His usual reaction included crying. If the situation continued, he would often become very resistive and hostile to the point of striking the clinician. After this he would frequently explain that he had made a mistake and he didn't want to cry but that he just couldn't help it. Behavior only improved after he experienced role playing situations in which errors and mistakes were deliberately included as part of the roles to be acted. From this point tolerance of his own errors increased and he moved ahead to assume responsibility for his own actions.

Nondirective Counselling

Some of the most helpful information relating to adjustment counselling is contained in the writings of Rogers (1942). His exposition points up the movement of the client from expressions of feeling concerning the problem, expression of faint positive impulses, the development of insight and self-acceptance, consideration of possible courses of action and ultimately, initiation of positive, constructive behavior. This progression is basically similar in all forms of adjustment counselling situations, whether the client is speech handicapped or emotionally disturbed. These steps can be used as a rough guide to progress of the counselling relationship. They are extremely interesting to observe and analyze, but it should be recognized that progress is the normal outgrowth of the relationship between the clinician and the client. The relationship permits emotional catharsis and expression of feelings without threat of reprisal or negative reaction by the counsellor. In addition, it must provide an atmosphere of true acceptance by the counsellor. Improvement occurs because the individual is able to examine and "feel" his behavior without the emotional concomitants and he is able to experience reactions more fitting to the situations encountered. It assumes a desire to be accepted and valued by others. Improved, effective behavior results from self-direction rather than from direct manipulation and instruction by the counsellor. The emphasis for counselling the speech handicapped lies in the areas of reactions to the speech disability and to the social experiences encountered. It is a communication and an exploration of these feelings and attitudes without the actual presence of the external threat encountered in real life situations. In this situation the clinician is always the objective listener never the evaluator, never the judge. By word or facial expression he should not convey messages of surprise, amazement, embarrassment, or displeasure.

The clinician should verbally reward and reinforce improved behavior as soon as the child can accept it, by noting the improved reactions of others to the new behavior. This procedure can often reduce the tendency toward ignoring the cause and effect relationship so important in social contacts. If the child fails to realize that others react to him because of the way he behaves, it is very likely that he will increase his negative social attitudes which, in turn, will be quickly reinforced. The mechanism of role-playing, to be described, is one of the most effective means of pointing up the cause-and-effect importance in human contacts at the affective or feeling level.

Catharsis

Experiences with children suggest that the discussion approach to counselling can be helpful to some speech handicapped children of school age, particularly at the later elementary and secondary levels. It has been surprising to see the open expression of feelings towards family, teachers, and classmates and the acquisition of simple insights which develop. Kyle, with a precocious younger sister who possessed classic female verbal skills, was one of these children.

> For many therapy sessions, Kyle seemed to resent the female clinician's frequent talking. He also showed much resentment towards his sister. These points appeared often in the counselling sessions until one day he exploded with a verbal torrent of abuse which included both sister and clinician. He then said, "You should go to speech class too — and my sister too." While the clinician searched her own speech pattern for some little defect, he added, "You talk too much."

Another boy, who told the clinician about his feelings during severe stuttering commented in the following way:

When I just told you about it, it didn't seem quite so bad. It felt bad when it happened, but now I don't think it would be so bad if it happened all over again.

Unfortunately however, for many children the progress of counselling often bogs down at the point of catharsis and expression of feelings when only verbal discussion is used. Catharsis alone is generally insufficient to achieve adequate emotional adjustment. It must be followed by an active trial and use of new modes of behavior and by experiencing new reactions to otherwise disturbing situations.

Discussion

One of the direct approaches to the solution of some specific and isolated problems causing conflict is through mutual discussion and analysis of that problem with the clinician. The technique has been used by many school mental health workers and guidance counsellors, especially for those problems which are school-centered. Problems centering around behavior at recess, hostile behavior towards a classmate, and difficult relationships with a specific teacher are examples. The clinician and child attempt an objective analysis of the problem, the long-term effect of such continued behavior, and alternative types of behavior which might be employed. This approach operates at the verbal level and usually must be supplemented with experiences at the feeling level.

Role-playing

Another approach which is generally more effective than verbal discussion and direct approaches makes use of the techniques of role-playing. These techniques are also used in sociodrama and psychodrama. They hold extremely high interest for all age levels and provide a vehicle for breaking the habit patterns of stereotyped emotional and behavioral responses. In role-playing, the clinician structures situations which may deal with problems common to the group or which are specific to one of the children. They may revolve around uncomfortable social situations such as being late for an important meeting, difficult parent-child situations, or other emotion-producing speaking situations.

Children are allowed to select or are assigned to the roles of parent, teacher, child, and other important persons in the scene to be enacted. No dialogue is supplied; instead, the general situation is outlined and the lines are elicited spontaneously according to the child's perception of the situation. When the brief scene is completed there is discussion of the ways in which each person reacted to the others. Was the person liked by the group or was he disliked? What words or tone of voice was used which made him liked or disliked? Did he seem angry and hostile or was he friendly and complimentary? When he played the role of being angry, how did the person to whom he was talking behave? Is this the way most people behave when they are angry or when someone attacks them through words? What phrases and words does he often use by habit which have positive effects on the listener? Are there some which are habitually used which produce negative effects? This type of analysis can and should be extended to actions of a nonverbal nature as well. By analyzing the roles played in this way, both the clinician and the children gain considerable insight into the way people react to specific types of behavior. Roles are frequently reversed, either by choice of the child or by judicious assignment of the clinician. At certain points in the counselling program it may be advisable for the inhibited child to play the role of the dominant teacher and parent.

Role-playing also makes possible the trial use of new forms of behavior. Many of these are suggested by the group or occasionally by the clinician. As more varying roles are attempted by each child, there is greater freedom of behavior and greater emotional insights into those forms of behavior which are most satisfying. It is usually preferable to present a choice of roles to the child so that he will have the experience of making his own decisions. Many children do not seem to understand that life presents numerous alternatives. Instead, they seem to feel that they are compelled to act in a specific and often harmful way. The simple method of presenting choices provides stimulation for the child to seek out the alternatives which are always present, to assist in the alleviation of stereotyped responses, and to avoid that "locked in" or trapped feeling common to many poorly adjusted children.

Referral

The speech clinician will also encounter children who are very severely disturbed and whose emotional problems go far beyond those relating to their speech disability. It is essential to recognize when the total psychological and environmental picture is so harmful that attempts at adjustment counselling by the speech clinician are insufficient. Responsibility must be assumed by the clinician for referral of such children to other agencies and services specifically designed to deal with them. When in doubt about the severity of the problem, it is imperative to seek all possible means for professional evaluation. It is indefensible to delay or block treatment of serious emotional problems through the provision of superficial and/or infrequent counselling sessions.

It is extremely fortunate that public schools within the past decade have made marked progress in the provision of services for evaluation and treatment of exceptional children, including those with emotional adjustment difficulties. Increasing numbers of special education programs utilize well-trained itinerant mental health workers, classroom or "crisis" teachers of the emotionally disturbed and personality matching of children and teachers. In many communities there are also child guidance clinic programs, family service agencies, and other professional workers who can be of great assistance. Utilization of these resources when indicated is an essential element of all quality programs.

Counselling Parents of Children with Speech Problems

Although many authors have discussed and advocated direct counselling of the parents of children with speech handicaps, the most convincing evidence of value was presented in a study by Wood (1946). In his study, the speech of children with functional articulation defects whose parents received adjustment counselling made significantly greater improvement than a control group whose parents did not receive counselling. Sommers (1964) and Shea (1958) in separate but similar studies present somewhat contradictory evidence that counselling, at least with respect to parent participation in the speech therapy program itself, has a demonstrable effect. Despite the lack or presence of demonstrated immediate effects in the speech pattern of the child, there are often many benefits which accrue to a counselling program, particularly in relationship to the improved emotional climate in the home and between the home and school.

The speech clinician can be an extremely effective liaison between school and home through a carefully conducted parent counselling program. As clinicians and school administrators experience more of the beneficial effects of parent counselling there is greater expectation that the clinician should have training and skill in this important area. Counselling is no longer an optional accessory; it is becoming a required activity of the effective clinician in many school systems. Numerous school administrators have expressed their conviction that programs with close and continuing parent contact are one of their most valuable public-relations tools. Parents who are aware of the school's interest in their child become enthusiastic and supportive, despite some academic and social problems which the child may experience.

It is also true that school programs involving parents are presented with the opportunity to impair public relations very significantly if carried on with any degree of disinterest, disorganization, or incompetence. Consequently, there is often some administrative reluctance to permit extensive parent contacts until the clinician has proven to be competent in this type of activity.

Most speech clinicians in schools with a case load of seventy-five to one hundred children cannot expect to provide continuing counselling opportunities to parents of more than a very few children. Therefore, it is necessary to select those to be included on some practical basis. The condition of limited openings has made some systems formulate exceedingly restrictive criteria for inclusion, such as the necessity for both parents to be in attendance at all sessions. Such restrictions are neither required nor practical. It is important, however, to center these counselling opportunities on the mothers because of their major influence on the development of the child's attitudes and emotions. Those to be selected should be those whose relationship with the child tends to produce speech anxiety and inhibitory speech behavior. In making this judgment, it is essential to be concerned with the relationship between the parent and child rather than between the parent and the clinician. Scheduling of at least one afternoon or evening group session per week is necessary, with other periods of time available for individual parents to schedule conferences with the clinician as either may desire. It is extremely important to set up a regular schedule of group meetings early in the school year without leaving the matter to chance and conflict with other meeting dates.

A few simple facts regarding parents, clinicians, and the counselling relationship are of value.

1. No parent can be completely objective and rational about his child or about himself.
2. Objective observations of the clinician about either the child or the parent have a reason for being discussed only if some benefit will accrue. The counselling relationship has no place for utterance of objective observations, facts, and other erudite analyses to satisfy the clinician's needs.
3. Parents as well as children will respond best to the clinician who has both sincerity and competency.
4. The counselling relationship always has the potential for expression of the feeling of parental guilt and the utilization of defense techniques.
5. Most parents are very unfamiliar with the terminology of clinical speech and require an explanation of complex ideas with simple vocabulary.

The Initial Contact with Parents

Contact with parents on an "in person" or at least an "in voice" basis, rather than through the use of parent letters which are routinely duplicated with space for the insertion of parent and child names, is strongly urged. Personal contact offers some advantages which can avoid barriers to a good counselling relationship. The initial contact should provide information about specific arrangements which the clinician desires to make with the parent, and it must also provide for a response to potential fears or concerns of the parent. Some parents after reaching the point of reasonable security in the counselling sessions have related an intense feeling of anxiety after the initial contact relating to the "real reasons" for the counselling sessions. One felt that counselling was a prelude to assignment of her child to a class for the retarded, while another thought the sessions were a type of compulsory night school and that she would in some way be graded on her performance.

Parents and teachers, when approached by a specialist often automatically assume a "problem set" born from past experiences in which the specialist expressed or conveyed some element of blame or incompetence. Defensive reactions are normal under these conditions. Unfortunately, these reactions direct one's attentions to rationalizations and explanations and make it very difficult to develop understanding of the speech problems and effective approaches to them. Consequently, it is important not only to minimize these implications, but also to actually build the self-image of the parent or teacher.

If such a problem set is displayed in the opening moments of clinician and parent or teacher contact, the visit should be limited to information gathering with questions directed to the parent or teacher designed to elicit his perception of the problem and the course of action which he may feel is important. The clinician can assist the respondent in formulating constructive thought by suggesting two or more major alternatives from which the person may choose. For example, the teacher or parent may be asked if, in his judgment, the speech errors persist because of a basic inability to hear differences between phonemes or because the child's habitual manner of producing speech developed strongly before fine discriminations were possible. Questions phrased in this manner show respect for the opinions and judgments of the parent and teacher which will make their involvement in the therapy program much easier.

Information Giving

Counselling sessions can effectively include information-giving by the clinician in addition to less formally structured opportunities for catharsis and discussion. Specific information relating to their child's particular speech problem is almost routinely requested by parents and should be provided in a simple, yet complete manner. Some carefully selected reference material can be used for study and later recall by parents in their own homes. Materials of greatest benefit are the small booklets designed for use by parents of the speech handicapped. Many clinicians and schools find it very helpful to have a supply of these booklets available for sale to parents when appropriate. As the counselling sessions progress, there is less need for information-giving. As the parents feel more secure, they will concern themselves more and more with problems which are real to them centering around their own feelings and techniques for aiding their children.

In addition to the information which should be available for each parent about his child's specific speech and behavior condition, it is helpful to communicate three major ideas early in the counselling sequence. First, few parents have an awareness of the complexity of the speech function or of human behavior. Consequently, there is the tendency to feel that the child should be able to alter his speech or behavior pattern simply by being instructed to do so. Parents have also been frustrated in their own direct attempts to alter the situation with this approach and may feel that the child is resistive or negative. A small amount of judicious explanation of the complex functions of encoding, decoding, association, memory, motor, and feedback components of speech can sometimes be helpful in relieving parents of their feelings of frustration and failure.

The second major concept relates to the effect of habit patterns on the maintenance and persistence of behavior once it is learned. Proper understanding of this aspect of learning not only helps the parent understand the discouraging persistence of the disorder, but more significantly, it is an effective inducement for the parents to plan realistic and frequent rewards for altered speech patterns. One mother pointed up the problems of many parents when she said, "I couldn't understand why he'd keep on doing it the wrong way. I tried to correct him over and over again, but it didn't seem to help. I accepted the good things that he did as a matter of course, but always criticized the things I didn't like." This mother began to use a planned program of occasional verbal rewards when her son made attempts to alter his speech. The results were almost immediately apparent as shown by heightened interest in therapy and rapid improvement in the speech pattern.

Third, it is essential to provide an overview of the course of the speech therapy program as it relates to the parent's own child. This must include basic oral explanation of the major aspects of the type of speech problem presented: stuttering, articulation, voice, or speech problems accompanying various organic conditions. It should include an explanation of the reasons for any special diagnostic assessments requested and a discussion of the structure and function of the speech musculature appropriate to the specific disorder. Booklets and selected references previously mentioned are an excellent supplement and extension of the oral explanation.

Dealing with Parents' Questions

As the counselling meetings continue, there will be many topics of significance which will be discussed. Parent concerns often relate to a fear of criticism and ridicule by the child's playmates and by the family's relatives and social contacts, expression of varying forms and degrees of guilt, inadequacy and failure, problems of selecting and evaluating competent medical advice and treatment, the fear of retardation or significant emotional disturbance, lack of understanding by the teacher, vocational prospects for their child, educational achievement questions, social relationship skills, and myriad other concerns. It is neither possible nor desirable to supply answers to many of these questions. Rather, it is essential to accept the concerns as real and to permit the parent to express the problem, and then progress toward a self-answer. Role-playing experiences, as previously described, are often very effective at this point. Many parents seem to get the first inkling of the fact that they can actually guide and manipulate the experiences of their children in a constructive manner several meetings after the first expression of their concerns.

There are, of course, some parents who are more likely to play the "take charge" role and who operate on the basis of "any action is better than nothing." The group process is especially helpful in developing insight for these parents since such an impulsive mode of operation is frequently subject to serious error. These are usually obvious to the other parents and provide much opportunity for group discussion.

Perhaps the most beneficial effect of the parent-counselling effort is the resultant sense of being freed from the imprisoning walls of our culture and society and its many judgments upon others. This sense of personal freedom and worth can be communicated to the speech handicapped child only when the important people in his environment possess it themselves.

The Parents' Role in Therapy

There are some differing opinions as to the efficacy of using the parent as a direct helper in the speech program. It seems very likely that the disagreement arises because it is so difficult to generalize about parents when involved in such a role. Many clinicians who have attempted to use the parent as an aide have quickly found that the procedure may be quite harmful unless very carefully structured. As an example, one clinician, after the lapse of nearly two weeks when the child was ill, found that the parent had used the time at home most effectively by teaching and habituating a seriously distorted phoneme. Similarly, another mother was used in providing ear-training work with her child when she possessed a "tin ear" with very little ability to make accurate discriminations of even gross auditory stimuli. The result, as could be forecast, was a heightened auditory confusion and habituation of error which caused the child to reject all such training.

Despite these and certain other problems, much success can be found in using the parent as an aide when the clinician understands those areas in which the parent can be most effective. It is often helpful to explain that there are two major divisions of the therapy program. First, the clinician must work towards the elicitation of new and correct speech behavior. The *parent* can and should do very little in this first phase. The understandings and approaches here are too delicate to permit anyone other than the speech clinician to attempt. Second, the program works towards habituation of new and correct speech behavior. The strength of thousands of habitually inaccurate productions with their defective auditory, kinesthetic, and tactile feedback sensations, must be replaced by greater strength for the accurate and competing speech patterns. A simple listing of these phases and activities follows. Many other therapy techniques can be classified in the same manner.

ACTIVITIES DIRECTED TOWARDS ELICITING NEW SPEECH PATTERNS
Sound identification
Sound isolation
Sound discrimination
Sound stimulation
Evaluation and treatment of oral structure
Development of motor functions
Articulator placement techniques
Self-analysis of symptom patterns
Reconfiguration techniques

ACTIVITIES DIRECTED TOWARDS HABITUATION OF NEW SPEECH PATTERNS
Use of nucleus situations and times for use of the new speech pattern
Use of special and consistent symbols of elicitation of the new pattern
Negative practice
Repetition of new motor and speech configurations
Use of rewards
Demonstration of newly acquired skills and others

Actual listing of activities in these two major divisions makes it explicit to the parent that techniques directed towards eliciting new speech patterns are highly skilled functions of the speech clinician. It also points up the critical and important role which the parent can play in stimulating use and habituation of the newly acquired patterns. It then becomes apparent that the clinician cannot go much beyond the first division of activities within the brief period each week which is available in the school therapy schedule.

Parents often inquire about the availability of additional therapy opportunities including camps and special schools. Usually this reflects an increased interest in providing all that is possible for their child. Similar inquiries are also made relating to medical and surgical evaluation and treatment. Competent advice in these areas depends upon a knowledge of resources which can only be gained by extensive contact with other professional personnel.

Educational Counselling and the Speech Clinician

The two most important environmental influences in the lives of young children are the home and the school. Just as the parents structure experiences and attitudes in the home, the classroom teacher structures the experiences and the attitudes of the school. The elmentary school child is in extremely close relationship to other children of his class. These children form his social world and provide the experiences for learning social relationships. He is subjected to varying degrees of social and academic stimulation. If this yields behavior which is successful and rewarding, favorable attitudes are built and strengthened. If the child's activities are permitted to produce a preponderance of unsuccessful attempts, inadequacies, or failures, the child will develop many attitudes predisposing him to failure throughout life.

Every speech clinician has worked with children whose class-room teachers have provided a restricting, inhibiting influence. Every clinician has also observed teachers whose classrooms are characterized by encouragement for participation and rewards for sincere attempts. Children fortunate enough to be in such class-rooms are apparent by their positive mental attitudes, their in-terest in learning, and their concern for the well-being of others. The effect of these two extremes on the emotional development of the child is directly related to the marked contrast observable in the classroom atmosphere.

Educational counselling activities of the clinician must deal effectively with the persons and conditions which affect the child's speech patterns and his approach to life. Kaplan, reviewing num-erous studies of emotional maladjustment in the public schools, points out that teachers are no more maladjusted than the general population, but that the role of teachers in the personality de-velopment of children is so critical that great importance should be attached to the mental health status of all educators. His conclu-sions are stated in the following paragraph:

> The problem of maladjustment among children is accentuated by the number of teachers who are ill-equipped to offer them any help be-cause of their own personal difficulties. While no exact data on malad-justment among teachers are available, research indicates that in 1957 there were at least 120,000 seriously maladjusted teachers in the na-tion's classrooms. A group almost twice this size could be described as being unduly nervous. Almost one fourth of the teachers now em-ployed are so unhappy that they would not again become teachers if they had a chance to start over.*

---

*Kaplan, L.: *Mental Health and Human Relations in Education*. New York, Harper, 1959 p. 68.

Occasionally the classroom atmosphere is so harmful to the child that reassignment to another teacher within the building or school district is absolutely essential for the preservation of minimal mental health. Although it is never the clinician's prerogative to effect such changes, it is the clinician's responsibility to make certain that these needs are known to the administrative authority. While mental health workers have often discussed the need for pupil-teacher matching on the basis of personality characteristics and emotional relationships, administrators are very reluctant to reassign pupils without an extreme measure of confidence in the person urging the change. Confidence of this degree comes not only from competence in the clinician's abilities, but also through continuing contact and discussion between the administrator and the clinician.

It is obviously inappropriate to attempt restructuring of the entire school situation to suit only the speech clinician's perceptions. Each year public schools are providing better education for increasing numbers of children. This requires added amounts of time for new curricular inclusions and more adaptation of existing time for many special service personnel including the speech clinician. Consideration of the load of the classroom teacher and the pressures under which he operates will also bring consideration for the clinician's program. Respect for the opinions and competence of other educational personnel must be communicated. Yauch (1952), in an article dealing with the role of the speech clinician, offers several suggestions for procedural approaches to cooperative scheduling and planning with the school staff. His proposal for a point-by-point "school relations plan" underscores the need for mutual understanding between the clinician and other school personnel.

Despite good procedural approaches to cooperative effort, the clinician will frequently meet special problems: the child is so far behind academically that he cannot afford time for speech work; speech class is always scheduled during the arithmetic lesson; little can be expected of him because his parents don't amount to much; if he does not participate in group discussion it is because he doesn't know much; children who resist or persist in certain behavior are stubborn or lazy; the best mental hygiene comes from mastery of subject matter. These attitudes have been expressed for many years. While they stem from a certain lack of understanding and perhaps from teacher maladjustment, it should be recognized that children with disabilities present many special difficulties for the teacher. There is no question but that the speech handicapped child, as well as other exceptional children, requires an inordinate amount of the teacher's time and energy. It is frustrating to find that the efficient learning of academic material is hampered by children in the group who have special learning problems. Speech handicapped children are particularly prone to present difficulties in the language arts, including reading and spelling. It may also be irritating to the teacher to find that many special arrangements must be made for consultation, discussion, and assistance for a small number of children.

The Teacher's Role in Therapy

With the majority of teachers whose classrooms provide emotional support and understanding, counselling will most often concern itself with providing specific information relative to the type of speech problem present. The teacher will often want to know if she should attempt to help the child in his speech efforts in the classroom. The answer to this question is generally affirmative, but the clinician will want to make certain judgments as to the manner of help which the teacher can provide. Success is much more likely when the basic therapy plan is explained and the two major divisions of therapy previously discussed are understood by the teacher. As in the case of parents, it is most desirable to request teacher assistance in the second phase of therapy relating to habituation of new patterns. Specific suggestions may include the use of some type of private signal between the teacher and child for correction of an error or for signaling the beginning of a one sentence "good speech time." The teacher will also be able to make judgments relating to the class activities in which to provide this type of stimulation. Although reading groups are often used for this purpose, there are some children whose reading abilities are such that correction at this time may have a very harmful effect.

It is legitimate to assume that one of the main tasks of counselling with educational personnel is the provision of professional and technical information. Here the clinician must provide and interpret the required information as appropriate. It is not realistic to expect the teacher to read extensively in the many areas of clinical speech. While the booklets previously mentioned for parents are the most helpful type of reference material for the teacher, it is also necessary to discuss salient points relating to individual children orally. It is often assumed that information-giving can proceed in a relatively straightforward manner because teachers are not emotionally involved with the children to any great extent. However, the way in which it is presented is highly critical because it frequently evokes emotional responses. Directives to the teacher are of little value. Information-giving must be a two-way street with understanding by both clinician and teacher. Asking questions such as Do you think Shari is ready to try her new sound before the group? or Does Sue seem to respond a little better when praised? are very useful. They assume an interest and a competence on the part of the teacher which will not quickly be discredited. Questions phrased in this manner are also useful in introducing consideration of teacher use of speech improvement, role-playing, and creative dramatics.

Phonics and Phonetics

The speech clinician and the elementary teacher have much common interest in reading and language arts instruction. The use of ear-training techniques by the clinician relates directly to the phonic approach to language arts used for instruction in reading and spelling. It is important for the clinician to know the early elementary teachers of her children and their philosophy and techniques in the area of phonics. Both are interested in the development of sound consciousness. Teacher-clinician discussion of the beneficial effects of such training and appreciation for its use should be expressed. Differences between the concept of "phonetics" as used by the speech clinician and those of "phonics" as used in the classroom should be minimized as much as possible.

Another area of concern for both teacher and clinician is

techniques and methods for the improvement of learning. Teachers know and understand that good students receive the greatest recognition and rewards, but that the poorer students need it the most. What may not be understood, however, is that the speech handicapped student typically needs acceptance and reward far beyond ordinary requirements because of the backlog of frustration and failure previously experienced. Similarly, this backlog dictates the need for understanding and planning a gradual approach to feared or unpleasant activities which maximize success opportunities. The techniques of "desensitization" as described by Van Riper (1959) have application to all learning situations.

The public school clinician typically has great freedom for the establishment and direction of the clinical speech program. This may breed an independence and isolation from the remainder of the school program which may be convenient, but which will interfere with effectiveness of the total program. The clinician may work with a child only one hour per week; the classroom teacher and other school personnel direct the child's activities, stimulate, reward or penalize twenty-five to thirty hours each week. The clinician has an intense interest in these hours. In the cooperative effort involved in the child's rehabilitation the speech clinician should do his part in making all of these hours productive for the child.

SUMMARY

Oral language presents a potential for emotional conflict to the child with a speech handicap. Frustration and impaired self-concepts frequently follow sensitization to public reaction in the presence of speech deviations. The child's behavior reflects his awareness of these reactions through avoidance and other symptomatic behavior which often follows a spiral development pattern.

Counselling the child focuses upon alleviating self-defeating behaviors, improving the self-concept, and exploring associated evidences of maladjustment. The speech behavior itself provides specific entry points for counselling. Some useful methods of counselling include direct verbal discussion of feelings, discussion of specific symptomatic behaviors, and techniques of role-playing. The effect of learning and habit in both speech and emotional behavior necessitates counselling which assists the child in selecting alternatives to break the stereotyped response pattern. Similarly, understanding of cause-and-effect relationships in positive social contacts can be provided at the "feeling" level.

Counselling with parents should be directed towards 1) provision of pertinent information relative to the various aspects of the child's disorder, 2) the effects of various parent-child interactions with special direction towards perceived success and failure, and 3) delineation of the point in the clinical speech program when the parent can contribute. The clinician's exclusive role is defined as that which elicits new patterns of speech production, while parents, teachers, and others can effectively aid in habituation of new responses.

Counselling with teachers and other educational personnel provides the clinician with additional insights and information and offers a vehicle for extending into the classroom the new behavior resulting from speech therapy. It also focuses upon the emotional climate of the classroom as it bears directly upon individual children with speech handicaps.

DISCUSSION TOPICS

1. Why is it that speech handicapped children with emotional problems find it so difficult to concentrate on altering their speech patterns?
2. In what ways does children's behavior reflect parental attitudes?
3. What signs are frequently present in behavior of children and parents which suggest that the discussion is approaching an emotionally sensitive area?
4. In what ways does children's behavior reflect parental treatment? Parental social attitudes?
5. What clues are present in the language behavior of children which give indications of a predominance of self-perceived failure?
6. What is the usual effect of asking numerous questions of a

child when he feels insecure? What type of questions can be used to build the self-concept?

7. What characteristics of your own personality are helpful in the counselling relationship? Which ones act as barriers?

8. The school administrator will hear varying reports of your counselling sessions. What steps and procedures would you follow to increase his confidence in the appropriateness of your efforts?

9. If it is true that children have a strong desire to be accepted by others, why do some with emotional maladjustments persist in behavior unacceptable to others?

10. Are you more effective in counselling with individuals or groups? Why?

REFERENCES

1. ANDERSLAND, P.: Maternal and environmental factors related to success in speech improvement training. *J Speech Hearing Res, 4:*79-90, March, 1961.

2. CHAPIN, A.: Parent education for preschool defective children. *J Exceptional Child, 15:*75-80, January, 1959.

3. GREENE, M.: *Learning To Talk.* New York, Harper, 1960.

4. IRWIN, R.: *A Speech Pathologist Talks To Parents and Teachers.* Pittsburgh, Stanwix House, 1962.

5. JOHNSON, W.: *Toward Understanding Stuttering.* Chicago, National Society for Crippled Children and Adults, 1958.

6. McDONALD, E.: *Bright Promise.* Chicago, National Society for Crippled Children and Adults, 1959.

7. McWILLIAMS, B.: Adult education program for mothers of children with speech handicaps. *J Speech Hearing Dis, 24:*408-410, August, 1951.

8. ROGERS, C.: *Counselling and Psychotherapy.* Boston, Houghton, 1942.

9. SHEA, W.: The effect of supplementary parental procedures in public school functional articulation cases. *Speech Monographs, 25:*142-143, March, 1958.

10. SOMMERS, R., *et al.:* Effects of maternal attitudes upon improvement in articulation when mothers are trained to assist in speech correction. *J Speech Hearing Dis, 29:*126-132, June, 1964.

11. SOMMERS, R.: Training parents of children with functional misarticulation. *J Speech Hearing Res, 2:*258-265, August, 1959.

12. SOMMERS, R.: Factors in effectiveness of mothers trained to aid in speech correction. *J Speech Hearing Dis, 27:*178-186, June, 1962.

13. TUFTS, L., and HOLLIDAY, A.: Effectiveness of trained parents as speech therapists. *J Speech Hearing Dis, 24:*395-401, November, 1959.

14. VAN RIPER, C.: *Teaching Your Child to Talk*. New York, Harper, 1950.
15. VAN RIPER, C.: *Your Child's Speech Problems*. New York, Harper, 1961.
16. VAN RIPER, C.: *Stuttering*. Chicago, National Society for Crippled Children and Adults, 1959.
17. WOOD, K.: The parent's role in the clinical program. *J Speech Hearing Dis, 13*:209-210, August, 1948.
18. WOOD, K.: Parental maladjustment and functional articulation defects in children. *J Speech Hearing Dis, 11*:255-275, August, 1946.
19. YAUCH, W.: The role of a speech correctionist in the public school. *Exceptional Child, 18*:97-101, February, 1952.

Chapter 6

THE SPEECH CLINICIAN – AS A RESEARCHER

OLIVER M. NIKOLOFF

SPEECH CLINICIANS OFTEN find themselves wearing many hats. The schools in which they function may expect them to serve as educators of teachers and parents, informal psychologists, and counsellors, as well as to provide therapy to children with speech problems. Increasingly, an even higher degree of sophistication is being required of the speech clinician in the decision making processes necessary for selecting principles, rules, best methods and techniques, and instruments for obtaining further knowledge. School speech clinicians will continue to be called upon to justify initiation, continuation, and expansion of clinical speech correction programs in the schools.

THE THREE R's OF DECISION MAKING

Persons engaged in the study of human behavior employ the same three R's of decision making as do workers in politics, medicine, or any other field (Ross and Stanley, 1960). These R's – rhetoric, reputation, and research – can be seen operating simultaneously in the broad area of education. School speech clinicians and others concerned with changing behavior, use these R's constantly, but not always with full awareness of on what their decisions are based.

Rhetoric

Rhetoric is perhaps the oldest of these methods and falls within the realm of classical speech study. In essence many decisions have been and will continue to be made on the basis of the most persuasive argument. From Grecian times to the present day, rhetoric has involved logical reasoning in the form of deductive processes. The syllogism (if a=b, and b=c, then a=c) was the

134

hallmark and keystone of this method and conjecture was frequently substituted for experimentation. Today in schools many procedures and curricula are presented because these seem to be "the logical" ways of doing business. Many a parent and teacher, unsophisticated in the area of speech, demonstrates this form of logic by requiring the child who stutters to "think about what you are going to say" or "go slowly."

Reputation

Reputation has played and continues to play a role in the decision making process in schools. In the past a quote from Aristotle or Benjamin Franklin was often good enough reason for accepting a goal or approving a procedure. Today at professional meetings of scholars the name-dropping of an eminent person as proof of merit is still a common and powerful technique. If Conant or even Rickover can be quoted as favoring a practice, it often requires substantial and convincing experimental evidence to the contrary to alter the practice.

Research

Yet, it is the third R, research, that is preeminent today in providing the substantial and convincing evidence needed to produce many educational decisions. True, not all educational decisions can be based upon research. The decision to provide clinical speech in schools, for instance, may be based partly upon the incidence of speech problems among the children. Ultimately, however, those in a position to make decisions must believe that speech therapy is worthwhile and is the task of the school — both *philosophically* based opinions. Research techniques are presently available which provide useful information bearing upon many types of educational decisions.

The Scientific Method

Research can be characterized in both simple and elaborate terms. In simple form it can be called a scientific or systematic method of observation that leads to more complete understanding of a situation, relationship, or cause. A more detailed description of the heart of the research technique usually includes the following steps:

1. Observation of pertinent facts concerning a problem.
2. Developing a hypothesis or hypotheses.
3. Experimentation or testing of hypotheses.
4. Generalization or conclusions.

This set of rules has come to be known as the scientific method.

The earliest application of the research approach in education is credited to a physician, Joseph Rice (1897), who reported an investigation of spelling practices employing more than 100,000 pupils. His investigation offers a useful contrast between the rhetorical and the research approaches. From early times it had seemed a reasonable and self-evident truth to educators that the amount of learning acquired was directly proportional to the time devoted to that subject. If the average pupil could learn to spell ten words in twenty minutes, then approximately twenty words could be learned by doubling the time on spelling. Employing the basic four steps of the scientific method, Rice identified classes of children in schools throughout the country that had been exposed to different amounts of time each day devoted to spelling (observation of pertinent facts), questioned whether increased amounts of time yielded greater spelling proficiency (the hypothesis), administered a uniform spelling test to all the pupils in all the classes that formed his sample (experimentation or testing of the hypothesis), and concluded that there was no difference in spelling mastery between groups of children who had only ten or fifteen minutes to practice and those who drilled for three or four times as long (the generalization or conclusion concerning spelling proficiency).

Rice's early research on spelling has been replicated by other investigators and today in most schools the recommended amount of time allotted daily spelling is approximately fifteen minutes.

Behavioral Science

Research is sometimes differentiated by classification and by purpose. While the general purpose of all research is to improve understanding, sometimes the subject of research is inanimate (as in such natural sciences as physics and chemistry) . When humans and animals are studied, the label "behavioral sciences" is attached. The major behavioral sciences are psychology, sociology, anthropology, and education.

Applied and Pure Research

"Applied" research and "pure" research represent different purposes. The name "applied" indicates that utilization or consumption has taken place. Pure research has as its purpose the acquisition of knowledge alone without specific consideration for economic or social application.

Phonetics, the science of speech sounds, seeks to discover and describe the sounds produced in the spoken forms of the various languages of the world. The researcher who records the sounds utilized in the Gungh-Ho Chinese dialect may be doing *pure* research. The researcher who used this knowledge to develop a new Chinese alphabet is engaging in *applied* research.

In a broad sense the term "research" has come to mean intensive investigation of a problem, and the search for a solution may be conducted by teams of highly specialized professional technicians or by a kindergartner who is undertaking his first organized and directed study. While there are objections raised to the notion that any intensive study that does not have as its goal unique or new knowledge is really research, the broadest view of research allows the term to signify both uniqueness as a product and uniqueness as a process. It is common practice at the college level for a student to conduct a research project that in reality is practice for the student in skill-building rather than a contribution to the body of knowledge in that student's field. In effect, then, the research effort in any given set of circumstances is governed by the researcher's level of skill and sophistication.

RESEARCH AND CLINICAL SPEECH

In undertaking a review of research as it applies to the field of clinical speech in particular, it is necessary to view the topic in general terms of methods (the major approaches and principles), or techniques (the ways of executing the investigative process), or instrumentation (the particular devices used for measuring).

Methods

There are three major methods or approaches in the research process. If the object of the study is chiefly the understanding of causations and probabilities, the label for the research method is "historical." If the object is chiefly the establishment of standards or norms, the method is called "descriptive." If principles or laws are the major subjects of study, the method of research is designaed "experimental." The methodology is not always clearly one type or another; sometimes a combination such as "historical-descriptive" is employed.

The Historical Method

The historical method is undoubtedly the oldest and perhaps the most widely practiced method of research. It gets its name from the effort of historians to understand past events from the standpoint of cause and effect. Original sources are used whenever possible; the Dead Sea Scrolls are considered an especially valuable Biblical resource because of their great age and consequent closeness to the events described. The Greek historian, Thucydides (460-400 BC), is given credit for bringing history into the realm of research by employing two techniques to explain the causations and circumstances of the Peloponnesian War. He attempted to portray the conflict with chronological precision and intensive investigation of the facts. He also rejected magical and mythical explanations of causation in deference to critical analysis of natural causes.

The speech clinician employs the historical method in specialized form almost daily. The case study is an intensive investigation of an individual in which the chronology of events is regarded as crucial and in which critical analysis by the clinician of his client's circumstances serves to explain the client's behavior. Consider the following six steps, outlined by Auer (1959), as essential elements of the historical method, as they apply to a typical referral to a speech clinician.

1. *Problem* (a selected person is the subject of historical review which includes pertinent information that bears on causes of behavior).

Steve is referred by his teacher to the speech clinic because he stutters when he is called upon to recite in class.

2. *Working hypothesis* (a theoretical explanation of the cause, or the means of arriving at a solution to the problem).

Steve's stuttering, hypothesizes the clinician, is probably the product of the circumstances or environment in his present classroom as they relate to some historical antecedents.

3. *Research design* (a plan for gathering information systematically from the primary source and secondary sources).

Steve (the primary source) must be interviewed, examined, and perhaps observed in several settings. Steve's teacher, parents, peers (secondary sources) must be interviewed, either in person or by means of documentation.

4. *Collection of evidence* (the procedures outlined in the research design are executed).

Steve and others are interviewed; the records of health and previous school experiences are consulted.

5. *Analysis* (the interpretation of the evidence that has been collected).

Have Steve and the secondary sources reported accurately in terms of their observations, their memories, and their verbalization? Can these reports be synthesized critically into patterns of Steve's stuttering in terms of time, place, and circumstance?

6. *Generalization* (explanation with direction toward solution of the problem).

Can Steve's stuttering be explained logically by his historical and environmental circumstances? Are solutions to his problem suggested? Should Steve be excused from recitation in class? Should therapy be initiated?

It should be apparent that the historical method is usually supplemented by further attempts to understand Steve's behavior. These efforts include both descriptive and experimental procedures. Yet it should be clear that one application of the historical approach plays a vital role in the understanding of behavior the speech clinician brings to bear in his job.

Occasionally other familiar applications of the historical method are made by the speech clinician. In advancing reasons for a new or expanded clinical speech program in a school system, it may be necessary for the clinician to compose a study of the development of the local program with documentation of its success and illustration of the need for improvements.

The Descriptive Method

Of the three methods of research discussed in this chapter, the most frequently employed by the speech clinician is probably the topic detailed here — the descriptive method. The major characteristic of this method is its power to ascertain what presently exists. What are the norms or frames of reference that we employ to describe a secondary stutterer or an articulation defect? If we know how frequently children enter school with cleft palates, or have major hearing losses, can we plan more effective special programs for them? Can we develop more suitable methods for individual or group therapy, knowing the frequency of improvement of children who have studied lipreading?

Descriptive research in the field of speech, according to Auer (1959), can be classified under four major headings: 1) studies of behavior, 2) studies of development and status, 3) analytical studies, and 4) methodological studies.

Studies of behavior are usually divided into two major classifications: survey and observation. Surveys are widely used in commercial as well as scholarly endeavor, and probably every reader of these words has been a participant in some capacity in a survey study — "What is your favorite TV program?" "Do you believe teachers should be permitted to use corporal punishment?"

Questionnaires or interviews are the typical methods of obtaining behavioral information. The questionnaire is a structured written instrument that usually permits the gathering of a limited amount of information from a large number of subjects. The interview is usually differentiated from the questionnaire in that personal contact takes place during the interview and further questions can be asked and clarifications can be made more easily by the interviewer. The number of interviews that can be obtained in a period of time is usually substantially fewer than the responses to a mail-out questionnaire. However, the quantity, quality, and reliability of the responses to the interview may be higher than that obtained through the questionnaire.

Observations, either direct or indirect, constitute the other major form of studying behavior. Systematic recording of impressions at the time and the studying of tapes, pictures, or audiograms at a later time are the methods used. The well-known anecdotal record is one of the most widely employed behavioral study techniques of the classroom teacher. The speech clinician commonly uses the tape recorder to permit later review of a session with a child or group of children.

Studies of development and status have already been reviewed in part in the previous discussion of the historical method. Case studies and genetic studies fall under the heading of status and development. The example of Steve, the stutterer, outlined the familiar elements of case study. Genetic studies are typically made of small groups over long periods of time with the objectives of understanding better the origins, development, rates of growth of the particular characteristics under scrutiny. By means of genetic studies, much has come to be known of the development of speech patterns. Perhaps the most ambitious and famous genetic study is that of Terman's (1925-26, 1930, 1947, 1959) gifted children. That investigation, begun in 1925, employing over 1000 elementary and junior high children, is continuing today. The periodic assessment of this group has provided enormous amounts of descriptive information about very bright people. Research that continues over long periods of time with repeated sampling of behavior is called longitudinal. In contrast, research that focuses on an isolated period of time is called cross-sectional. If the school speech clinician examined a sample of third graders with the purpose of discovering how many had voice problems, this kind of research would be called cross-sectional. The group is being examined at one particular time without direct reference to past or future. If this group of third graders were examined again as fifth graders and again as seventh graders or on some similar consistent periodic basis, this kind of research would be called longitudinal.

Analytical studies have gained greater attention from researchers in speech during the past decade. Content analysis is basically the classification of the frequency of occurrence of designed symbols or signs in a communication. Thus, infant speech sounds could be classified or slang vocabularies of high school seniors analyzed.

Methodological studies are perhaps the most valuable and at the same time the most difficult to execute in any scientific field. Studies of this variety produce both criteria for evaluating and instruments for measuring. How do we know what "good" speech is? What constitutes a stuttering or articulation "problem"? These are called criterion issues. Establishing norms or typical performances is essential in dealing with criterion issues. How can it be established that a child reaches the norm or is defective in some aspect of speech or hearing? Instruments or tests are of direct use in this endeavor. The speech clinician is a consumer of many devices, and he may develop instruments independently. Independently developed devices rarely meet standards of adequacy in terms of validity and reliability. These qualities, the first meaning that the instrument measures what it purports to measure and the second indicating the consistency of measurement, are technically difficult to obtain without considerable statistical sophistication on the clinician's part. Most school speech clinicians must be satisfied in the realm of methodological research to be wise employers of instruments rather than creators of such devices.

The reader will recall that the historical method of research employs significant events of the past as the criterion for making judgments and predicting future events. The descriptive method provides frames of reference or norms by which we could compare alternatives in making judgments and predicting future events.

The third major research method is labeled "experimental," and its chief characteristic is the control of all variables except the one in question. By holding all but one (sometimes several variables are experimental) factor constant a systematic study of operation and effects takes place.

The Experimental Method

A more detailed examination of the experimental method reveals that three major concepts underlie this procedure. The principle of "causation" is the first of these. If cannon balls of different sizes and weights are dropped from the Leaning Tower and fall to earth with the same speed, it is concluded, after repeated trials, that there is a cause-and-effect relationship between falling bodies and the earth. Human behavior is almost always more complex than the famous cannon-ball illustration. Single cause leading to single effect is not usually sufficient to explain why Steve stutters or why Sarah's *th* sound is misarticulated. Several determining factors (multiple-causation) leading to the effect are nearly always involved. Yet, the experimental method exists on the premise that the causes for the effects may be isolated and identified.

In order to isolate the cause leading to the effect the concepts of *independent* and *dependent* variables are employed. In its simplest form the independent variable is the one that is manipulated or changed by the experimenter, and the dependent variable is responsive to the manipulation of the independent factor. If time devoted to articulation drill is varied — one group receives fifteen minutes a day, another group thirty minutes once a week — *time* is the independent variable. *Improvement* in an articulation performance is the dependent variable.

The third major concept in the experimental method is called control. The principle of constancy of environment, except for the elements being scrutinized, is not foreign to either the historical or the descriptive method of research. Most experimentation in the fields of speech involves the use of groups rather than individuals. A variety of schemes have been devised to provide the balancing of environmental circumstances. Among the most popular are the following:

1. The matched pair technique — two groups are identified with pairs having nearly the same characteristics — identical twins are the best illustration.
2. The equated group technique — the average characteristics of each group in many dimensions are the same.
3. The single group technique — the same group receives different treatments at different times.
4. The rotated group technique — a refinement of the single group procedure. Each group receives the same treatments in a mathematically balanced order.

After the experimenter has completed the collection of his data, how does he know if there is a genuine cause and effect relationship? The answer to the question is never absolute — either Yes or No. All experimentation is based on the principle of probability of occurrence. When a relationship between independent and dependent variables is viewed as being unlikely to occur by chance alone, a conclusion is drawn that a cause and effect relationship exists. The reader reasonably will ask, How unlikely is unlikely? The answer to this question is more complicated. The decision to declare a cause-and-effect relationship to be genuine rather than the product of a set of "fluky" circumstances is arbitrary. In most behavioral sciences the likelihood of the apparent relationship's happening five or fewer times in one hundred by chance (fluky circumstances) is considered fair evidence to substantiate the reality of cause and effect. The answer to the relationship question is always, then, a qualified statistical one (At the end of the chapter a brief statistical resume will be given).

Consider these questions, Is it possible that the sun will *not* rise tomorrow? Is it possible that Steve, who has stuttered every day for five years, will awake tomorrow and *never* stutter again? In the statistical sense we would have to concede that it is possible that either of these events will occur tomorrow, but we would probably insist that each is extremely unlikely (or more unlikely than five times in one hundred). Yet we cannot be absolutely certain. Certainty in the scientific realm can only be considered as a definition. If we label a chair by that name, or an audiometer by that name, these objects are not estimated to be so in terms of chance — they are absolutes (until we change the label).

Although the discussion of probability, popularly known as the law of chance, has been focused on the experimental method of research, the theory of probability is used to test hypotheses based on the historical and descriptive methods as well.

MEASUREMENT

It should be clear that in order to make inferences about cause-and-effect relationships or differences between individuals or groups, a measuring system of some kind needs to be assigned to the phenomena being observed. It is assumed that the numbers used represent the phenomena in a meaningful and orderly fashion.

Stevens (1951) describes four levels of measurement that are commonly employed in the behavioral sciences. The lowest or simplest scale of measurement is dichotomous — Steve is a stutterer or he is not a stutterer. The statement is true or it is false. In a more refined form of nominal scaling, Sarah could be categorized or classified in one of five levels of severity of articulation difficulty. In these illustrations there is no mathematical relationship between categories except as each is considered to be different and distinguishable from the other.

The next degree of refinement in measurement is called ordinal scaling. The essential quality in this form of measurement is the *ranking* of phenomena. Sarah, who was earlier identified on a nominal scale as being a level-three articulation problem, could be identified *within* this category as being less severe than Sally, but more severe than Joyce. We do not know how much less severe an articulation problem Sarah is than Sally or how much more severe than Joyce, but we know her position, and the *position* of all the other people on the scale in relation to one another.

The interval scale indicates not only Sarah's, Sally's, and Joyce's position in relation to one another, but it assesses the distance between each person. Suppose, for this third level of refinement of measurement, the intelligence quotients for Sarah, Sally, and Joyce are 150, 100, and 75 respectively. It is not only obvious that Sarah, Sally, and Joyce can be ranked, but that there is a *calibrated* distance between persons. However, can we say that Sarah is twice as bright as Joyce or that Sally is two-thirds as intelligent as Sarah? The answer to each of these questions is almost certainly No. In fact, if Sarah and Joyce were both ten years of age, Sarah's vocabulary might be five times larger than Joyce's rather than twice as large. What reliance, then, can be placed in an interval scale for which the units are not really equal? Many behavioral traits can be conveniently placed on interval scales which have no absolute zero points or properties that make them suitable to complete algebraic manipulation. The attractive feature of interval scaling is the suitability of powerful statistical applications when the characteristics of the intervals on the scale (though not equal) are known.

If the scale has characteristics of absolute equality between units, the fourth and most refined level of measurement has been reached. Very few traits in the domain of the behavioral sciences can be assessed on ratio scales. In school settings Sarah's height or weight could be compared to Sally's and it could be determined that one was two-thirds as tall as the other. But measures of this kind, though the most *precise* in terms of refinement, are not characteristics that the school speech clinician is likely to be interested in from a research viewpoint.

The nature of the research problem determines the method of scaling to be employed. Many times the behavioral researcher must be satisfied with relatively crude measuring applications because his data are not amenable to great refinement.

Speech clinicians are likely to use a combination of measurements. Imagine that a study is set up in which a group of children having had nursery school and kindergarten experiences is compared at third grade level with a group whose schooling started at first grade. The speech clinician seeks to determine whether or not significant differences exist between groups in the number and degree of severity of speech problems. In this illustration, years of schooling can be measured very precisely — on a ratio scale. The degree of refinement involved in measuring the number of children and degree of severity of their speech problems will probably be quite crude, — perhaps in three categories: no problems, mild problems, or severe problems.

SAMPLING

A feature of research that is intimately related to the measurement process is known as the sampling problem. Almost never does the researcher have opportunity (because of time, cost, or simple unavailability) to observe or measure the complete population that is to be studied. The speech clinician who wishes to ascertain the prevalence in per cent of children in his school system who have voice problems may not be able to interview every one of three thousand pupils. Instead he may have to be satisfied to interview one hundred children who represent adequately the entire school population.

The process of sample selection is based on a premise that if a fair and unbiased method is employed with a large enough sample that a much smaller group can be representative of the entire population. The accuracy of modern sampling procedures is exemplified by the success of predicting the outcome of most recent presidential elections involving millions of votes. The representative sample included only thousands of statements by people of how they thought they would vote on election day.

Two systems of sampling are commonly employed. The least complicated is called random sampling; this method is typically used when little is known about the population.

Random Sampling

If three thousand children form the population of a school system from which one hundred are to be randomly selected, all children's names from the attendance roster could be placed on slips of paper, placed in a waste basket and shaken, and one hundred drawn from the container. A random selection for ascertaining the prevalence of voice problems could thus be obtained. The essential quality involved in the selection process is that everyone of the three thousand children had an equal chance to be selected. A more efficient method for obtaining the names of the one hundred children is by use of a table of random numbers — a set of numbers that serves the same purpose as drawing names from a waste basket or a hat.

Restricted Sampling

The second sampling technique, restricted sampling, includes *stratified, quota,* and *selective* methods. A stratified sample from three thousand children might prescribe random selection of ten children at each grade level. Because of known characteristics of a graded school organization, the researcher might want his sample to include an equal number from each grade.

As is quite likely, there are more children in the elementary grades than in the twelfth grade (sixteen-year-olds who drop out reduce the upper-grade population), and a quota sampling method might be employed which called for twelve sixth graders and eight twelfth graders to be chosen.

Selective sampling would be employed if a particular characteristic were thought to be associated with voice problems in the school population. From the school medical records, all children with frequent colds might form a group from which the one hundred would be randomly chosen.

The determination of the size of the sample is dependent on a number of factors. The representativeness of each respondent, the difficulty of obtaining accurate responses, the size of the entire population are among the most important considerations. The school speech clinician would be wise to seek the advice of a statistically sophisticated person before research is begun which employs sampling techniques. A basic flaw in much otherwise adequate research design is the use of biased or inadequate sampling techniques.

STATISTICAL METHODS

Although the school speech clinician may have a modest background in the domain of statistics and may need to consult with a specialist on complicated techniques, the basic measures of central tendency, variation, and correlation should be within the clinician's repertoire.

Central Tendency

The two measures that are most commonly used to portray the typical or "average" characteristic or person in a group are the *median* and the *mean*. The median is the midpoint in a group of measures when these are arranged from highest to lowest. Suppose the clinician has administered an articulation test to one hundred children and he wishes to know the typical or average number of errors for that group. By stacking the papers in a pile, placing the paper with the fewest errors on the bottom and completing the stack with the paper or papers with the greatest number of errors on top, the task of systematic measurement has begun. To find the midpoint or halfway mark, the fiftieth and fifty-first papers need to be identified; two piles are thus separated (as are modern superhighways) by the median. The formula for finding the median is the following: $N + 1 \div 2$ (N represents the number of persons or characteristics in the sample). In the illustration above, $100 + 1 \div 2 = 50.5$, the point halfway between the fiftieth and fifty-first papers. The median is a stable measure of central tendency; it is not affected by extremely high or low scores, and it is simple to obtain even without aid of distribution tables, desk calculators, or computers. In school settings, particularly on standardized tests of achievement, the median is the most popular descriptive measure of central tendency.

The arithmetic mean is obtained by summing the scores in a distribution and dividing the sum by the number of cases (N). The formula for obtaining the mean is as follows: $\Sigma X \div N$ (Σ stands for "sum of"; X, for each individual score). In the illustration of one hundred cases used in the preceding paragraph, each score is accumulated until the sum of the one hundred articulation-error papers has been obtained. That total is then divided by 100. It is not necessary to put the scores in order using this method of calculating the mean; however, when a large N is involved, a frequency distribution technique is often employed. The frequency distribution is a systematic method of grouping scores by intervals for convenience of handling. Thus, if the grouping interval is 5, all articulation-error papers from 0 errors to 4 errors would be collected together as a single package that is identified by the frequency or number of cases within. The 0-4 frequency interval might include three cases; the 5-9 interval, seven cases.

The arithmetic mean is sensitive to extremely high and low scores and may portray with some distortion the "typical" or "average" case. When the mean is "pulled up" by very high scores or "pulled down" by extremely low scores, the distribution is called skewed. Despite these limitations, the arithmetic mean is preferred by statisticians because it can be used for inferential as well as descriptive purposes. By comparing the means of two groups of students, one from a suburban and one from an urban area who had been given an articulation-error test, it would be possible to infer which group "averaged" more errors. The median is not amenable to such interpretation.

The *mode* is a third measure of central tendency, but it is seldom used except as a very gross yardstick. The mode is simply the score occurring most frequently.

Measures of Dispersion

Dispersion or *variability* of scores in a group is sometimes of greater interest than the central tendency measures. The school speech clinician who is giving group therapy to eight children may be more concerned about the range of different problems than the typical problem of his group.

The most popularly employed measure of variability is called the standard deviation. It is the companion measure to the mean and it is measured from the mean. If a score is one standard deviation above the mean, it marks the point above which 16 per cent of the scores fall (one standard deviation below the mean extends down to the bottom 16 per cent). It is possible to use this measure of dispersion to calculate two or more standard deviations or parts of standard deviations. The method of obtaining the SD will not be detailed here, however, the reader who has not had a formal course in statistics will find an excellent introduction to this and other statistical measures in the booklet *Shortcut Statistics for Teacher-made Tests*. Not only does the SD provide a consistent distance measure from the mean for a single distribution of scores, but its properties can be interpreted and translated for other sets of scores — there is a "standard" quality about it.

The other frequently used measure of variation is related to the median. The distribution is first divided into one hundred parts, called percentiles. The uppermost quarter is marked by the 75th percentile and the lowest quarter is marked by the 25th percentile. These points are called the third and first quartile. The term "interquartile range" denotes the distance between the first and third quartiles and measures the middle 50 per cent of the distribution. Scores beyond the two quartiles are the more extreme or deviant scores in the distribution. It is possible, using the percentile method of description, to identify not only the quartiles but also the scores at points of the distribution.

Graphs

One of the most illuminating ways of understanding statistical data is to see these data plotted in graphical form. The following illustration shows the distribution of one hundred students who were administered the articulation-error test.

Figure 7 is called a histogram or block graph. The number of errors ranges from 0 to 7 on the base line. The one hundred students are grouped in intervals of 4 in the vertical direction.

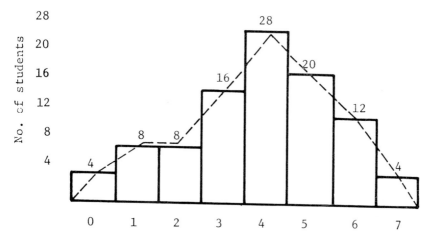

Articulation Errors

FIGURE 7. A histogram and frequency polygon of 100 students who were administered an articulation-error test.

To find the mean apply the formula $\Sigma X \div N$. $(384 \div 100 = 3.84)$. To find the median apply the formula $N + 1 \div 2$ $(100 + 1 \div 2 = 50.5)$. The score 50.5 is one below which half the students fall and above which half fall. Thirty-six students made three or fewer errors, and thirty-six students made five or more errors. The halfway mark or median is located exactly halfway between three errors and five errors at 4.

The mean in this distribution is below or smaller than the median and indicates a degree of "negative" skewness. Several extremely low error scores were not counterbalanced by a similar distribution of high error scores. A lack of symmetry of distribution was produced, indicated by the longer "tail" of scores on the left side of the histogram. Had a longer tail been produced on the right hand side of the distribution, it would have been labeled "positively" skewed. Skewed distributions are quite common when small samples such as the one illustrated above are involved. The appropriateness of the mean or median and the measures of variability, as well, are related to the degree of skewness. When the distribution is greatly skewed, the mean and standard deviation are less reliable descriptions.

Another commonly used method of presenting a graphical picture of a distribution of scores is called a frequency polygon. Note the dotted lines on the previous histogram. This method shows a smoothed rather than a blocked picture of the scores.

Many statistical applications are designed to do more than offer descriptions of groups or individuals within groups. Earlier in this chapter it was pointed out that the researcher is frequently interested in determining whether one group differs from another in, for example, the incidence of stuttering or tongue-thrust difficulty, as these features may be related to environment. Urban versus suburban comparisons or individual versus group therapy are often the criterion variables.

Correlation

The other statistical question that is commonly posed by the researcher concerns the relationship between variables. A typical question might concern the nature of the relationship between measured intelligence and the prevalence of articulation errors for a group of five-year-olds. In order to answer such a question with statistical satisfaction, measures of the variables of intelligence and articulation would need to be obtained on the same group of children. These two distributions of scores could then be compared, the degree of relationship determined and an index of relationship presented. Statisticians have a number of indices that they employ to show such relationships, however, the most commonly employed is called the Pearson product-moment correlation coefficient (r). This index is calculated basically by using paired scores for individuals. The detailed explanation of the computation can be found in any elementary statistics text (see references at end of chapter).

The Pearson r as an index ranges from +1.0 to −1.0. An r = +1.0 indicates perfect positive relationship or going-togetherness. The child who scored highest on the intelligence test also scored highest on the articulation test, and every other child maintained the same rank and distance on both scales. If the child who was highest on the intelligence test scored lowest on the articulation test and every child reversed the position he held on the intelligence test, the r would equal −1.0. In real life neither perfect positive nor perfect negative relationships exist, except under the most unusual circumstances. An r = .0 indicates no relationship between variables. For instance, toe length and scholastic aptitude have consistently shown no relationship. Between an r of 0 and 1 all gradations of relationship can exist. The researcher, naturally, prefers to discover a high relationship between variables because predictions can be made with greater accuracy and confidence and cause and effect relationships more readily inferred. The researcher needs to be particularly cautious, however, in concluding that *cause-and-effect* relationships necessarily exist merely because a high correlation is found. An illustration of jumping to conclusions may be shown in the widely publicized correlation between car ownership and low grades in some high schools studied. Many newspapers (and educators who should know better) immediately assumed that car ownership by high school students *causes* low grades. Before this conclusion can be reached, many other questions need to be answered. How does the scholastic aptitude of the car owners compare to that of non-car owners? If, as a group, the car owners have lower IQ's than the non-car owners, then the cause of the low grades needs to be recalculated.

A high statistical correlation between domineering mothers and stuttering children may be shown to exist, but to demonstrate that the mothers cause the stuttering would require much additional information.

The previous section on statistical methods gave the reader a brief review of several measures of central tendency, dispersion, correlation, and the use of graphical statistical data. Although this section offers only the most rudimentary introduction to statistics, the beginning researcher needs at least this minimal background before considering the tasks that are described in the final section.

WHAT THE SPEECH CLINICIAN CAN AND CANNOT DO IN RESEARCH

In order to define the research tasks that are within the realm of manageability, it is necessary to describe the situation in which the typical speech clinician finds himself in the public school setting. The kind and quality of research that can be undertaken is largely dependent upon the availability of facilities and subjects, the cooperative atmosphere provided by teachers, administrators, and parents, and the amount of time that can be spared without interfering with the clinician's regular job.

The clinician often begins his research effort in solitary splendor. While it is true that speech clinicians get together on occasion for district or regional meetings (in large school systems schoolwide meetings for specialists are frequently scheduled), for the most part the speech clinician operates as an itinerant individual who is not in close contact with his colleagues on a daily basis. For this reason the development of common research ideas as products of consultation with colleagues is not easy for the speech clinician. Despite the typical circumstance of semi-isolation, the clinician-researcher frequently is able in the course of his daily chores to generate questions that are suitable for investigation. In fact, it is not a paucity of questions that confronts the clinician as he makes his daily rounds, but rather the problem is that of focusing on topics which are amenable to solution in light of clinician background and available facilities. The neophyte researcher, often after several successful clinical experiences, may feel, for example, that he has discovered a general technique for the remediation of stuttering. Problems of this magnitude are virtually never amenable to attack by less than a corps of highly trained research specialists funded by thousands of dollars over a time schedule of several years' duration. A basic recommendation for beginning researchers is to restrict and confine the initial undertaking. A clear-cut solution to a small problem is nearly always more rewarding and useful than having a large array of partial pieces of information about a more extensive problem.

HOW THE CLINICIAN MAY IDENTIFY
A GENUINE PROBLEM

In addition to the general approach of attacking problems on a modest scale, the quandary of identifying a genuine problem often occupies the clinician's mind. A number of guides are available to assist the clinician-researcher in judging the merits of his problem. Here are several from a list of twelve offered by Krumboltz. If a "yes" answer can be given to each of the following questions, then chances are good that the problem is worthy of further consideration.

1. Is the problem truly important? (Is it frequently encountered in real life? What methods are presently being employed to solve problems like this?)

2. Is the problem interesting to others? (Ask several colleagues.)

3. Does the problem display originality and creativeness? (Review research on the topic.)

4. Can the problem be stated in the form of an hypothesis that is testable? (Try to state the problem in terms of behaviors that can be measured.)

5. Can something new be learned from the problem? (What has previous research produced?)

6. Will some other person be able to replicate this study? (Is the research design appropriate?)

7. Will the proposed data-gathering instruments actually give the information wanted?*

SOURCES OF RESEARCH PROBLEMS

It was previously suggested that a major source of ideas for investigation is the clinician's professional experience in the form of his day-to-day contacts with problems.

There are additional sources of research problems that are also fruitful. It is almost a universal characteristic of speech clinicians to continue their graduate educations. This academic training often presents the clinician with "hothouse" environmental conditions and contact with colleagues that produce many research ideas. The direction of the college instructor also serves as a source of refinement of research ideas. Opportunities may arise for cooperative graduate student-college instructor research

---

*MacAshan, H. H.: *Elements of Education Research*. McGraw, 1963, pp. 31-32.

projects, with the graduate student providing the entree into the school system and the college instructor providing expertise and access to computer time.

Another major source of research ideas is found in the form of research literature. There are periodically updated research summaries that are available for many of the subfields of speech. These summaries are typically reviewed by experts in the field, and suggestions are often made for further investigation. There are reports of theses and dissertations completed during the year and these reports are published annually. Perhaps the most valuable periodic reports of research are found in *Speech Monographs*. There are specific articles that are presented by authors on topics of their choosing. These authors frequently conclude their individual research review with suggestions for further research.

Finally, there are many studies worthy of replication. Will this author's findings hold true in another situation? Will this method, found effective with suburban children, prove equally effective with deprived-area children, with children with cerebral palsy, or with Indian children in a reservation school?

SOME ILLUSTRATIVE PROBLEMS

Pronovost reported in 1961 a study of public school speech and hearing services that still has great applicability today for directing research effort. Three major areas of needed research were identified as follows:

1. Collection of longitudinal normative data on speech, with special reference to articulation, voice, and fluency characteristics.
2. Comparative studies of program organization, including evaluation of the number of times sessions are held weekly, combinations of intensive and less intensive therapy, and the block system of scheduling.
3. Comparative studies of the use of different remedial procedures with children of various ages presenting different types of disorders.

In addition to the three areas of greatest priority, Pronovost listed six other major research needs:

4. Development of standardized tests of normal and impaired speech and voice.
5. Development of criteria for selection of primary grade children for inclusion in clinical programs.
6. Comparative studies of speech improvement and clinical programs.

7. Comparative studies of the effectiveness of group, individual, and combined group and individual therapy programs.
8. Studies of children's language usage, personal adjustment, and social adjustment in relation to changes in speech during participation in therapy programs.
9. Comparative studies of different curricula and clinical training programs for prospective public school speech and hearing personnel.

It is obvious that several topics listed above are only amenable to large-scale research efforts. The development of standardized tests of normal and impaired speech and voice (number 4) is much too ambitious for the single speech clinician or even a group of clinicians who have full-time jobs to perform. It is by no means beyond the realm of feasibility for the working clinician to involve himself in projects which demonstrate by means of descriptive research his school system's situation in the dimensions of numbers of children with various types of articulation, voice, or fluency characteristics (number 1); the kinds and quality of in-service programs offered in his school system for teachers by clinicians, and to clinicians by outside experts (number 6); the availability and adequacy of community resources for supplementing the speech program; the careful documentation of the case load of the clinician to demonstrate need for expansion of staff (number 2). These examples are primarily research which is descriptive in nature. A particularly illuminating selection that the beginning clinical-researcher may find useful to supplement these brief illustrations of descriptive research and to add illustrations of historical and experimental designs may be found in Auer (1959).

A FEW PRECAUTIONS

It has been frequently noted by ringside boxing observers that the most entertaining and masterly performances presented among the evening's bouts may not be those that are featured and beamed throughout the nation via television. Instead, the non-publicized preliminary bout is sometimes the most worthwhile. Analogously, the nonpublished, bread-and-butter, local research performed by the school speech clinician may be the most significant contribution that can be made in improving the quality of the program in his school system. It cannot be stressed too emphatically that, like charity, good research begins at home. The clinician who is conscientious maintains accurate, up-to-date records and files. He periodically evaluates the features of his program in light of its goals and the often rapidly changing needs of his school system. He is in regular contact with other programs and other approaches to problems. Good housekeeping is the basis for good research.

There is little question that there is a glamorous and perhaps mystical quality attached to the person who is "doing research" whether he be physicist, biologist, or social scientist. While there remains vast unexplored areas within the domain of clinical speech, there is much knowledge that has been reliably identified, but, unfortunately, is not being employed. It is of paramount importance that the speech clinician be a sophisticated interpreter and an energetic applicator of current research knowledge. One of the most stinging criticisms that is directed towards education as a broad field concerns the "research gap," the time discrepancy between knowing and doing. The field of clinical speech is not immune from the ailment of clinging to traditional methods and "sabertooth" curricula long after the research evidence has clearly pointed to new approaches. The task, then, for the research-oriented speech clinician is that of employing current knowledge as well as discovering new knowledge.

SUMMARY

Research as it is undertaken by the speech clinician is characterized by qualities that are found in other disciplines. The scientific method, utilizing observation hypothesis, experimentation, replication, and generalization is described as it would be applied to clinical speech. Applied and pure research are compared and the three major methods of approach to research — historical, descriptive, and experimental — are outlined. Problems of research design including sampling techniques and basic statistical approaches are introduced. The final section of this chapter includes the most pressing current research needs in the clinical speech domain and several illustrations of research problems that the public school speech clinician can reasonably undertake. Several recommendations concerning the acquisition and dissemination of research findings conclude the discussion.

DISCUSSION TOPICS

1. Why should the speech clinician be interested in research?
2. How can he utilize research to improve his clinical program?
3. Why is the importance of research increasing?
4. What type of research is the average speech clinician most apt to engage in?
5. Why do research if the clinician does not plan to publish the results?
6. What areas of research are most lacking in the clinical speech field?
7. What areas have received the most research attention?
8. How do you explain the above?
9. When research is done in the schools, why is it important that it be done well?
10. Should the speech clinician evaluate research published — the literature? Why? How?

REFERENCES

1. AHMAN, D. S., and GLOCK, M. D.: *Evaluating Pupil Growth*, 2nd ed. Boston, Allyn & Bacon, 1963.
2. AUER, J.: *An Introduction to Research in Speech*. New York, Harper, 1959.
3. Educational Testing Service: *Shortcut Statistics for Teacher-made Tests*. Evaluation and Advisory Service Series, Number 5, Princeton, New Jersey, 1961.
4. MacAshan, H. H.: *Elements of Educational Research*. New York, McGraw, 1963.
5. PRONOVOST, W. L., *et al.*: Research: Current status and need. *J Speech Hearing Dis, Monograph Suppl, 8*, July, 1961.
6. RICE, J.: The futility of the spelling grind. *The Forum, 23:* 1897.
7. Ross, C., and STANLEY, J.: *Measurement in Today's Schools*, 3rd ed. Englewood Cliffs, New Jersey, Prentice-Hall, 1960.
8. STEVENS, S. S.: *Handbook of Experimental Psychology*. New York, John Wiley, 1951.
9. TERMAN, L., *et al.*: *Genetic Studies of Genius*, vols. 1-5. Stanford, California, Stanford, 1925-1926, 1930, 1947, and 1959.
10. THORNDIKE, R., and HAGEN, E.: *Measurement and Evaluation in Psychology and Education*. New York, John Wiley, 1961.

UNIT III

The Professional Planning of the
Speech Clinician

Chapter 7

PROGRAM SCHEDULING

ROLLAND J. VAN HATTUM

Tıme ıs a precıous commodıty to all of us. It is not unusual to see the slogan "Time is money" posted conspicuously in manufacturing plants or business offices. Time may not be money to the speech clinician, but it certainly is an important aspect of the clinician's planning. The budgeting of time may be even more important to school personnel than to business or industry because of the traditional limitations of the school day and school year. Each school day is usually no longer than six hours in duration, and each school year is usually approximately one hundred eighty school days or a potential total of 1,080 hours. Not only is this lack of time alarming to one attempting to provide services to children in school environments, but the holiday seasons further subtract potential work time. Anyone who has attempted to present instruction or therapy during the periods immediately preceding and following Halloween, Thanksgiving, Christmas, and Easter well understands this point. The festive mood preceding and following holidays is hardly an inducement for productivity by children.

Yes, time is precious and must be used wisely. There are three important aspects of the usage of time facing clinicians working in schools. The first two, scheduling the week and the year, will be discussed in this chapter. The third, planning the time of each clinical day, will be covered in the next chapter.

SCHEDULING

Scheduling is a professional responsibility which should be determined by the clinician. Unfortunately, other persons often make the decision as to the type of scheduling utilized. As Irwin (1953) points out, sometimes boards of education are most anxious that the clinician see all the children with speech and hearing defects in the school district and, therefore, indirectly determine the scheduling system. The effectiveness of the program is apparently judged as being less important than public relations. The clinician has the professional obligation to resist pressures which contradict his clinical judgment. The best way to do this is to provide evidence of the soundness of his planning. This is most efficiently accomplished by educating administrators.

The clinician's time is often insufficient for the task confronting him. Eisenson and Ogilvie (1963) point out several ways in which the clinician attempts to meet this problem: giving a little assistance to all the handicapped, taking care of those who are most urgently in need of treatment and will receive the greatest benefit from it, and working with children in schools in one geographic area one year and in another the second year. None of these solutions seems appropriate. Perhaps the best solution is for the clinician to avoid impossible situations by not accepting employment in them.

It is unlikely that a clinician can operate the type of program which would truly benefit the speech and hearing handicapped where the ratio of clinician to school enrollment is greater than 1 to 2500 and where the number of schools to be served is greater than six. Even six schools exceeds the more desirable number of four. These figures are general guidelines and are further dependent on other factors such as the distances between schools (travel time between schools based on traffic, throughways, and other impediments), the enrollment in each school building, the socioeconomic status of the neighborhoods served, whether both elementary and secondary schools are being served, whether a program has existed in the past, and the degree of sophistication of classroom teachers in regard to speech problems.

These same factors are among those important in determining the type of scheduling to be utilized. Ideally, scheduling should be totally dependent on the needs of each child. Under a system such as this, a certain child might be seen for an hour a day, every day. Another child might be seen every day for an hour for a week or two and then seen for half an hour two times a week. Still another child might be seen initially once a week for several weeks and then seen daily. The possible combinations are infinite. Anyone working in the schools knows they are also impossible. Scheduling is related to many factors in the schools. Being realistic, the final system of scheduling selected by the clinician usually represents a compromise between the program which best meets the needs of most of the children and the one that the school environment, administration, and teaching personnel desire and can accommodate.

NO BLOCK SYSTEM

Most of the discussion in the literature about scheduling revolves around comparisons between so-called traditional systems known variously as the "regular," "itinerant," and "intermittent" system and "the block." Discussion and debate takes place on professional programs, in the professional literature, and among clinicians. This is ironic since there really is no such thing as *"a block program."* There are an infinite variety of systems of scheduling which are more intensive in nature than the twice a week system, but they vary to such an extent that they cannot be lumped together under a single term.

The National Study, (Bingham, Van Hattum *et. al.,* 1961), revealed that most clinicians and supervisors had not used both systems and so could not make comparisons. Others who reported indicated a slight preference for the regular system. Since there was some indication that there might be confusion regarding the definition of the term "block," a follow-up study was performed. One hundred questionnaires were sent out and seventy-five persons responded. Of this number, ten did not know the meaning of the term "block." When those who did profess to know the meaning of the term responded with their conception of how the block operated, they described no fewer than twenty-six different variations of procedure. The study reports as follows:

> Most respondents described the block as a concentrated or intensive program varying in length from two weeks to a full semester. Most stated that the system involves therapy sessions four or five times per week, but some described it as involving a period of therapy in one group of schools with two sessions per week followed by a shift to another group of schools.

The clinician should be most cautious in evaluating literature making comparisons between various systems of scheduling without carefully noting the description of the systems described rather than the labels applied to the systems. For example, one clinician described his program as a block program by saying he went to one block of sixteen schools during the first semester and saw children either once or twice a week. Then, during the second semester, he went to another block of fifteen schools. This hardly would seem to meet the criteria of intensive therapy.

There really is no such thing as *"a block system"* unless it is defined as intensive scheduling or as some system by which the school year is divided into shorter periods of time, during which certain schools are visited more frequently than twice a week. This, however, is rather awkward. In truth, scheduling exists along three continua. The first continuum includes the number of weeks the clinician spends in a school consecutively. This might vary from two weeks, which was the minimum reported in the study previously described (Bingham, Van Hattum *et al.*, 1961), to the entire school year, which would hold true, for example, in the traditional system.

The second continuum pertains only to those scheduling systems whereby the entire school year is not utilized and concerns the number of times the intensive periods are repeated. For example, a person may go to one group of schools for six weeks, then to another group of schools, then return to the original schools. This may occur several times.

The third continuum pertains to the number of times per week children are seen, which varies from one to five times per week, assuming they are seldom if ever seen more than once a day. If these three continua can be visualized, the infinite varieties of possible methods of scheduling which can be utilized can be seen.

Research Relating to Scheduling

In addition to the considerations mentioned above, several research studies have been reported, some in literature which is not easily accessible to all. Although the research methodology employed in many of these studies may be open to question, for one reason or another, the results obtained do bear consideration.

Van Hattum (1959) reports that five years of records were available for the Rochester, New York, schools utilizing the twice-a-week method of scheduling. Dismissal rates under this system were from 18 to 21 per cent. A similar period of time, utilizing an intensive system of two six-week sessions per school, yielded dismissal figures of from 38 to 41 per cent. In addition, the clinicians reported that they preferred it, and that there were administrative advantages. The children and teachers found it easier to remember when therapy was scheduled. The room was in daily use during that period. The clinician could concentrate materials and supplies in a few schools, rather than several. Clinicians became better acquainted with school staffs. Finally, in therapy, the clinicians found it easier to plan and execute a program of therapy when children were seen daily. They reported better remembering of planning on their part and on homework on the part of the children.

Ervin (1965) reports that the study in Arlington County, Virginia, found the block more effective in terms of improvement for functional disorders of articulation at second and third grade levels. Two days a week for a twenty-week period constituted the program of cycle therapy, while the block program consisted of therapy four days a week for two five-week periods, one in the spring and one in the fall. Ervin cautions that further generalizations concerning other types of speech disorders of organic etiology and higher grade levels remains open to investigation.

Weaver and Wollersheim (1963) conducted a study in the Champaign, Illinois, schools. Both systems allocated three weeks for screening. The intermittent system then proceeded in the "usual manner," according to the authors. The block system consisted of three five-week periods. When the school was not on the scheduled block, service was given one day a week; otherwise it was four days a week. Results indicate greater improvement under the block system than the intermittent system. Also, a questionnaire submitted to teachers and principals revealed that the principals preferred the block and commented on such things as ease of scheduling, working relationships between the speech clinician and the school faculty, and improved motivation. Of the forty teachers who reported, two stated no preference and thirty-four of the remaining thirty-eight preferred the block. They, too, referred to such things as ease of scheduling, increased speech benefits, and better motivation. Even some of the teachers preferring the intermittent system pointed out these factors, but were more concerned about the disruption of classes which they felt was more noticeable in a block program.

MacLearie and Gross (1966) reported on five studies conducted on scheduling in Ohio. In the Brecksville study (Weidner, 1966), children received help either under the traditional method (defined as two one-half-hour periods per week, throughout the school year) or under the "intensive cycle plan" (defined as four times per week for six consecutive weeks in two separate six-week cycles during the school year). Results indicate that more children received help under the cycle plan, reducing the waiting list. More children were dismissed as corrected, although the percentage was only slightly higher, and it appeared that there was less remission of improvement among the cycle group when examined again in September following the June dismissal. Of thirty-five teachers surveyed, thirty preferred the cycle method, two had no opinion, and three preferred the traditional method.

The Cleveland study (Norris, 1966) defined traditional therapy as two one-half-hour periods per week, although it continued for five weeks. Intensive therapy was defined as daily thirty-minute therapy sessions for two weeks. In Program A, intensive therapy was followed by traditional therapy. In Program B, traditional scheduling was followed by intensive scheduling. Under the traditional scheduling, notebook lessons were taken home every night to be reviewed by child and parent, while the notebooks were kept in school for the intensive cycle scheduling. The reason for this is not stated. The researchers report that the difference in average gain, while favoring the intensive method was not statistically significant. Children improved significantly under each system. All groups made their greatest gain in their first therapy program, regardless of the scheduling method. The "intensive program first" group had a greater average gain than the "traditional method first"; although the results were not statistically significant. However, the "traditional therapy second" had a better average gain than the "intensive therapy second." The researchers report that the optimum program may be intensive therapy followed by traditional therapy.

The Crawford County study (Irwin, 1966) compared three groups. Group I had two half-hour sessions per week for one school year. Group II had three half-hour sessions per week for one school year. Group III had four half-hour sessions for an eight week period, followed by once-a-week therapy for the second eight-week period. The findings indicated that there were no significant differences among the three groups following eight weeks of therapy. A connected speech sample score which was used as one measure was the only one to reveal a significant difference among the groups. Although all groups showed gains, the greatest gain was made in Group III (four half-hours per week). Group II (three half-hours per week) made more progress than Group I (two half-hours per week). Twice-weekly scheduling for sixteen weeks resulted in more improvement on total speech scores than four times per week for eight weeks. Each group had thirty-two classes during the period studied. Following sixteen weeks of therapy, no significant differences existed among the groups. Following thirty-two weeks of therapy, no significant differences existed between Group I (two times a week) and Group II (three times a week). The researchers summarize that all groups showed improvement on all test measures from time period to time period and that all groups made the greatest gains early in therapy during the first eight-week period. Other factors noted were that intelligence made a difference, children in grades two through eight made equal progress, nonsense syllable stimulation scores were not effective prognostic indicators, and the poorer the pretherapy score, the greater the gains at the end of eight and sixteen weeks. They conclude, "Gains shown by the group scheduled four times per week were only slightly greater than the gains of the other two groups, but not significantly so." Also, twice a week was as effective as three times a week but not significantly so, and the lack of gain between eight and sixteen weeks was thought to be a result of a plateau of learning rather than scheduling.

The Dayton study (Beitzel, 1966) compared the traditional plan (two half-hour periods per week throughout the school year) and the intensive plan (four half-hour lessons per week) as to the age at which children respond best to intensive cycle scheduling, the type of speech problem for which intensive scheduling seems most effective, the optimum length of time for a block of speech therapy, and the feasibility of scheduling both systems concurrently in one building. The study was conducted from 1961 until 1964. Best results were obtained with articulation problems of children in grades four, five, and six, while seventh and eighth graders revealed the least improvement. Intensive scheduling was less effective with organic problems. A greater number of children received speech therapy with the intensive program. Beitzel further reported that the intensive cycle accomplished a number of other things: better integration of speech therapy with the total school program, more frequent contacts between the clinician and school personnel, reduction in the effect of absenteeism on speech progress, shortening of the time allotted to speech screening, more conferences with parents and teachers, and fewer problems in scheduling upper elementary children, since they could be seen at times which best suited their programs.

The East Cleveland study (Holderman, 1966) examined the relative effectiveness of the traditional and intensive short term plans of scheduling with defective sibilant sounds in grades two through six. In this study the traditional plan was defined as two half-hour periods, two days a week, for twelve weeks, while the intensive plan was defined as therapy received in four half-hour periods, four days a week, for six weeks. The researchers comment, "The data appear to indicate a decided difference in the rate and/or degree of progress. The judges' evaluation showed improvement in the experimental group twice as large as in the control group. Thus, within the limits set forth in the study, a favorable result is found for the short-term, intensive therapy plan."

Another study on scheduling was performed in Chicago (Fein *et al.*, 1956) and compared results of speech help once a week throughout an entire school year with speech help twice a week for one semester. The results were judged to be similar and the conclusion is drawn that neither system is superior to the other. One statement in the study is somewhat confusing in that it states that the block was rejected as being too unwieldy administratively to be considered. First of all, as mentioned earlier, some school administrators have reported that they prefer the block administratively. Secondly, this statement lends support to the often-heard criticism that the school environment is more interested in convenience than in progress. It is hoped that the latter statement is not true.

Research reports relating to scheduling are usually confusing and seldom conclusive. Further, research methodology, due to the complexity of the problem and the number of variables involved, is often open to question. In fact, one of the major problems may be that too many variables are altered in a single study. However, based on the available information, it would seem that the following observations are defensible.

1. Systems of scheduling which provide speech therapy four or five days a week appear to yield higher dismissal rates for articulation problems than traditional methods. Because of the high percentage of clinicians' case loads devoted to articulation problems, this would suggest strong consideration of the use of some type of intensive system.

2. These intensive systems do not appear to be as successful with speech problems associated with organic conditions. Although these may constitute a smaller proportion in numbers, the severity of the problems deserves special weighting.

3. Numerically, more children receive clinical attention in intensive systems.

4. The greater gains appear to take place early in therapy, regardless of the system employed. This should have implications for the clinician's planning.

5. Speech clinicians, in reporting advantages of intensive scheduling systems, point to such factors as teachers and children not forgetting time scheduled for therapy; clinicians and children not forgetting therapy content; reduced necessity for transporting equipment, materials, and supplies, and reduced need for transportation time.

6. School administrators and teachers indicate that intensive scheduling is easier administratively and are impressed with the increased opportunity for the clinician to function as a member of the school staff.

The available evidence appears to favor intensive systems of scheduling, but the lack of solid evidence to support any system

conclusively is an indictment of the entire profession for not fulfilling its responsibility for research in the schools.

Factors to be Examined in Scheduling

From the results of the meager research available and from
reports of clinicians working in schools, there are twenty factors
to be considered in determining the system to be utilized. All of
these factors do not carry equal weight but are worthy of examination. Let us briefly discuss each of the twenty factors.

1. Laws, Rules, and Regulations

State laws or rules and regulations of the state department of
education often dictate certain requirements such as the number
of times per week a child must be seen, the number of minutes per
week a child must be seen, or the number of weeks throughout the
school year that the child must be seen. In addition, other factors
such as required case load may indirectly have a bearing on the
type of scheduling which will qualify for reimbursement. In these
instances it is unfortunately true that clinicians have little opportunity to exercise professional judgment. The ideal answer professionally would be complete freedom to come and go as one
pleases and to schedule according to need as do, for example, members of the medical profession. No one would even imagine legislation, similar to that controlling scheduling of clinical speech in
many states, which would force physicians to spend as much time
treating pneumonia as the common cold, or as much time minis-
tering to a cut finger as to a heart attack. Yet, this is frequently the
situation confronting the speech clinician. An important factor,
then, that determines scheduling methods is often state regulations, particularly where state reimbursement is dependent on
complying with these regulations.

Similarly, local rules and regulations may function in the same
way. For example, in some cooperative programs either written
agreements or understandings may exist which tie a clinician's
expenditure of time to the number of pupils in each cooperating
school or to the proportionate share of monies expended by each

school in support of the program. Little can be done in such instances except that professional speech and hearing organizations on local, state, and national levels should work towards the elimination of such restrictions.

2. *Tradition*

This factor as a controlling force in policy should never be underestimated. In fact, it is often the most difficult factor to change. It is not unusual for a clinician to be confronted by a supervisor who has used a particular method and prefers it for no other reason than that. This is not to belittle the supervisor who *has* tried various systems, objectively, and has reached a decision based on experience. It would be hoped that it is not necessary for each generation to repeat the mistakes of the last, although it sometimes appears that this is true.

However, it must be recognized that most of us are hesitant to depart from the methods we have used and with which we feel comfortable. It is only after we can clearly see advantages to an alternate method that outweigh the difficulties involved in change, that we are willing to accept change. Incidently, we usually are more willing to accept change when it is on a "trial" basis because this implies a possible return to the known and more comfortable. Thus, a clinician contemplating program changes would do well to build a case for a change and then sell it thoroughly by talks and circulated reports before attempting to implement it. Even then it is wise to utilize an experimental basis, as indeed it should be. Change for change alone is not only valueless but can be disrupting. Some persons possess a need for continuous change in order to cope with their own boredom. Although they may be successful in meeting their own needs, it may be at the expense of many frustrated teachers and administrators.

Where tradition is so strong that all change is impossible, the clinician has the choice of accepting this gracefully and going about his business as efficiently as possible under existing conditions or changing positions. However, it is seldom that a situation exists where solid evidence fails to gain support over a period of time.

3. Number of Schools and Number of Changes Required

The smaller the number of schools assigned to the clinician, the more the flexibility in scheduling. As the number of schools increases, the difficulty in scheduling increases and the likelihood that the program will provide significant help to children decreases. Also, the more schools assigned, the lower should be the total enrollment in these schools. Where secondary schools are involved, additional weight must be given to them, since it is more difficult to schedule at this level due to the lack of flexibility of the students' programs.

4. Number and Severity of Speech Problems

The prevalence of speech problems can vary considerably from state to state, from city to city, from community to community, or even from school to school within a community. Probably the biggest single factor is socioeconomic status. Children from deprived areas tend to have poorer models and poorer motivation. However, on the other hand, it is usually also true that the standards applied to them are often less rigorous. In addition, differing philosophies of the definition of a speech defect can cause widely divergent reports in one school if clinicians change from one year to the next. One clinician may report all children with speech errors in the primary grades as needing speech help and report a figure perhaps five times greater than his predecessor who viewed many of these children as being in the process of speech maturation and not in need of speech help.

In addition, sometimes a clinician finds himself confronted by fewer problems but with problems of considerable severity such as those associated with cleft palate, cerebral palsy, or hearing loss; or, he may find himself assigned to a school building where several special education classrooms are located. All these factors, in addition to the number of children enrolled in the schools, can make a difference and need to be taken into consideration when total numbers of children are being considered.

5. Distance Between Schools

Anyone who has had experiences in both city and county pro-grams will recognize the importance of travel time. Although not always the case, city schools may be a matter of a few blocks and a few minutes apart while a clinician may drive twenty miles or even considerably more between some rural schools. However, miles are not the only factor. It may be possible to drive the twenty miles in rural areas more quickly than the "few blocks" in the city. Furthermore, some city systems attempt to give the clinician a variety of experiences by assigning schools from varying socio-economic areas. This prevents one clinician from having all children from an upper or a lower socioeconomic area with a resultant greater variety of speech problems. Travel time is in-creased under this policy since the socioeconomic status tends to increase as one moves from the central core of the city. In this situation it is likely that the clinician has one school downtown and another on the outskirts requiring considerable travel.

6. Equality of Time Assigned to Schools

Where a clinician has a school population of 2000, for example, it is not necessarily true that this number of children will be equally distributed in four schools of 500 pupils each. It may well be that the clinician will have one school with 1000 enrollment, one with 500, one with 300, and a fourth with 200. It would not seem wise to distribute time equally. Rather it would seem more defensible to divide the number of children with speech problems by the number of therapy hours available, or the number of pupils by the number of therapy hours available.

Under the first, and recommended, system, let us suppose that the clinician utilized a half day for office time and devoted the other 27 hours to therapy. If the school with an enrollment of 1,000 was found to have 53 speech problems, for example; the school with 500, 18; the school with 300, 12; and the school with 200, 11, this would total 94 speech problems. Dividing this figure by the 27 hours available for therapy would yield an approximate ratio of one hour of therapy time for each 3.5 speech problems.

Thus, the school with 1,000 pupils would be assigned 15 hours; the school with 500 would be assigned 5 hours; the school with 300 would be assigned 3.5 hours; and the school with 200 would be assigned 3.5 hours also. Travel time would be deducted from time assigned to schools.

Under the second system, the total school population of 2,000 would be divided by 27 hours available for therapy and this would reveal a result of one hour of therapy for each 75 pupils. The school with 1,000 pupils would receive 13.5 hours of therapy; the school with 500 would receive 6.75 hours of therapy; the school with 300 would receive 4 hours; and, the school with 200 would receive 2.75 hours of therapy. One might wonder why the total enrollment would be used rather than the number of children with speech problems. One conference with a building principal determined to get his fair share of services, according to his judgment, would answer this matter.

7. Office Time

Office time, or coordination time, is that time designated for the clinician to work on records and reports; conduct parent interviews; consult with classroom teachers, administrators, and special education personnel; advise or consult on speech improvement, and administer diagnostic evaluations. It is definitely not a luxury but an integral and necessary part of the clinical program. It should be recognized as such by the clinician and school administrators. Most clinicians recognize that it is not coffee time, time for personal business, nor time for social visits. The few clinicians who have viewed it as such have made it difficult for those professional clinicians who have used the time to the advantage of the program. It is a factor such as office time that determines whether a clinician finds professional satisfaction in the schools because he can function as a clinical specialist or whether the school environment seems only to offer a succession of problems without the time necessary to work on their solutions.

8. Needs of Various Problems

No one has clearly indicated the ideal scheduling system for various types of speech problems, for children with various levels of intelligence, or for children of various age levels. We do assume that the more therapy an individual receives the sooner his problem will be alleviated. However, there certainly is a saturation point, and spaced learning and paced learning are also factors to be considered. It has been mentioned previously that, while intensive speech help appears advantageous for articulation problems, spaced assistance may be better for problems of stuttering or speech problems accompanying certain organic conditions. It was also stated that intensive therapy followed by spaced therapy may be a desirable method. However, this is admittedly based on more empirical than research evidence. The research need cannot be overstated. Until it occurs, each clinician is forced to follow his own particular prejudice.

9. The Forgetting Factor

The forgetting factor applies to the clinician, the student, and the teacher. In regard to the clinician, it concerns whether he can remember the goals of therapy for each child, the techniques which seem most successful with each child, and the point at which the previous therapy session ended and the next should logically begin. Where a large number of children are scheduled, this may be impossible. Some clinicians, faced with unrealistically large case loads, use a shotgun approach in which they are hopeful that something they are doing will be of benefit to someone, although they are not really certain. This would seem to be one point where there would be little doubt that an intensive system seems superior. When children are seen daily, the clinician is better able to remember the child, his individual needs, and the program deemed desirable for him.

In regard to the child, the opportunity for forgetting may be due to the infrequency of weekly sessions or, in the case of an intensive system, the length of time between the intensive periods. In other words, if a child receives speech therapy once a week, he has six days to forget. If he receives help every day, he has much less opportunity to forget new skills. However, if his program is interrupted for long periods while the clinician is away at other schools, there is an opportunity for forgetting also. It depends on how much improvement and carry-over has occurred before the clinician leaves the school and whether there is periodic reinforcement of the new behavior. This needs to be considered in various systems of scheduling.

In regard to the teacher, forgetting may be involved in getting the child to "speech class." The clinician who daily must go to Mrs. Eymer's room or send another child there before she can begin her therapy session is well aware of this problem. Generally, the more frequent the sessions, the better able the teacher is to remember. Also, the better able the teacher is to aid in carry-over in the classroom.

10. *Amount of Help Throughout the School Year*

In considering various systems of scheduling, it is usually helpful to compare programs on the basis of the amount of time each child receives during a total school year rather than at any given time during a year. For example, screening may take the first twenty days, or four weeks, leaving the equivalent of thirty-two weeks. Under the traditional method, if each child receives speech help twice a week for half an hour, this would mean a total of thirty-two weeks x two times per week x one-half hour per session, or a total of thirty-two hours of therapy for a year. To have an equivalent amount of therapy time in an intensive system, the clinician would have to schedule four times a week, one-half hour, for sixteen weeks. However, several of the studies previously reported have indicated that the children appeared to achieve greater gains under an intensive program; although the actual number of therapy hours per year were slightly fewer.

11. *Extent of Gains Noted*

As stated in the previous paragraph, it is less important to compare actual therapy hours than to compare gains made. Under which system will children make better progress? We do not yet know the final answer to this question. Some research reports better gains for articulation problems with intensive systems and better gains for speech problems accompanying organic conditions under traditional systems. It may be, as Lauder (1966) states, that the improvement is more related to the competency of the clinician than to the scheduling method utilized. Or it may be true that the children make greater gains for a given clinician when the clinician is using the system of scheduling with which he feels more comfortable and which seems more efficient to him.

12. Availability of Room

One of the major concerns of clinicians is the facilities in which they work. It is difficult enough to find satisfactory work space at any time. Complicated scheduling can make this even more difficult. All the evidence in the world can be gathered to indicate one system is superior to another, but if a room is not available to accommodate the system, it will probably not be possible to use it. For example, some administrators are unwilling to have a room vacant for several weeks while a clinician is away at another school. Although the room may be in use the same number of hours throughout the school year, it may not seem so to the administrator unless this is pointed out to him. Also, where facilities are shared, the scheduling of other multiassigned specialists may determine the speech clinician's schedule, in part. In one school system, the intensive program seemed so successful to the superintendent that he asked other itinerant personnel to examine their programs to see if intensive scheduling would be possible for them. A schedule was finally established whereby the school psychologist, school social worker, and speech clinician all used the same room on an intensive basis.

13. Ease for Teachers and Administrators

In addition to the availability of a room, other factors may make one system more efficient, or at least seem more efficient, to teachers and administrators. For example, some teachers feel that the intensive system causes children to miss certain aspects of the program every day for a short period of time and cause them to fall behind during that period to a greater extent than they would if missing only once or twice a week even though over a longer period. Sometimes the "ease" factor is secondary to the previously mentioned tradition. One principal continually complained that the intensive program in his school seemed less efficient to him; although he was never able to explain why. It just seemed less efficient to him.

14. Amount of Time the Clinician is Gone

Because of the problem of forgetting, which was discussed before, and because of the public relations aspect, it is better for the clinician not to be absent from a school too long, regardless of the scheduling system chosen. This suggests that the periods of time should not be too lengthy, or at least some provision should be made for periodic visits to a school even when it is not being provided intensive help. Spending part of a day in a school makes school personnel feel that someone is near at hand to assist them and advise them, if need be. One of the major disadvantages of an intensive system is the feeling that teachers and administrators report that there is no one to assist them. When a teacher or administrator wants advice, he is similar to all of us in that he wants it immediately. Waiting several weeks is a frustrating experience for him. This is often particularly true at the beginning of the semester when a school is waiting for a clinician to initiate his program there. To wait several weeks may seem like an eternity to the teacher with a stutterer daily reminding her that speech help is not available.

It has been stated that every teacher might prefer the intensive system—as long as they were included in the first period.

15. Opportunity to Relate to School Staff

Clinicians using the intensive system often state that one of the major advantages is the opportunity to better relate to the school staff. This is supported by the results of the research studies reported. Seeing the staff daily, eating with them, attending school functions, and socializing with them, all appear to be easier to accomplish under the intensive systems. Although the service rendered may be clinical in nature, it is extremely important that the clinician relate to the educational personnel, reveal an interest in the total school program, and gain the cooperation of the educators in the clinical speech program. Communication is important in any work environment and this is particularly true for a specialist such as a speech clinician who is viewed as "part time" by the permanent staff. To know their concerns and to have their support is critical. This can only be accomplished if the clinician wishes to "belong" and makes an attempt to do so. Even if this is best accomplished in an intensive program, as has been suggested, it must be accomplished in any system selected.

16. Number of Staff to Relate To

Perhaps one reason an intensive program seems to make it easier to relate to the staff is that there are fewer to relate to at any one time. It is difficult for a clinician to get to know sixty teachers at one time. However, if it is only necessary to become acquainted with fifteen teachers at one time, the task seems easier.

17. Interest of Clinician and Children

Under the traditional system the children and the clinician may begin to appear somewhat bored with the program in May or June, according to their reports. This is understandable, since seeing the same large group of children for ten months is a difficult task. The clinician feels obligated to plan new and different activities every week for approximately thirty weeks. Under an intensive system, both the clinician and the children can look forward to a change of schedule every few weeks. Also, the clinician can feel free to repeat activities used during a previous period.

18. Public Relations

Although not the major factor professionally, it is important that the community be satisfied with the selected system of scheduling. Also, as taxpayers they must be satisfied with the way their monies are being expended. One PTA worked diligently to have a program utilizing the intensive system of scheduling changed back to the former traditional system because one of their influential members was convinced, and succeeded in convincing others, that the traditional system was better for her son. Sometimes the number of children scheduled favors one system over another. For example, using the traditional system one clinician was able to schedule one hundred children. When he changed to an intensive system he scheduled sixty children during each of three periods for a total of 180 children per year. Thus, although he did not feel overburdened at any one time, he was able to see almost twice as many children. This was sufficient evidence to sell the program to the board of education on a permanent basis. Dismissal rates are also good public relations.

19. Ability to See "Half Day" Children

The children in kindergarten who are at school only half a day can create a scheduling problem in certain schools. This is particularly true if, for example, the older children attend in the afternoons and the younger group in the mornings, as is often the case. Or, in other instances, the children north of the school may attend in the morning and those south of the school may attend in the afternoon. School administrators can seem remarkably inflexible when it comes to changing a child with a speech problem accompanying cleft palate from the morning kindergarten to the afternoon so he can be there when the speech clinician is. The speech clinician should attempt to understand that, in the first instance, the child may be placed with a group that does not meet his social needs if a change is made, and in the second instance, the clinician may be asking for a considerable change in the transportation system to accomplish the change. A program that allows for the clinician to be at the school during the other half day at least once a week can resolve this problem in part.

One way of accomplishing this and preventing children from missing too much of a given subject matter is to reverse mornings and afternoons during alternate periods. For example, if the clinician is at School A in the morning and School B in the afternoon during the first period assigned to these schools, on his return he can schedule School B in the morning and School A in the afternoon.

20. Elementary and Secondary Schools

Finally, the level of schools assigned is a major consideration in scheduling. Junior and senior high schools are not set up in such a way as to function well in an intensive program. It tends to be too disrupting to the student's overall program. Elementary schools are much better able to tolerate various systems of scheduling. Elementary school schedules are less complicated and more flexible.

Scheduling at the junior and senior high school levels is usually best accomplished on a two-visits-a-week basis. In the traditional system, where a clinician is assigned both elementary and secondary schools, it is not unusual to note that elementary schools are scheduled two times a week and secondary schools only once. It is difficult to understand why pupils in high school are thought to need less therapy time than those in elementary school. Pure speculation would probably reason that the reverse is true. Actually, it is probably true that this system is another concession to the difficulties involved in scheduling at the secondary level, even once a week.

Many factors need to be considered when planning a schedule for the year. Some of them are related to the needs of children but many are unfortunately, but realistically, related to necessity. Which of these factors applies to a given situation only the individual clinician can determine. If at all possible, the needs of children should be the first factor considered. Where it is not possible, it should serve as a goal for the clinician to pursue.

SAMPLE PROGRAMS

Although, as previously stated, an infinite variety of possible scheduling systems exist, let us examine several of these representative systems. Some comments on the strengths and weaknesses are presented. No attempt is made to present all of the possible comments.

The school year consists of approximately 36 weeks or 180 days. Three considerations have been stated. These are 1) the number of weeks the clinician spends in a school consecutively, from two weeks to the entire school year; 2) the number of periods of therapy a school receives per year. In the traditional system this is one, while both this factor and that mentioned above are highly variable in intensive scheduling, and 3) the number of times per week children are seen or, similarly, the number of times a school is scheduled each week. The traditional system most often utilizes a two-times-a-week system, although it may use only one or, less frequently, three. Intensive systems usually use four times a week as a base but, on occasion, a system uses five times a week.

In the following examples, the top line will present the yearly schedule with the number of periods and the length of the periods, expressed in weeks, below the line. The bottom box shows a typical weekly schedule with the five days of the week, the morning and afternoon program, the letters A to H representing schools, and O designating office time.

1. Four Schools on a Twice-a-Week Schedule

YEARLY SCHEDULE

September |————————————————————————| June
Same Schedule

WEEKLY SCHEDULE

	Mon.	Tue.	Wed.	Thu.	Fri.
A.M.	A	C	A	C	O
P.M.	B	D	B	D	O

Advantages. Each school receives an equal amount of time. Children receive help throughout the school year. Teachers and administrators become accustomed to a speech clinician's availability. The clinician has office time for the many responsibilities he has to fulfill at that time. The room can be saved on a regular basis throughout the school year. It can also be shared with other itinerant personnel.

Disadvantages. It does not take into account the varying needs of various speech problems. There is much forgetting possible; for example, from Wednesday until the following Monday. This applies not only to children seeking to master skills but to the clinician attempting to carry out a program of therapy with continuity. Also, the case load is usually large.

2. Eight Schools on a Twice-a-Week Schedule

YEARLY SCHEDULE

September |————————————————————————| June
Same schedule

WEEKLY SCHEDULE

	Mon.	Tue.	Wed.	Thu.	Fri.
	A			A	D
A.M.	B	D	F	B	F
			G	C	G
P.M.	C	E	H	E	H

A, B, G, and H are smaller schools.

Advantages. Provides service to a large number of schools. Each school receives help throughout the entire school year. Teachers and administrators become accustomed to the speech clinician's partial presence. The room can be saved on a regular basis. The administration and board of education may be impressed with the large number of schools served and, possibly, with the large case load served.

Disadvantages. There is obviously a great deal of changing schools required, resulting in loss of time for therapy. There are a large number of teachers and administrators for the clinician to relate to. There is an additional burden in preparing reports and notifying persons regarding such matters as change of schedule. No time is allocated for the important paper work, telephoning, and clinical activity the clinician should engage in. The forgetting factor is present and is greater for the clinician than in the previous program. The case load probably is larger.

3. Eight Schools on a Once-a-Week Schedule

YEARLY SCHEDULE

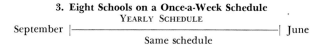

September |————————————————————————| June

Same schedule

WEEKLY SCHEDULE

	Mon.	Tue.	Wed.	Thu.	Fri.
A.M.	A	C	E	G	O
P.M.	B	D	F	H	O

Advantages. Several schools receive token help. Boards of education may be impressed with the number of schools one clinician is serving. Children are visited throughout the school year. A full day of office time is available.

Disadvantages. All those listed under the above-mentioned program. In addition, it is unlikely that children with serious speech problems would receive any significant help. The schools cannot observe what an efficient and successful clinical program can do for a child. Boards of education are unlikely to add additional personnel when the needs of children appear to be met, even only on paper.

Note: approximately the same result would be achieved if System 1 were utilized for one semester and then four new schools were added for the second semester.

4. Four Schools and a Junior and a Senior High School

YEARLY SCHEDULE

September |——————————————————————| June

Same schedule

WEEKLY SCHEDULE

	Mon.	Tue.	Wed.	Thu.	Fri.
A.M.	A	Jr	D	A	D
P.M.	B	C	B	Sr	C

Advantages. Children receive attention throughout the school year. The clinician has experience with a variety of age levels. A complete program from kindergarten through twelfth grade exists. Teachers and administrators become accustomed to the availability of the clinician. Rooms can be allocated on a regular basis throughout the school year.

Disadvantages. There is something contradictory in the premise that elementary children must be seen at least twice a week, while secondary school children require therapy only once a week. This differs from System 1 only to the extent that the secondary schools substitute for office time. Thus, not only does the clinician lose these valuable hours, but additional case load is added and additional personnel to relate to.

5. Four Schools on an Intensive Basis

YEARLY SCHEDULE

	1	2	3	4	

September |————|————|————|————| June

9 wks 9 wks 9 wks 9 wks

WEEKLY SCHEDULE FOR PERIODS 1 AND 3

	Mon.	Tue.	Wed.	Thu.	Fri.
A.M.	A	A	A	A	OB
P.M.	B	B	B	OA	B

WEEKLY SCHEDULE FOR PERIODS 2 AND 4

	Mon.	Tue.	Wed.	Thu.	Fri.
A.M.	C	C	C	C	OD
P.M.	D	D	D	OC	D

Advantages. Children receive intensive therapy for eighteen weeks. Teachers become familiar with the schedule. The clinician becomes better acquainted with the staff. Articulatory problems seem to respond well to this type of program, and the dismissal rate is reported to increase sharply. There is less forgetting by children and clinicians of the program and the therapy. Equal time is provided each of the four schools. Relatively little time is devoted to travel. The clinician has office time. Children in morning or afternoon kindergarten can be seen at least once a week. For half the school year the child's classroom program is not disturbed at all.

Disadvantages. The room must remain vacant for half the school year in most cases. This is difficult for administrators to accept. Forgetting may occur when the clinician is not at the school. Children who move may be missed entirely. Children miss certain aspects of their classroom programs daily for a period of time. More severe problems do not receive speech help throughout the school year as may be advisable. Some schools must wait nine weeks for speech help to begin, and all schools experience nine-week gaps.

6. Six Schools on an Intensive Basis

YEARLY SCHEDULE

September |—2—|—5—|—5—|—5—|—5—|—5—|—5—|—2—|—2—| June
(periods 1 2 3 4 5 6 7 8 9)

WEEKLY SCHEDULE FOR PERIODS 1, 4, AND 7

	Mon.	Tue.	Wed.	Thu.	Fri.
A.M.	A	A	A	A	A
P.M.	B	B	B	B	B

WEEKLY SCHEDULE FOR PERIODS 2, 5, AND 8

	Mon.	Tue.	Wed.	Thu.	Fri.
A.M.	C	C	C	C	C
P.M.	D	D	D	D	D

WEEKLY SCHEDULE FOR PERIODS 3, 6, AND 9

	Mon.	Tue.	Wed.	Thu.	Fri.
A.M.	E	E	E	E	E
P.M.	F	F	F	F	F

Advantages. A number of schools receive speech help. This help is equally distributed among these schools, at least in terms of time. Clinicians become acquainted with the staffs. Children receive twelve weeks of intensive speech help. There appears to be less forgetting by children and clinicians. The clinician distributes office time throughout the week rather than scheduling it all on one day. Less time is devoted to travel than in other systems. A large and a small school can be scheduled together if the clinician chooses not to change schools at noon.

Disadvantages. Some teachers and administrators object to frequent changes of schedule. Some schools wait for seven weeks before therapy begins. Children with severe problems have frequent interruptions in their therapy program. The room must be kept vacant while the clinician is gone.

7. Five Schools with All Schools Screened First

YEARLY SCHEDULE

September |—1—|—2—|—3—|—4—|—5—|—6—| June
       6   6   6   6   6   6

WEEKLY SCHEDULE FOR PERIOD 1

	Mon.	Tue.	Wed.	Thu.	Fri.
A.M.			Screening		
P.M.	A	A	A	A	A

NOTE, it is suggested that the smallest school be designated School A.

WEEKLY SCHEDULE FOR PERIOD 2

	Mon.	Tue.	Wed.	Thu.	Fri.
A.M.	B	B	B	B	B
P.M.	C	C	C	C	C

WEEKLY SCHEDULE FOR PERIOD 3

	Mon.	Tue.	Wed.	Thu.	Fri.
A.M.	D	D	D	D	D
P.M.	E	E	E	E	E

WEEKLY SCHEDULE FOR PERIOD 4

	Mon.	Tue.	Wed.	Thu.	Fri.
A.M.	A	A	A	A	A
P.M.	B	B	B	B	B

WEEKLY SCHEDULE FOR PERIOD 5

	Mon.	Tue.	Wed.	Thu.	Fri.
A.M.	C	C	C	C	C
P.M.	D	D	D	D	D

WEEKLY SCHEDULE FOR PERIOD 6

	Mon.	Tue.	Wed.	Thu.	Fri.
A.M.	E	E	E	E	E
P.M.	A	B	C	D	O

Advantages. Each child has twelve weeks of intensive speech help but his program is interrupted at one time for only six weeks. All screening is done early so that teachers have the feeling that the speech problems in their room are known to the "expert." The clinician can quickly screen small school A and begin a program there while continuing to screen at the other four schools. Children in morning or afternoon kindergartens can have at least six weeks of help.

Disadvantages. Two schools do not begin their therapy programs for six weeks, and two do not begin for twelve weeks. Teachers and administrators may not like having to make adjustments to the frequent change of program. It may be difficult to have a room available in the morning for part of the semester and for the afternoon for another part of the school year.

8. Six Schools on a Combined Basis

YEARLY SCHEDULE

September |———|———|———|———|———|———| June
　　　　　1　　2　　3　　4　　5　　6
　　　　　6　　6　　6　　6　　6　　6

WEEKLY SCHEDULE FOR PERIOD 1

	Mon.	Tue.	Wed.	Thu.	Fri.
A.M.	A	A	A	A	A
P.M.	B	C	D	E	F

WEEKLY SCHEDULE FOR PERIOD 2

	Mon.	Tue.	Wed.	Thu.	Fri.
A.M.	B	B	B	B	B
P.M.	A	C	D	E	F

WEEKLY SCHEDULE FOR PERIOD 3

	Mon.	Tue.	Wed.	Thu.	Fri.
A.M.	C	C	C	C	C
P.M.	A	B	D	E	F

WEEKLY SCHEDULE FOR PERIOD 4

	Mon.	Tue.	Wed.	Thu.	Fri.
A.M.	D	D	D	D	D
P.M.	A	B	C	E	F

WEEKLY SCHEDULE FOR PERIOD 5

	Mon.	Tue.	Wed.	Thu.	Fri.
A.M.	E	E	E	E	E
P.M.	A	B	C	D	F

WEEKLY SCHEDULE FOR PERIOD 6

	Mon.	Tue.	Wed.	Thu.	Fri.
A.M.	F	F	F	F	F
P.M.	A	B	C	D	E

Advantages. Children are seen throughout the school year and also receive intensive speech help. This combines features of both types of programs. Each school receives equal opportunity for speech help. A number of schools receive speech help. The clinicians become acquainted with schools staffs and also see them throughout the school year. Articulatory problems and other types may respond well.

Disadvantages. Intensive period of therapy may not come in the stage of the child's therapy when it would be most beneficial for him. Some schools wait for some time before significant help is scheduled for them. Rooms must be available on varying schedule. Children must continually readjust. The clinician must travel considerably.

9. Six Schools on an Intensive Basis

YEARLY SCHEDULE

September |—|—|—|—|—|—|—|—|—|—|—|—| June
1 2 3 4 5 6 7 8 9 10 11 12
3 3 3 3 3 3 3 3 3 3 3 3

WEEKLY SCHEDULE FOR PERIODS 1, 4, 7, AND 10

	Mon.	Tue.	Wed.	Thu.	Fri.
A.M.	A	A	A	A	A
P.M.	B	B	B	B	B

WEEKLY SCHEDULE FOR PERIODS 2, 5, 8, AND 11

	Mon.	Tue.	Wed.	Thu.	Fri.
A.M.	C	C	C	C	C
P.M.	D	D	D	D	D

WEEKLY SCHEDULE FOR PERIODS 3, 6, 9, AND 12

	Mon.	Tue.	Wed.	Thu.	Fri.
A.M.	E	E	E	E	E
P.M.	F	F	F	F	F

Advantages. Children receive several intensive periods of therapy. The clinician becomes acquainted with school staffs. The room is not vacant for long periods of time. Teachers and administrators become familiar with the daily schedule. There is less forgetting by the clinician and children when the clinician is at the school and periods are short enough so not much forgetting occurs while clinician is away. Help is spaced throughout the school year.

Disadvantages. The school program is disrupted since therapy seems to be constantly starting and stopping. The gaps in-between do allow for forgetting; although it may be minimal. Teachers and administrators may have difficulty remembering when the clinician is at school.

Selecting the Most Appropriate System

These are only a few examples of the infinite variety of ways in which the school week and school year can be arranged. Each has advantages and disadvantages. The systems presented here can be combined in a number of ways, or other systems devised. Add to this the ways in which each day can be arranged, and the importance of the decisions of the clinician are clearly evident. The clinician should examine his particular situation from all the aspects and make the determination as to which system best suits his situation. It is not an easy decision. Perhaps that is why so many clinicians ultimately decide on the traditional system. It is hoped that in the near future, research will provide more definitive answers to aid clinicians with such decisions.

SUMMARY

Because of the limitations of the school day and the school year, the professional time available to the speech clinician is an especially valuable commodity. The manner in which the clinician uses this time in planning his program for the week and for the year is referred to as "scheduling" in this text. Rightfully, this should be the responsibility of the clinician but, unfortunately, other factors or persons sometimes influence the final decision. The clinician should resist pressures that prevent him from exercising his best judgment.

Comparisons often are made between the scheduling systems that are considered basic. Although known by several labels, the traditional system is that which consists of visits to schools once or twice a week throughout the school year. The other supposedly basic system has been called the "block." However, there is no such single system. Rather it refers to any system which does not function as the traditional system in that shorter and more intensive periods of clinical speech are scheduled in the schools. There are an infinite variety of scheduling systems. These can be visualized along three continua. The first continuum includes the number of weeks the clinician spends in certain schools consecutively; the second pertains to those systems in which the entire school year is not utilized and concerns the number of times the intensive periods are repeated, and the third pertains to the number of times per week children are seen.

Some research has been conducted on the various systems of scheduling, and the results appear to indicate that the intensive systems do result in higher dismissal rates for functional speech problems, in less forgetting by clinicians, teachers, and children, in better integration into the school staffs by clinicians, and in more children being scheduled. Much research is needed, however, to provide more definitive information.

In determining which scheduling system to utilize, the clinician has many factors to consider: legal aspects, tradition, number of schools and changes required, number and severity of speech problems in the schools, distances between schools, equality of time assigned to schools, office time, needs of various problems, the forgetting factor, amount of help throughout the school year, gains noted, room availability, ease for school personnel, amount of time the clinician is gone, ability to relate to school staffs, number of staff members to relate to, interest, public relations, ability to see half-day children and elementary and secondary school considerations.

Realistically, the final system of scheduling adopted is usually a compromise. Hopefully, the needs of children will continue to take precedence over other factors in this decision.

DISCUSSION TOPICS

1. Rank the twenty factors in the order of importance you feel appropriate.

2. Are there factors included that you consider to be unworthy of inclusion in this list? Why? Are there factors omitted that should have been included? Why?

3. Do other professions have to contend with some of the restrictions in planning that the speech and hearing profession does? If you can think of similar problems, discuss them.

4. How can the speech and hearing profession as it functions in the schools have more freedom to plan and execute programs in the way it considers most efficient and effective? What barriers do you see to this?

5. Is there any justification for operating programs to please school administrators, boards of education, and state department personnel?

6. Under each of the systems presented, add to the list of advantages and disadvantages.

7. Plan several additional programs. Schedule four schools using eight-week periods. Schedule three schools and a junior-senior high school using a combined method and five-week periods. Schedule five elementary schools with the following enrollments and approximately equal prevalence of speech problems: 1200, 250, 500, 300, 300.

8. What criticisms can you see in the studies on scheduling?

9. Set up a research study on scheduling which would add to our knowledge of the relative effectiveness with functional articulation problems and problems related to organic factors.

10. Give advantages and disadvantages of office or coordinating time always falling on the same half day, of this time being distributed throughout the week. How important do you consider this time to be? Why?

REFERENCES

1. AINSWORTH, S.: *Speech Correction Methods.* Englewood Cliffs, New Jersey, Prentice-Hall, 1948.

2. BEITZEL, B.: East Cleveland study. In *Experimental Programs for Intensive Cycle Scheduling of Speech and Hearing Therapy Classes.* Columbus, Ohio, Ohio Department of Education, 1966.

3. BINGHAM, D. S.: *Program Organization in Public School Speech Therapy.* Des Moines, Iowa, Department of Public Instruction, State of Iowa, June, 1962.

4. BINGHAM, D. S.; VAN HATTUM, R. J.; FAULK, M., and TAUSSIG, E.: Public school speech and hearing services: IV Program organization and management. *J Speech Hearing Dis, Monogr Suppl 8,* June, 1961.
5. BLACK, M. E.: *Speech Correction in the Schools.* Englewood Cliffs, New Jersey, Prentice-Hall, 1964.
6. COATES, N. H.; GARBEE, F. E., and HERBERT, E. L.: California's public school programs for speech and hearing handicapped children dilemmas and horizons. *J Calif Speech Hearing Assn Monogr Suppl,* May, 1963.
7. EISENSON, J., and OGILVIE, M.: *Speech Correction in the Schools,* 2nd ed. New York, Macmillan, 1963.
8. ERVIN, J. E.: A study of the effectiveness of block scheduling versus cycle scheduling for articulation therapy for grades two and three in the public schools. *J Speech Hearing Ass Virginia, 6* (2), Spring, 1965.
9. FEIN, B. G.; GOLMAN, M.; KONE, H., and McCLINTOCK, C.: Effective utilization of staff time in public school speech correction. *J Speech Hearing Dis, 21:*283-291, September, 1956.
10. GARBEE, F. E.: *The California Program for Speech and Hearing Handicapped School Children.* Sacramento, Bulletin of the California State Department of Education, Vol. XXXIII (4), December, 1964.
11. HOLDERMAN, B.: East Cleveland study. In *Experimental Programs for Intensive Cycle Scheduling of Speech and Hearing Therapy Classes.* Columbus, Ohio, Ohio Department of Education, 1966.
12. IRWIN, R. B.: Crawford County study. In *Experimental Programs for Intensive Cycle Scheduling of Speech and Hearing Therapy Classes.* Columbus, Ohio, Ohio Department of Education, 1966.
13. IRWIN, R. B.: *Speech and Hearing Therapy.* Englewood Cliffs, New Jersey, Prentice-Hall, 1953.
14. LAUDER, C.: "Speech and Hearing Services in Schools: Organization and Administration of Programs." Paper presented at Council of Exceptional Children Convention, Toronto, 1966.
15. McCAUSLAND, M.: A public school speech program. *Speech Teacher, 11,* March, 1962.
16. MACLEARIE, E. C., and GROSS, F. P.: *Experimental Programs for Intensive Cycle Scheduling of Speech and Hearing Therapy Classes.* Columbus, Ohio, Ohio Department of Education, 1966.
17. MACLEARIE, E. C.: *The Ohio Plan for Children with Speech and Hearing Problems.* Columbus, Ohio, Ohio Department of Education, rev. 1964.
18. NORRIS, D.: Cleveland study. In *Experimental Programs for Intensive Cycle Scheduling of Speech and Hearing Therapy Classes,* Columbus, Ohio, Ohio Department of Education, 1966.
19. VAN HATTUM, R. J.: Evaluating elementary school speech therapy. *Exceptional Child, 25:*411-415, May, 1959.

20. WEAVER, J. B., and WOLLERSHEIM, J. P.: *A Pilot Study Comparing the Block System and the Intermittent System of Scheduling Speech Correction Cases in The Public Schools.* Champaign, Illinois, Champaign Community Unit 4 Schools, May, 1963.
21. WEIDNER, W.: Brecksville study. In *Experimental Programs for Intensive Cycle Scheduling of Speech and Hearing Therapy Classes.* Columbus, Ohio, Ohio Department of Education, 1966.

Chapter 8

PLANNING TIME AND FACILITIES

LEE I. FISHER

T WO IMPORTANT DETERMINANTS of the success of the clinical speech program in the schools are the use the clinician makes of the time available to him and the way he plans and arranges the facilities in which he carries out his clinical program. Both of these matters bear careful consideration and planning. Efficient use must be made of the limited time available to the clinician and professional, and efficient office and therapy space must be secured, in addition to equipment, materials, and supplies. The first section of this chapter covers the aspect of planning the use of time. The second section discusses the facilities.

THE USE OF TIME

In the last chapter the scheduling of the year and the week into its many possible basic forms was discussed. After the type of system to be utilized is selected and the clinician has decided on how many days will be spent in the schools each week, he still must decide how the hours of the week and of each day will be spent.

Planning Time for the Week

Overall Considerations

The study by the American Speech and Hearing Association (Knight, Hahn *et al.,* 1961) revealed that school clinicians work an average of 35.20 hours per week on their jobs. This time is divided as follows: therapy, 23.09 hours; travel, 2.68 hours; conferences, 2.53 hours; writing reports, 2.12 hours; preparing lessons, 3.23 hours; and, other duties, 1.55 hours. These are averages compiled from the reports of several hundred clinicians and are not suggested as recommendations by the association. However, they do suggest current practices, which may be assumed to be those the clinicians considered to be desirable. In other words, clinicians currently spend approximately 65 per cent of their time in providing therapy, approximately 13 per cent in office types of activities such as reports and conferences, approximately 9 per cent in preparation for therapy sessions and, unfortunately, 8 per cent for travel. This 8 per cent is equal to about 32 minutes a day and, although it is unfortunate that valuable time must be spent, this is an admirable minimum for this unproductive activity.

In addition to those activities mentioned above, nearly all school clinicians put in many extra hours before and after the scheduled periods. Professional clinicians spend many evening hours in additional lesson planning, preparing materials, conferring with parents, speaking to groups, attending school functions, writing reports and remaining current in the professional literature. These persons also spend time extending their professional skills through course work, workshops, meetings, and conventions.

Coordinating Activities

Adequate time must be reserved for coordinating activities as the weekly unit of time is being planned. One full day each week is certainly not an unrealistic amount of time to spend for planning, for preparing records and reports, for keeping current in correspondence, and for conferring with office personnel, administrators, and parents. According to the survey of school clinicians (Knight, Hahn *et al.*, 1961), 13 per cent reported the use of one full day each week for coordination, 52 per cent reported using one-half day each week, and 18 per cent reported that they did not have work time for coordination activities. Experienced clinicians have found that one-half day each week is not really a sufficient amount of time for office work. However, it is extremely unfortunate to have less than one-half day each week for coordinating activities.

Time for Testing

When time units are planned, careful consideration is given to the amount of time that will be used for testing, therapy, conferences, professional growth, and in-service training. The amount of time that is used for testing will depend on which screening and diagnostic procedures are used, the number of children to be screened and evaluated, and the number of children who are in need of direct or indirect remediation. The actual amount of time that is used for screening and diagnostic evaluation varies a great deal. For example, one clinician may have only one hundred children to screen; whereas another clinician may have nearly a thousand children to evaluate. The amount of time that is used for screening also depends on which grade is screened. It takes more time to screen a first grade child than it does a third grade child if similar screening techniques are used.

Whenever testing, the clinician should take sufficient time to complete an adequate evaluation. Unfortunately, the tendency is to hurry through the testing procedures as there are so many children to evaluate. During screening, conversational speech should be evaluated in addition to any specific pictures or sentence articulation test that may be used. This is particularly important when second or third grade children are screened as they often make conversational errors which they do not make on specific test items. Listening to a child's connected speech also provides a good opportunity to evaluate the child's fluency and voice characteristics. It takes two to three minutes to screen a child's speech. Some clinicians take up to five minutes to screen each child. A clinician may be able to make an adequate diagnosis of a minor speech problem in a few minutes but it often takes several hours to thoroughly examine, evaluate, and diagnose a child with a severe speech problem.

There is the possibility of taking too much time for testing just as there is the possibility of taking insufficient time for this purpose. At this point, the major caution is to guard against overtesting or testing repeatedly without sufficient reason. However, it is important to remember that periodic reevaluations need to be made to assess progress and determine current severity of problem.

Adequate time must be reserved for testing at the beginning of a new program, at the beginning of each school year, periodically throughout the school year, and at the end of the school year.

Sufficient time needs to be reserved for screening, evaluating referrals, and reevaluating children with known speech problems who have not been scheduled for therapy.

TIME FOR THERAPY

Public school clinicians spend most of their time in therapy. As a rule clinicians schedule at least four days of therapy each week. For example, if a four-week period of time is used at the beginning of the year for a survey of the program needs, and a two-week period is used at the end of the year for records and reports, there are approximately thirty weeks of the school year left for therapy. A clinician who follows this plan spends at least 120 days in therapy during the year. If only ten therapy sessions are held each day, the clinician will have to prepare for at least twelve hundred therapy sessions.

A clinician must remember that when a child is selected for therapy he will likely miss some of his classroom instruction. Consequently, the clinician must accept the challenge to make effective use of the child's time in therapy. A therapy session is indeed a short amount of time. The events and interactions which occur during these few minutes can be very meaningless or very meaningful. Experienced clinicians set present and long-range goals and then plan objective ways to reach these goals. The amount of therapy time is cumulative for each child. For example, if sessions last one-half hour and a child is seen twice a week for thirty weeks, the child will receive thirty hours of therapy in a school year. A great deal can be accomplished in this amount of time.

TIME FOR CONFERENCES

Time must be reserved for conferences throughout the year. Conferences with administrators are essential to effective planning and management. There is no better way to gain acceptance and support than to confer frequently with the school administrators. Clinicians should confer with the administrators at the beginning of each school year to discuss procedures, facilities, and schedules. After screening and diagnostic testing are completed, it is wise to discuss the results with the school administrators. A copy of test results may be given to the administrator at this time for his records so he will have appropriate information about the current status of the therapy program. Administrators may be invited to participate in teacher and parent conferences. Conferences may also be held to explore problem areas or to propose improvements. However, administrators vary in their desires for conferences with special service personnel. The clinician should not be discouraged if an administrator indicates a lack of interest in a conference. Continued offers should be made for conferences in spite of this. The choice is the administrators. The time suggested may be a factor. The first weeks of school, midsemester, and the end of the school year are particularly busy for administrators, and clinicians should make every effort not to impose on them at these times.

Conferences with the classroom teachers are essential. Coordinating speech therapy with classroom training and experience is necessary for effective management of all children with speech problems. One of the reasons for holding these conferences is to inform the teachers of the results of diagnostic evaluations, therapy goals, and progress in therapy. It is important to confer regularly with the teachers to make specific suggestions for helping the speech impaired children in their classroom. One can also obtain information from the teachers regarding a child's speech improvement in the classroom. The teacher's role in the therapy process has changed recently. More emphasis is currently being placed on the need and value of including the classroom teacher in the therapy process. This trend is significant from the standpoint that the classroom teachers know their children better than the clinician and they are with the children five days a week. Therefore, teachers have many opportunities to help the speech impaired children in their classrooms. Nearly all teachers are eager to help, and if they are given a little guidance by the clinician, their help can be very significant. For example, a child who has progressed to the point where he is using a sound correctly in connected speech needs help daily. The teacher may be asked to listen for correct sound production during reading class or other periods of the day. She may be instructed to praise the child for correct production or may call errors to the child's attention in a number of ways. Furthermore, the teachers can often provide a great deal of helpful information about a child's attitudes and motivation.

The severity of the problem, stage of therapy, and rate of improvement determine how frequently the clinician will meet with the teachers. The frequency of teacher conferences also depends on the knowledge, skill, and desire of each teacher. For example, some teachers need more guidance than others and some desire to help more than others. Before a child is scheduled for therapy, the clinician should ask the teacher if she has a preference as to the time of day when the child should or should not be scheduled. Teachers usually do not like to have their children miss certain time periods, for example reading and recess.

A conference should be held to inform teachers of the results of diagnostic evaluations. Another conference may be held after the children have been in therapy for a few weeks for the purpose of discussing reactions to therapy. Many clinicians prefer to hold conferences every few weeks to discuss progress in therapy. At the end of the school year it is advisable to confer with the teachers to summarize progress and to inform the teachers of the current diagnosis of each problem.

The conferences may be formal or informal. When formal conferences are held, the date, time, and place should be specified in advance. The classroom teacher should also know when others are invited to participate in the conference. The purposes and objectives of the conferences should be planned before formal conferences are held. An informal conference is a brief meeting of the clinician and teacher and may be held for the purpose of conveying a single item of information or suggestion. Such a conference may take place any time during the day and does not need to be planned in advance. In the survey of public school clinicians (Knight, Hahn *et al.*, 1961), 51 per cent of the school clinicians prefer informal meetings with teachers. Teacher conferences last anywhere from one minute to one hour or more. The majority of teacher conferences probably should not exceed one-half hour.

Parent conferences are equally important. Parents may be

overly concerned about their child's speech problem, or they may be unaware of the problem. They certainly need guidance in helping their children with their speech improvement at home. Sommers (1959, 1962, 1964) has reported significant results when parents are trained to assist in the therapy process. In the future, more emphasis will likely be placed on involving the parents in the therapy process.

One of the major deterrents to parent conferences at the present time is that clinicians do not have sufficient time to meet with all the parents of the children who receive therapy. The clinician and parents may meet before therapy is initiated, periodically, at the termination of therapy, or a combination thereof. In the survey (Knight, Hahn *et al.*, 1961), 40 per cent of the clinicians felt that the public school clinicians should establish contact with all parents. Finding a time to meet with parents is a real problem. Many schools have parent conference days, and the parents are scheduled to come at a specific time. One may use this opportunity to meet with parents. However, if the clinician desires to meet with both parents it is better to schedule the conferences after work in the afternoon or in the evening. There is much to be said for meeting with the parents in their homes. These parent conferences should be arranged in advance. If possible, both parents should be present. Such visits help one understand the home environment and the family. Suggestions resulting from home conferences may be more helpful to the child than suggestions that are made in a school office where parents are often uncomfortable. Where individual meetings with parents are impossible, group meetings may be a possible solution or telephone conversations may be "third best" substitute. However, telephone conversations may supplement conferences when additional information is desired from the parents or when the clinician wishes to provide information.

IN-SERVICE TRAINING

A small amount of time should be reserved for in-service training and meetings. Many school districts have regular in-service training programs scheduled throughout the year. Administrators frequently ask the clinician to participate in these general training sessions. Participation time may vary from a few minutes to an hour or more. It is often wise to request time to talk with the administrators and teachers. At these general training sessions the clinician may describe any aspect of his services. These meetings may be held during orientation day, at regular teachers meetings, or at county or area teachers meetings.

Responsible clinicians take the initiative to organize special parent and teacher training sessions. These training sessions may be held during school hours. Freilinger and Shine (1964) developed a teachers' workshop for the purposes of describing their services, coordinating services with classroom training, and training teachers to help the speech handicapped children in their classroom. In 1962 they developed a manual, *Practical Methods of Speech Correction for the Classroom Teacher,* to use in conjunction with these workshops. Following the workshop, the teachers may use the manual in their classroom.

Planning Time for the Day

As in the yearly and weekly schedule, many variations of the daily schedule are possible, depending on the number of children scheduled individually and the length of therapy sessions. Every program is dependent on the number of hours children are available which seldom exceeds six hours. Because of the shortness of the school day, as much of this time should be devoted to actual therapy as possible.

Effective Use of Time

A basic rule to follow is to be in the schools during school hours. The clinician who arrives and leaves with the teachers will be accepted much more readily than the clinician who arrives just a few minutes before the first therapy session and leaves before school is dismissed. Frequently, clinicians are required, or they find it helpful, to go to a central office before and/or after school. Clinicians who have followed this practice have found that this is a very good time for correspondence, conferences with office personnel, changing therapy materials, and similar duties.

Even though school clinicians are very busy, it is relatively easy to waste work time during school hours. Ineffective use of time can result from poor planning or from deliberate acts. It is important to have a reasonable amount of time for a brief rest each morning and afternoon. A reasonable amount of time is considered to be ten to fifteen minutes each half day. However, one should guard against spending too much time in the lounge drinking coffee, wasting time between therapy sessions, and permitting time to pass by with meaningless activities or games during therapy. School days pass rapidly. The person who really plans to use all of his work time effectively will discover a real challenge. Those who accept this challenge will find their work much more enjoyable than the person who does not carefully plan the use of his time.

LENGTH OF THERAPY SESSIONS

Good clinicians plan their daily work time very carefully. The length of therapy sessions is the primary consideration in planning this unit of time. The tendency is that therapy sessions last twenty to twenty-five minutes in the schools. Individual therapy sessions should not be shorter than fifteen minutes, and group sessions should not be shorter than twenty minutes. The maximum amount of time for either an individual or a group session probably should not exceed thirty minutes. The reason for this is the number of children in need of assistance. If the therapy sessions last thirty minutes, only eight or nine sessions can be held during the same amount of time. However, if more time is available or if case loads are reduced, it may be possible and advantageous to work with some children for more than half an hour at a time. Actually, there is no reason for therapy sessions to be of uniform length. It may be advantageous for some groups to meet for forty-five minutes while an individual child may be seen for fifteen minutes. It is very helpful to schedule a five-minute interval between therapy sessions. This is realistic since many teachers do not send their children to therapy and it takes the clinician about five minutes to get the children. When the teachers send them on time or they remember to come by themselves, this five minute period may be used to prepare for the next therapy session.

General Considerations
Informing School Personnel

Employers, administrators, and teachers often observe a clinician's work habits. They know that clinicians plan their own time schedules, and classroom teachers occasionally are resentful of this fact. Administrators and teachers may not understand the diverse responsibilities of the itinerant clinician and wonder where he spends most of his time. Therefore, it is important to inform the administrators and teachers of the clinician's whereabouts during the school year. During the first weeks of school while screening, diagnosis, and scheduling are in process, the clinician should prepare a schedule for the school administrators. As soon as the permanent schedule for the year is completed and approved, it should be mimeographed and distributed to the administrators and teachers in the district. School personnel are much more apt to understand the clinician's busy schedule if it is distributed. If this is not done the administrators and teachers may raise questions or make harmful comments.

Policies and Time

Administrators and the board of education set major policies pertaining to the overall responsibilities of school employees. Some of these responsibilities definitely pertain to budgeting time. It is within this framework that a clinician needs to have definite freedom to budget his own time. Clinicians must have the responsibility to plan their own diagnostic and therapeutic schedules. The clinician also has the responsibility for selecting the children to be scheduled for therapy, and should have the primary responsibility of determining the size of the case load. This is a factor that should be examined before accepting a contract. When there is serious objection to one or more of the policies which are in effect, the objection should be brought to the attention of the appropriate personnel for discussion and possible revision.

Contracts

The employing superintendent, board of education, special education director, and the head speech clinician all may contribute to guidelines for the clinicians employed in their district. These may include not only factors relating to time and scheduling but also policy on length of annual contract, daily and weekly hours, office hours, and assignment of clinicians to specific schools. A contract may also stipulate policy on sick leave, vacation periods, convention participation, work on Saturdays, travel allowance. It is extremely important that all of these stipulations be understood and acceptable before the contract is signed. Two offers, while offering the same salary, may be vastly different in worth to the clinician when the length of contract and fringe benefit differences are evaluated. It is unfortunate that some clinicians still work without a formal written contract.

FACILITIES

The Therapy Room

Physical facilities are an integral aspect of the overall therapy program. Clinicians spend the majority of their working time in the confines of their therapy rooms; therefore their physical facilities are of extreme importance. Space is at a premium in public school buildings all over the country with our rapidly expanding school population. Many school buildings throughout the country are crowded and lack adequate classroom facilities and space for their teachers and special personnel. This is particularly true of many older school buildings, as they were not built to accommodate the many special services that are provided in today's education. Clinical speech is only one of many special services in competition for available work space. For example, one clinician recently said that the school nurse, elementary consultant, psychologist, hearing clinician, music teacher, reading specialist, and the speech clinician were all working in the same school building on the same day.

Clinicians work in every room and space imaginable in the public schools. Many clinicians still work in the storage room, teacher's lounge, nurse's office, library, lunchroom, gymnasium, stage, another teacher's office, principal's office, music room, hallway, janitor's closet, furnace room, or one of many other possibilities. In fact, many clinicians do not have a room to call their own in any of their assigned schools. This is really not too surprising when one realizes how many demands there are on the available facilities, and when one contemplates the fact that many clinicians go to a given school only once or twice a week.

The adequacy of therapy rooms may run on a continuum from extremely unsatisfactory to ideal. Since the majority of speech clinicians work in a number of buildings, they often find a variety of facilities available for their use. As a result of a recent survey by the American Speech and Hearing Association (Knight *et al.,* 1961) it was reported that only 36 per cent of the school clinicians felt their facilities were adequate, and 50 per cent of the school clinicians reported their therapy rooms were inadequate.

It is not surprising that many school clinicians have adopted the attitude of "I will work wherever I can." The clinician who is willing to do this is frequently well aware of the fact that "wherever I can" may not be a satisfactory working area for the children and himself. However, it is felt a good clinician can adapt his clinical services to the physical facilities that are available. When a school is denied clinical speech services because adequate work space is not available, it should be remembered that it is the children who suffer and not the administrators.

Importance to Therapy

Why is the speech clinician's room so important? Clinicians who have worked in a variety of facilities for several years report that there is a definite relationship between the quality of physical facilities and the results of therapy. Poor facilities tend to minimize motivation of both the child and the clinician; whereas good facilities have a tendency to improve motivation. Poor facilities may create undesirable attitudes, be distracting to the children, and in some cases create fear within the children when they must work in small, dirty, junky, dark, and/or noisy cubbyholes. This is not to say that an effective clinician cannot observe some very significant improvement in some of the children he works with in even the poorest of facilities. The clinician can do very little to change the size and the shape of the facilities, but he can do a great deal to improve the appearance, equipment, and furnishings.

In general, school administrators are well aware of unsatisfactory physical facilities and, in most cases, do their best to help improve the situation. They realize that a clinician cannot provide effective services in poor physical facilities and will often give the clinician a choice of rooms or spaces that are available. One way in which the clinician may improve physical facilities is to make an issue of his needs.

The clinician should take the initiative to secure the best available working area. This can be done by talking with the special education director, school administrators, and the board of education. These people need to be informed by the clinician and/or supervisor if physical facilities are unsatisfactory as some of them may not be aware of the unsatisfactory working conditions. The clinician who attacks this problem tactfully and energetically by talking with these individuals and by preparing written reports and suggestions for improving the facilities is sure to improve his working conditions to some degree. When new school buildings are being planned it is important to discuss physical facilities with the architect as well as with the board of education.

The following suggestions are offered for those who are interested in improving their facilities, or in assisting in the planning of new facilities. The therapy room should be centrally located, easily accessible to classrooms, relatively quiet from extraneous noises, and near rest rooms.

Size of the Room

Clinicians working in the public schools throughout the country have reported that their therapy facilities are too small. Unfortunately, small storage rooms are often converted into a place to work for the speech clinician and other school personnel. The clinical speech room should contain a minimum of 150 square feet as this is the smallest room that will comfortably accommodate a clinician and a group of at least six children. Movement is restricted and activities must be limited if the room contains less than this space. A clinical speech room that is designed for a new school should contain at least two hundred square feet of floor space. Of course, a room that is also used for other school activities may contain several hundred square feet of floor space. For example, vacant classrooms are often adapted for speech therapy.

FIGURE 8. This is a picture of a very attractive therapy room that has been designed for speech and hearing services. The clinician's office is located in the therapy room. This arrangement has proven to be very satisfactory in many situations. Photo courtesy of Speech and Hearing Services, University Hospital Schools, Iowa City, Iowa.

Other Factors

The room should be well lighted with both natural and artificial lighting. It should be properly heated and should contain a thermostat to regulate the heat. Likewise, the room should be properly ventilated. Windows that can be opened for fresh air are preferable to windows that cannot be opened. The room must have at least one electrical outlet. Sound-treating materials should be used for ceiling and wall construction. A one-way mirror for observation purposes may be included.

The room should contain a table and sufficient chairs of appropriate sizes and heights. A chalk board, bulletin board, and a large wall mirror are considered to be necessities. The mirror should measure at least two feet by four feet. The room should also contain a cabinet for storing materials, and a small file cabinet that can be locked for storing records. A lamp, clock, calendar, and one or two framed pictures are also very appropriate in the clinical speech room.

The room must have a professional appearance. The furniture should be arranged appropriately. The clinician can do a great deal to create a pleasant, neat, cheerful, clean, and comfortable room. Ingenious clinicians take time regularly to continually improve the appearance of their therapy facilities.

The following report on recommendations for housing in the schools was prepared by a subcommittee on housing, of the Committee on Speech and Hearing Services in the Schools of the American Speech and Hearing Association.* This report was subsequently edited by the Committee on Speech and Hearing Services in Schools.† The final report of the committee is available through the American Speech and Hearing Association.

————————→

†Engnoth, G., *et al.*: *Report on Housing.* Committee on Speech and Hearing Services in Schools, November, 1967.

*Farquhar, M., *et al.*: *Report of the Subcommittee on Housing.* Committee on Speech and Hearing Services in Schools, American Speech and Hearing Association, November, 1966.

Item	Minimal	Acceptable	Ideal
		ROOM	
Location	Near elementary classrooms and relatively quiet	Near lower elementary classrooms and relatively quiet	Near lower elementary classrooms and relatively quiet. Near administration unit with accessibility to waiting area, secretarial services and other special service personnel
Size	150 sq ft	200 sq ft multipurpose room	250 sq ft to be used exclusively for speech and hearing services
Number	One	One	One room and adjoining office
Lighting Artificial Natural	50 foot candles One window	50 foot candles One window with shade	60-75 foot candles, indirect, plus floor lamp Two windows with blinds and draperies
Heating	Adequate central heating or space heater	Adequate central heating	Central heating with thermostat which can be controlled by clinician
Ventilation	One window which can be opened	One window which can be opened	One window which can be opened or air-conditioning
Acoustical Treatment	None	Acoustical treatment of ceiling	Acoustical treatment of ceiling, door and walls, draperies, carpeted floor

Item	Minimal	Acceptable	Ideal
Electrical power supply	One 110 V double plug	Two 110 V double plugs conveniently located	Three 110 V double plugs conveniently located. Dimming mechanism to facilitate use of audiovisual equipment
Intercom	None	None	One listen/talk unit, connected to administrative offices
Rest room facilities	Available	Available	Adjoining rest room(s) facilities — for exclusive use of speech and hearing room only
Chalkboard	One 3' x 3' mounted or portable	One 3' x 5' mounted on wall at appropriate height for children	One 3' x 8' mounted on wall at appropriate height for children
Bulletin board	None	One 4' x 4' mounted on wall	One 4' x 6' mounted on wall
Mirror(s)	Small hand mirrors	Small hand mirrors plus one 2' x 4' mounted on wall at appropriate height for children	Small hand mirrors plus one 3' x 5' which can be covered mounted on wall at appropriate height for children
Observation facilities	None	None	One-way-vision window 3' x 5' with listening facilities
FURNITURE			
Desk	None	One small office desk	Two four-drawer office desks (one for room and one for office)
Chairs			
Adult	One chair	Three chairs, one office chair, two folding chairs	Two office chairs, two lounge chairs
Children	Six chairs that can accommodate both lower and upper elementary cildren	Six chairs that can accommodate both lower and upper elementary children	Five chairs appropriate for lower elementary children and five chairs appropriate for older children
Table	One approximately 32" x 48", 24-30" high	One approximately 32" x 48", 24-30" high	One table appropriate size and height to accommodate younger and one appropriate size and height for older children

STORAGE FACILITIES

Storage space	Two shelves	Small locked cabinet	Large locked cabinet, preferably in a small storage closet adjoining therapy room
File cabinet	None	Two drawer file cabinet with lock	Four drawer file cabinet with lock
Bookcase	None	Wall mounted or stand. Approximately 4' linear space	Wall mounted or stand. Approximately 8' linear space

EQUIPMENT

Auditory training equipment	None	None — if portable unit is available to clinician	One master control unit with 4-6 headsets and microphones
Tape recorder	None — if portable is available to clinician	One assigned for exclusive use of clinician	One or more assigned for the exclusive use of the clinician. Mechanical use of machine should be designed for remote control so child will not be distracted
Phonograph	None	One 3-speed monophonic available in building	One 3-speed monophonic with record supply assigned to clinician
Telephone	None	One	One — direct outside line in speech and hearing office and extension in clinician's room
Typewriter	None	Available	One manual or electric
Electric clock	None	One	One with second hand
Wastebasket	One	One	Two
Stopwatch	None	None	One
Miscellaneous	None	Not included in this report but extremely useful to clinicians is a growing list of recently developed electronic equipment such as Echorder, Phonic Mirror, Language Master.	

Equipment, Materials, and Supplies

There is no doubt that equipment, materials, and supplies aid the speech clinician in his work. Some clinicians desire very little equipment and very few materials. Others prefer to use a great deal of equipment, an abundance of materials, and many supplies. Some clinicians do their best therapy with only a pencil and paper, blackboard and chalk, or with a mirror, but most clinicians need much more equipment and a variety of materials. The quality of materials that are available and the manner in which they are used determines, to a major degree, how effective one is as a clinician.

One of the problems of the speech clinician in the public schools is that he provides service to several school buildings. Ideally, duplicate equipment should be available for his exclusive use at each of the assigned buildings. However, budgeting limitations often make this impossible. Therefore, the clinician must usually carry his equipment and materials from school to school. Even though equipment and materials are often cumbersome and heavy, most clinicians can carry enough equipment and materials with them for a day of therapy. Before leaving the central office each morning, the clinician should go through the materials he has packed in his bag the previous day, sort out the ones that will not be used during the day, and add other items to use.

Commercial Materials

Until recently there has been very little material that has been designed specifically for clinical speech work. However, the picture is rapidly changing and, at present, there are some very good materials available. The progressive speech clinician will experiment with what is available, will search for new materials that can be used effectively, and design new materials for specific purposes. He should use whatever works to accomplish the goals that have been set forth. No material is highly effective or ineffective in and of itself, but the effectiveness of the materials depends upon the clinician's resourcefulness in using what is available. Some very simple materials can be used to reach the desired goals.

Clinicians should begin to accumulate materials as soon as they begin to work with children in their training. This is the proper time to begin to select and evaluate materials. When interviewing for a position, the clinician should definitely find out what equipment, materials, and supplies are available.

Budgeting

The majority of school districts have funds available for professional equipment and materials. Program supervisors generally formulate special education budgets. The clinician who inquires about the amount that can be spent annually during his initial interview can begin to plan for the utilization of these funds. The clinician who sets up a new program should prepare a list of equipment, materials, and supplies that are needed to begin the program. After this list is prepared, cost estimates should be obtained for everything on the list for the purpose of determining the total cost of these items. Certain items may be given priority if sufficient funds are not available for purchase of all of the desired items.

Budgets for equipment, materials, supplies, and a professional library should be planned. The amount of money that is available in different school districts varies from a few dollars to several thousand dollars in some cases. When funds are limited, the clinician might create an increase in available funds by promoting the need for new equipment and materials. After one determines how much can be spent, it is wise to investigate specific kinds of equipment, materials, and supplies that can be purchased from program funds.

It is necessary to confer with the superintendent and special education director to discuss how much money can be spent annually. In many school districts it is necessary to plan for major expenditures one or two years in advance of the purchase of the items as budgets are often planned well in advance. After selecting the desired equipment, materials, and supplies the list should be presented to the board of education or to the purchasing agent for approval. In some school districts consumable materials such as notebooks, index cards, and paste are ordered through each school, while specific speech materials such as books and equipment are ordered through the central office.

In addition to the program budget most clinicians plan a personal budget for purchasing equipment, materials, and supplies. Clinicians in training usually purchase some materials even though they make most of their own materials. Clinicians in the public schools are extremely busy and have little time to prepare homemade materials. Every clinician needs to decide if he will make personal expenditures for equipment and supplies and, if so, how much will be spent. Of course, the answer to this question is often determined by the amount of money that is available in the program budget for this purpose. Many clinicians purchase some of their own equipment and materials to supplement board of education purchases. This has the added advantage of making it possible for the clinician to retain the equipment and materials with which he is familiar should he change employment.

Professional Library

Professional people have a definite need for their own library. Speech clinicians who work in the schools are no exception. In fact, a public school clinician's library is of paramount importance for continuous professional growth. All clinicians acquire a number of professional books during their training but these textbooks should only be the beginning of a well-planned library. The publications of the American Speech and Hearing Association and the state speech and hearing association in which the clinician is working should certainly be an integral part of his library. *The Cumulative Indexes of the American Speech and Hearing Association* (Willis, 1962) are particularly helpful in locating articles of interest.

A clinician can plan the development of his library by preparing a list of the professional books and journals he should have in addition to a list of books he would like to acquire. The clinician should plan a schedule and a means by which these books can be acquired. Some clinicians buy a professional book each month; whereas others may purchase a book for their library every few months.

A professional library cannot extend a clinician's professional effectiveness unless the library is used. Professional reading should be done on a regular basis so as to enable the clinician to keep abreast of the explosion of knowledge in our profession. The clinician who sets aside a specific time each week to do professional reading will likely become a much better clinician than a person who does little or no professional reading on his own. Some clinicians set aside one evening each week for professional reading while others do their professional reading on weekends. It is important to remember that motivation and desire to learn through professional reading will ultimately improve clinical ability and skill. Set aside a regular time to do professional reading and use that time effectively!

List of Equipment and Materials

Following is a list of some of the most important items of equipment and materials that may aid school clinicians in their work.

Automated teaching machines designed for therapy such as the Ar-tik' Speech and Hearing Recorder, Echorder Speech and Language training aid, and the Phonic Mirror.

A good portable lightweight tape recorder with an adequate number of tapes. Thirty-minute recording tapes are suggested for therapy. A number of smaller tapes might be used to record speech samples at the beginning of therapy. After the initial recording, the tapes may be filed until the end of the year when a similar recording is made and the tapes are compared.

A portable pure tone screening and threshold audiometer is an important item of equipment for the school clinician to have unless the hearing testing program is done entirely by a hearing clinician or the school nurse.

Film projectors, both filmstrip and 16 mm, are very useful along with a small portable screen and a well-developed filmstrip file. Sixteen-millimeter films for parent and teacher education and therapy can be rented from many university and college audiovisual departments.

A portable record player with various speeds and a library of appropriate records for therapy.

A portable auditory training unit and table model amplifiers are vital equipment if hard of hearing children are served in the therapy program.

A pair of battery-operated telephones.

Six hand mirrors which measure about 10" x 12."

A pen flashlight.

A supply of tongue depressors.

A large durable carrying case for transporting materials.

Office supplies such as scissors, paste, construction paper, stars, crayons, slate, chalk, and rulers.

Charts, diagrams, and miscellaneous materials.

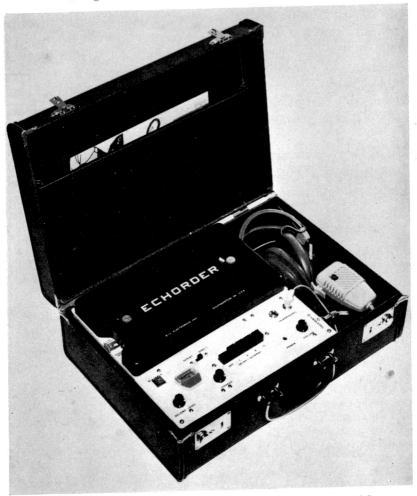

FIGURE 9. The Echorder is an example of an automatic speech and language training aid that can be set to play back speech and language under various time delays. Sommers (1964) outlined the usefulness of this training aid in a comprehensive manual. Photo courtesy of RIL Electronics.

Selection of Materials

Every clinician should exercise good judgment in the selection of materials that are purchased either personally or with program funds. All materials must be appropriate for use with children. Some materials are selected for a specific purpose while others are chosen for their versatility and can be adapted for multipurpose use. A variety of materials should be selected for use with different purposes, age groups, and stages of therapy. Maturity and speech development must also be considered when materials are purchased.

Choose materials that are basically speech centered. Certain games can be used during therapy if they are speech centered. Speech clinicians working in the schools are professional people but they should never become professional game players. When traditional games are used, the clinician should not say to the children, "Today we are going to play a game," but rather should announce, "Today we have an activity to use to help improve your speech. The purpose of this activity is to . . . ." Material should be selected that can be used with short, simple instructions. Children should be able to complete a given activity at least once during a therapy session and "learning the game" should occupy an insignificant part of the therapy session. Another important factor in choosing materials is to purchase durable materials which are sturdy, rugged, and lightweight as they need to be transported constantly.

SURVEYING COMMERCIAL MATERIALS

A few years ago there were very few commercial materials available for speech therapy. During the last few years, the trend has changed and there are many materials available at the present time. Some of the material on the market is poor, so it is imperative to evaluate all new materials carefully before they are purchased. One way to gather this information is to keep a file of brochures received through the mail. The clinician may request additional information from the publishing companies. This is a helpful means of gathering information, but commercial advertising should not be the sole criterion for selection as advertising can be misleading.

Materials are often displayed at the American Speech and Hearing Association conventions, state association meetings, and local group meetings where the clinician can examine what is available. One of the best ways to evaluate various materials is to meet with several clinicians in the surrounding area and look over each others' motivational devices, discuss how they are used, and talk about their effectiveness.

CLINICIAN-MADE MATERIALS

Public school clinicians generally do not have sufficient time to make their own materials. Homemade items are usually inexpensive, but they are time consuming to prepare. However, elementary teaching materials can often be adapted or revised for therapy, so it pays to be curious about the materials that elementary teachers use in teaching language, speech, and phonics. The clinician can design specific materials and sometimes needs to in order to accomplish a particular goal or to use with certain children.

Many speech clinicians use speech workbooks for at least some of their children. Speech workbooks or notebooks can be used very effectively if they are planned carefully. The primary purpose of a speech notebook is to serve as a means of helping a child reach the desired goal of improved communication. A child with a stuttering problem may record information obtained during therapy that will be helpful to review. A child with an articulation problem may be given assignments or practice material on a regular basis.

Speech workbooks need be nothing more than notebook paper stapled together or folded in half and stapled. A cover designed by the child adds to the personality of the workbook. This also provides good public relations and may better enlist the parents' and teacher's cooperation in the program as the child carries it to his classroom and to his home.

Public school clinicians often use worksheets as they provide a multitude of practice material and aid in motivating the children during therapy. Worksheets may be a part of a child's speech notebook or they may be used separately. In either case they may serve as an effective means of communication between the clinician and the children, and between the therapy process and the teachers and parents. Worksheets may also provide an excellent means of language development. Some examples of clinician-made worksheets are as follows.

———————————→

Dear _____,

I AM

WORKING

ON   THE

_____   SOUND

IN

SPEECH   CLASS

PLEASE

☐   Help me find _____ pictures with this sound.

☐   Listen to me say this sound correctly.

☐   Say this sound correctly for me if I make a mistake.

☐   Read me a story so I can practice listening to my sound.

Thank you, _____

FIGURE 10. This is an illustration of a worksheet which may be sent with the child to the teacher or parents. This worksheet can be used successfully to inform them of the sound being emphasized and to enlist their help.

Write some words or
draw some pictures in
the bubbles that have
your sound in them.

FIGURE 11. A very versatile worksheet which can be used for any sound. After the children draw pictures in the bubbles, the worksheet may be used for practice.

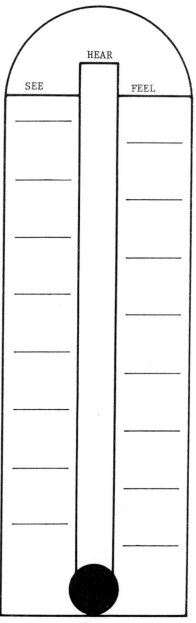

Start at the bottom.

Fill the blanks with

words containing your

sound.

Circle your sound in

each word.

Say each word twice.

Make the Thermometer rise!

FIGURE 12. Illustration of a worksheet for practice words for any sound. The child can practice his sound in a variety of ways after he has filled all the blanks with words containing his sound.

SOUND DISCRIMINATION

DIRECTIONS: Some of the following words begin with the *l* sound and some begin with the *w* sound. Circle the correct letter at the beginning of each word. In some cases you will have to circle both the *l* and the *w*.

w
  ed
l
	l
	  ee
	w
		w
		  et
		l
			l
			  ood
			w
				w
				  ong
				l

w
  ax
l
	l
	  ast
	w
		l
		  ock
		w
			w
			  ittle
			l
				l
				  ove
				w

w
  ane
l
	l
	  amp
	w
		w
		  ill
		l
			l
			  ot
			w
				w
				  eg
				l

l
  ap
w
	w
	  in
	l
		l
		  ike
		w
			w
			  amb
			l
				l
				  ing
				w

w
  ead
l
	l
	  id
	w
		w
		  ater
		l
			l
			  ay
			w
				w
				  ake
				l

FIGURE 13. This is an illustration of a discrimination worksheet for the *l* sound. The clinician can go over the worksheet with the child after he circles the correct letter (s) in each box.

WORDS THAT BEGIN WITH THE *R* OR THE *W* SOUND

The following pairs of words may begin with either the *r* or the *w* sound. The words in these pairs sound the same except for the first sound, so you must be very careful how you say the first sound. Say these rhyming words slowly and try to make the beginning sound of each word correctly. Can you SEE, HEAR, and FEEL that the *r* and *w* letters DO NOT make the same sounds? Practice! Good luck!

r
  ake
w
	w
	  ing
	r
		r
		  ag
		w
			r
			  eed
			w
				w
				  age
				r

w
  on
r
	r
	  eek
	w
		r
		  ig
		w
			w
			  ise
			r
				w
				  ave
				r

w
  ail
r
	w
	  ipe
	r
		r
		  it
		w
			r
			  ent
			w
				w
				  ide
				r

r
  ound
w
	r
	  ed
	w
		w
		  est
		r
			r
			  ay
			w
				r
				  oof
				w

FIGURE 14. An example of a worksheet which has been designed for discrimination between *r* and *w*. Since so many children substitute *w* for *r*, this worksheet is very useful.

SOUND PRACTICE

The following words contain your sound. Pronounce these words before a mirror at home. Watch your tongue and your mouth to see how and where your sound is made. Listen carefully to each word as you say them. If you make the sound incorrectly the first time, try again!

Ask your mother or another family member to listen to you say your sound correctly in these words. If you make an error, the person listening should say the sound correctly in the word for you. Try to say your sound correctly the second time.

You should go over these words several times making sure that you can say all the words correctly. Next use each word in a sentence. Then you can put all the words into a story. Use a pencil to check off the words as you say them in your story. Don't forget to thank the person for helping you. Good luck on your improvement!

Words containing the *s* sound:

At the beginning	In the middle	At the end
see	grocer	yes
so	seesaw	miss
some	answer	box
Sue	missing	face
sing	history	goose
sap	mister	grass
saw	possible	this
sold	outside	house
suit	myself	us
sign	lesson	mouse

FIGURE 15. This worksheet has been designed for home practice. It can be used for any sound. The directions stay the same but the words change. The advantage is that the worksheet and directions become familiar to both child and parent as many children work on a number of sounds during the therapy process.

Cautions Regarding Materials

While materials are very essential, some cautions are in order. The first caution pertains to the competitive factor of material. One should be very careful whenever using highly competitive materials since they may be distracting to therapy and may place the emphasis on competition itself. Competition may not be desirable for many children in the therapy program. Some mention has already been made of the fact that if games are used as materials they should be couched in terms of activities rather than talked about as games per se. Games must remain speech and language centered if the clinician expects to accomplish speech centered goals.

Another caution is to avoid using the same materials over and over for the same children. The children and the clinician lose interest when the same materials are used repeatedly. This is one reason why it is so important to develop a good variety of materials. Another caution pertains to using the same materials session after session during the day regardless of the purpose, goals, or stage of therapy. Unfortunately, some clinicians have been known to take one activity with them and use it over and over throughout the day. A wise clinician will use a variety of materials every day. The last caution is to guard against using materials which are too time consuming. A given activity or material probably should not take more than three-fourths of any therapy session. The remaining time can be used effectively to review and give assignments.

SUMMARY

Clinical speech service in the schools implies thorough examination, detailed diagnosis, meaningful prognosis, and functional long-range plans for direct or indirect remediation. Consequently the clinician needs to use his time effectively and select his case load accordingly. School administrators and classroom teachers must be informed about many aspects of the clinical program. Teachers should always have a therapy schedule for their children. Clinicians plan the daily, weekly, and annual time budgets.

Weekly scheduling alternatives are considered after a survey of the program needs has been completed. One day each week is recommended for coordination activities. The clinician has the responsibility to select the case load and to determine the length of therapy sessions. Time is reserved for testing, therapy, conferences, and in-service activities in all clinical programs. Conferences with administrators, classroom teachers, and parents are essential to the provision of effective service. Teachers and parents should be trained to assist in the therapy process.

Therapy facilities are an integral aspect of the overall therapy program. Clinicians should be prepared to work in a variety of rooms. Poor facilities are distracting and may delay therapy progress. The clinician should take the initiative to secure the best available working area. The clinical speech room should contain a minimum of 150 square feet of floor space.

Appropriate equipment, materials, and supplies need to be selected by the clinician. Selection should be started as soon as one begins therapy. Budgets for equipment, materials, supplies, and a professional library should be planned. A professional library is encouraged and time should be reserved for using the library. Good clinicians exercise wise judgment in the selection of materials and avoid the use of games in therapy. Various cautions regarding the selection and use of materials are offered.

DISCUSSION TOPICS

1. Discuss the rationale and advantages of a case load of less than one hundred children in a clinical speech program.
2. Discuss the implications of a clinician's freedom to budget his own time in view of the fact that clinicians are considered to be professional persons.
3. List and discuss the advantages of meeting with all of the school administrators at the beginning of each school year.
4. Develop and discuss a speech screening test for first and third grade children.
5. Develop and discuss an outline for a teacher's workshop.
6. Discuss the view presented in this chapter that a clinician should have parent conferences in the children's homes.

7. The clinician needs to assume the role of a politician when locating and improving therapy facilities. Discuss this point of view.
8. Prepare a list of therapy materials which you feel you will need to begin full-time work. Discuss your list with others.
9. Discuss the idea that the clinician should never be a professional game player.
10. Develop a list of one hundred therapy books to begin your professional library. Share your list with other student clinicians.

REFERENCES

1. BINGHAM, D.: *Program Organization in Public School Speech Therapy.* Des Moines, Iowa, Iowa State Department of Public Instruction, 1962.
2. ENGNOTH, G., *et al.*: *Report on Housing.* Committee on Speech and Hearing Services in Schools, American Speech and Hearing Association, November, 1967.
3. FARQUHAR, M.; FISHER, L., *et al.*:*Report of the Subcommittee on Housing.* Committee on Speech and Hearing Services in Schools, American Speech and Hearing Association, November, 1966.
4. IRWIN, R. B.: *Speech and Hearing Therapy.* Pittsburgh, Stanwix House, 1965.
5. KNIGHT, H.; HAHN, E., *et al.*: Public school speech and hearing services, II The public school clinician: Professional definition and relationships. *J Speech Hearing Dis, Monogr Suppl 8,* June, 1961.
6. SHINE, R. E., and FREILINGER, J. J.: *Practical Methods of Speech Correction for the Classroom Teacher.* Davenport, Iowa, Gordon Printing, 1962.
7. SHINE, R. E., *et al.*: The priceless gitf of better speech, *N.E.A. Journal, 53*:36A-36B, January, 1964.
8. SOMMERS, R. K.: Factors in the effectiveness of mothers trained to aid in speech correction. *J Speech Hearing Dis, 27*:178-186, May, 1962.
9. SOMMERS, R. K., *et al.*: Training parents of children with functional misarticulation. *J Speech Hearing Res, 3*:258-265, 1959.
10. SOMMERS, R. K., *et al.*: Effects of maternal attitudes upon improvement in articulation when mothers are trained to assist in speech correction. *J Speech Hearing Dis, 29*:126-132, May, 1964.
11. SOMMERS, R. K., and BRADY, D. C.: *A Manual of Speech and Language Training Methods Using the Echorder.* Southampton, Pennsylvania, RIL Electronics Co., 1964.

12. VAN DUSEN, C. R.: Public school speech clinic rooms, equipment and supplies. *Execptional Child, 6:*226-227, 1940.
13. WILLIS, C. R.: *Cumulative Indexes of the Journal of The American Speech and Hearing Association, (1936-1961).* American Speech and Hearing Association, Washington, D.C., 1962.

Chapter 9

CASE FINDING, CASE SELECTION, AND CASE LOAD

RONALD K. SOMMERS

Prior to the initiation of the therapy program, the speech clinician is called upon to make a number of important professional decisions regarding program organization. What methods should be employed to find those children in need of help? Which of those found to be in need of help should be selected for therapy if this is necessary? How many children should be scheduled for speech help? The decisions the clinician makes will have important implications for the type of program the clinician operates, the values which the children receive from the program, and the degree to which the program is judged by others to be successful.

In professional terminology the methods employed to locate children in need of help is called case finding; the system used to determine which children are scheduled is called case selection, and the number of children scheduled is called case load.

CASE FINDING

Effectiveness and Efficiency

Locating those children who require clinical speech services is a type of problem solving. Of the many proposed methods for solving this problem, those utilized must meet the criteria of effectiveness and efficiency. The term "effectiveness" denotes the successful arrival at intended goals, while the term "efficiency" has a different meaning, characterizing a technique or procedure which is not wasteful of time, effort, or information. Of the many case finding techniques which have been suggested or used by speech clinicians in the schools, most fail to meet one or both of these criteria. One technique, the survey method, may be amenable to modification so that it has both effectiveness and efficiency. Perhaps it might be well to examine a number of proposed techniques of case finding in light of these criteria.

Class Visitation

An early technique, described by Johnson (1956) but currently not widely used by speech clinicians in the schools, consists of having the speech clinician visit classrooms during periods in which oral recitation is conducted. This class visitation technique is dependent upon hearing each child recite. It is obviously highly inefficient, since many trips to the same classroom may be necessary before each child is heard, and it is not characterized by effectiveness because it lacks control over the context of speech. This lack of a standard sample of speech may affect the outcome of the case finding, since the articulation of younger children is often inconsistent and the particular context of a child's speech from minute to minute varies to such a degree that certain speech sounds may not be articulated. This would imply that some children would not be located and the class visitation technique would tend to be ineffective in arriving at its intended goal of locating all those with speech problems.

Teacher Referral Technique

This method depends upon the classroom teacher's ability to recognize and report children having speech problems. Typically the speech clinician either visits each teacher early in the school year and asks which children require speech testing or may need speech therapy, or this information is requested on a form which is then returned to the clinician. Only those children referred by the classroom teacher are examined and considered for therapy, except in cases where parents request a speech examination or principals, school nurses, or out-of-school agencies bring attention to the speech needs of children. Occasionally, only special groups of teachers are selected as referral sources. The reading teachers at the elementary level may serve as the clinician's source of referrals and English teachers at the junior and senior high levels may similarly be chosen. The clinician may reason that both such groups of teachers have a common interest in speech and communication and both groups sample the speech of most children at these different grade levels.

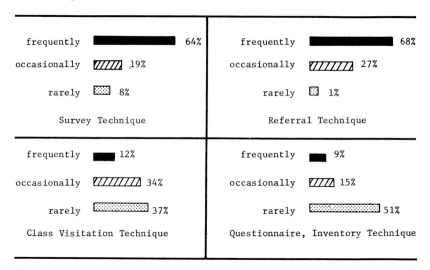

FIGURE 16. Relative frequency of use of four procedures for locating speech problems as reported by clinicians in nationwide sample (N = 705).

The teacher referral technique has enjoyed widespread popularity among speech clinicians working in schools (Roe *et al.,* 1961) . This technique was reported as being most popular in certain geographical areas of the United States, namely, in the West Coast and Southwest-Mountain-Hawaii regions; whereas, in the same study, it was found that the survey technique was much more commonly used by speech clinicians working in schools in the Midwest. In the nationwide study of speech and hearing services in the schools (Roe *et al.,* 1961) , 705 speech clinicians indicated their use of four different techniques of case finding. The results, seen in Figure 16, show that the teacher referral technique was most widely used, with the survey technique a close second.

These preferences by speech clinicians were mirrored in the results of a questionnaire study of 141 supervisors of speech and hearing. The results, contained in Table I, also support the fact that the referral technique was slightly more popular than the survey technique.

TABLE I
FREQUENCY OF USE OF FOUR LOCATING METHODS

| Method | Frequency of Use | | |
	Frequently	Occasionally	Rarely
Survey	72	19	5
Referral	78	16	2
Class visitation	19	33	43
Questionnaire or inventory	11	28	57

Relative frequency of use of four methods of locating children with speech problems as reported by 141 supervisors of speech and hearing programs. Values represent percentages of respondents replying as indicated.

The popularity of a technique of case finding does not attest to the ability to meet the criteria of effectiveness and efficiency. In fact, some evidence exists that a very popular case finding technique which is heavily dependent upon teachers' judgments regarding speech problems may, indeed, be ineffective in locating such children. This may be true regardless of the age of the child, his grade level, or whether or not teachers have received some degree of training in locating such children. It may be particularly true if the speech clinician is interested in knowing about the existence of numbers of children with important but less severely handicapping speech problems.

Diehl and Stinnet (1956) investigated the abilities of second grade teachers in Kentucky to identify speech and voice problems in children. Based upon a population of 3200 second grade children, the participating teachers were found to miss two out of every five children determined by two speech clinicians to have speech problems. Although the children with severe speech problems more often were located by teachers than were the children with lesser degrees of difficulty, two out of ten severe problems were not reported by teachers. Only four out of ten children with minor speech problems were identified and reported by teachers. The results of this investigation supported the opinion that the teacher referral technique of case finding was lacking in effectiveness. Although these investigators did not report information concerning the efficiency of teachers' referrals, experienced clinicians using this method have commonly observed that many of the children referred by classroom teachers do not have speech defects;

rather, these children often tend to be slovenly in speech. In this regard, the technique may be inefficient, since it takes time for the speech clinician to examine such children, report results to teachers, and clarify the differences between slovenly speech and speech defects. Diehl and Stinnett (1956) speculated that the effectiveness of the teacher referral technique might be enhanced by a training program for teachers which would serve to orient them to speech problems. This same idea had previously been presented by Ainsworth (1948) and Irwin (1953).

Although some research evidence tended to demonstrate that the teacher referral technique was rather ineffective in identifying speech problems at the elementary level, other evidence, previously cited, indicated its popularity as a case finding technique. The reasons for this seeming paradox are not clear; however, this technique may have some virtues not overlooked by some speech clinicians, and these same virtues may make it even more attractive at the secondary level. First among these is the ease for the speech clinician. It is obviously far simpler and less time-consuming to ask teachers to compile and submit names of children who they believe have speech problems than it is to examine a population of school children and make this determination. Also, in many school districts it has become accepted practice to have classroom teachers refer certain children to specialists for remedial teaching, special health needs, psychological testing, and for other reasons. Therefore, the teacher referral technique for locating speech problems tends to follow a traditional pattern. In this regard, both school administrators and teachers may readily agree to the use of this technique and may challenge the necessity for the use of more elaborate techniques.

A second reason for this popularity may reside in efforts of the speech clinician to formulate good working relationships with teachers by establishing an area of joint responsibility—a point where the classroom teacher and the speech clinician work together to help boys and girls with speech defects. The teacher finds the problems, and the speech clinician corrects them. Since some speech clinicians tend to have limited contacts with teachers, they may be reluctant to discontinue this method of case finding for fear of losing professional contacts and acceptance.

Many experienced clinicians establish a survey technique of case finding in the elementary grades but rely exclusively on a teacher referral technique for children at the secondary school levels. Presumably, the reasons for this are the same as those cited for the use of this technique in general. An additional reason, however, may stem from the fact that far fewer children with speech problems are served at the secondary levels (Bingham *et al.*, 1961), and this may indicate that many speech clinicians feel that time limitations preclude the scheduling of only the most severe problems and that a teacher referral technique will be effective in locating them.

A series of studies were completed in Montgomery County, Pennsylvania, schools to determine the effectiveness of teacher referral at the secondary level and to explore the benefits of orienting a select group of teachers to the identification of speech problems. These studies challenged the assumption that secondary teachers were capable of identifying a satisfactory percentage of students having severe, moderate, or mild speech defectiveness.

The results of these studies, summarized in Table II, were based upon referrals from 438 secondary teachers and the testing of over 10,000 students during a two-year period.

The procedures in these studies were similar to those used by Diehl and Stinnet (1956) except for differences in testing materials. The local speech clinician submitted to each secondary school teacher a form which asked the teacher to list the names of all students whom he felt might have speech problems. These completed forms were returned to the principal by each teacher. After all completed forms were returned, a staff of speech clinicians entered the secondary school and examined all children. Testing was normally accomplished by having one speech clinician assigned to every English class. Speech clinicians recorded the type of speech problem according to the categories of articulation problems, rhythm problems, or voice problems and rated these according to defectiveness, i.e. severe, moderate, or mild. In addition, a

further category consisted of students found with poor diction or
slovenly speech.

TABLE II
RESULTS OF A SECONDARY SCHOOL SPEECH SCREENING

Type and Severity of Speech Problem	Number Found by Teachers and Confirmed by Clinicians (A)	Number Found by Clinicians (B)	Percentage B/A (C)	Number Found by Clinician and Not reported by Teachers (D)
Articulation disorders:				
Mild problems	44	131	33.6%	87
Moderate problems	46	112	41.1%	66
Severe problems	8	14	57.1%	6
Voice disorders:				
Mild problems	4	62	6.5%	58
Moderate problems	12	21	57.1%	9
Severe problems	9	14	64.3%	5
Rhythm disorders:				
Mild problems	16	27	59.2%	11
Moderate problems	18	24	75.0%	6
Severe problems	14	17	82.3%	3
Total	171	422	40.5%	251

The results of a secondary school speech screening, comparing the effectiveness of
referrals from 438 teachers with the findings of nineteen speech clinicians. Total
N = 10,122 students drawn from five senior high schools, two combined junior-
senior high schools, and three junior high schools.

Before the inception of these studies, training sessions were
held to increase the percentage of agreement among the speech clinicians who served as testers. Tape recordings of both elementary
and secondary school children evidencing various degrees of speech
defectiveness were played and each tester indicated independently
whether a child had an articulation, rhythm, or voice problem and
whether this was severely, moderately, or mildly defective. Following the final training session, the intragroup mean agreement for
all testers was as follows: 1) articulation problems, 91 per cent
agreement concerning degrees of defectiveness and 96 per cent
agreement about the type of problem; 2) rhythm problems, 85 per
cent agreement about the degree and 98 per cent agreement about
the problem; and 3) voice problems, 81 per cent agreement
about the degree and 97 per cent about the problem. In general,
the reliability thus determined appeared adequate for research
purposes.

A comparison of the results of the Montgomery County studies with those of Diehl and Stinnett (1956) for elementary subjects shows some striking similarities in the abilities of teachers to identify speech problems. Both of these investigations show that teachers in general can locate many of the children with severe speech defects, but they overlook a sufficient number to throw the entire technique into jeopardy. For example, Diehl and Stinnett (1956) found that teachers could locate 81 per cent of the children with severe speech problems in second grades, while this percentage at the secondary level in the Montgomery County study was found to be 67.9 per cent, indicating that almost one of three secondary students with a severe problem was not identified by teachers. Diehl and Stinnett, in the same study, reported that second grade teachers had succesfully identified 60 per cent of all degrees of speech defectiveness; the Montgomery County study found this overall precentage of correct identification to be only 40.5 per cent at the secondary level. In this latter study secondary teachers were successful in locating 57.7 per cent of the students with moderate and 33.1 per cent with mild degrees of speech defectiveness.

Early findings in the Montgomery County studies showing the ineffectiveness of secondary teachers in identifying speech defects led to an additional investigation. The notion of Ainsworth (1948), Irwin (1953), and Diehl and Stinnett (1956) that teachers might become more effective if trained to identify speech problems was explored. The entire English and foreign language department, consisting of fourteen teachers from a high school of 1250 students, volunteered to learn more about speech problems and agreed to attend two one-and-one-half-hour training sessions after the close of school. Training took place approximately one week before the teachers were asked to submit names of students whom they felt had speech or voice defects. The teachers appeared interested in the lectures, discussions, and tape recordings of different types and degrees of speech problems which comprised the two orientation sessions. One week after the conclusion of these orientation meetings, all of the teachers were asked to complete the referral forms. Those submitted by the fourteen trained teachers were analyzed twice, once along with those from all teachers and then independently from those submitted by the untrained teachers. The results of this investigation, obviously limited by a small sample and a singular approach, are presented in Table III.

Generally speaking, it appears that neither the effectiveness of the technique of teacher referral nor its efficiency was improved as a result of this training program. In fact, it can be seen in Table III that the number of students referred from the trained teachers was proportionately greater, but the quality of these referrals in locating the real problems was hardly any better than that of the untrained teachers. This means, of course, that the efficiency of the technique decreased since more false referrals were made to the speech clinicians. Said differently, it appears that the stimulated interest of the fourteen trained English and foreign language teachers did not result in better quality referrals, merely in more referrals. The limitations of this small study are obvious; however, it does cast some doubt upon the validity of the concept that teachers without extensive training can be used to accurately identify speech problems. More comprehensive studies are needed to determine the validity of these findings.

With the exception of Irwin (1953), who reported that the questionnaire-inventory method was an accurate way of locating speech problems in the schools of Ohio, almost all other authorities have endorsed the survey technique of case finding (Ainsworth, 1948; Johnson, 1956; Van Hattum, 1958; Van Riper, 1954). A simple plan for this speech screening has been presented by Ainsworth (1948). He proposes two different types of surveys—the initial survey and the annual survey.

TABLE III

EFFECTIVENESS OF TRAINED AND UNTRAINED TEACHERS

Teachers	Real Problems Located by Teachers	Real Problems Missed by Teachers but Found by Clinicians	False Referrals to Clinicians from Teachers
Trained (N=14)	6	31	45
Untrained (N=41)	9	28	15

A comparison of the effectiveness and efficiency of trained versus untrained high school teachers in locating speech problems.

THE INITIAL SURVEY

The more basic of the two is the initial survey in which each child is interviewed personally by the speech clinician. The clinician asks his name, age, grade, and other items of information in order to elicit a sample of his speech. Older children are asked to read special materials. Ainsworth suggested that this initial survey should take about two minutes per child, and he further suggested that a speech survey record be completed for each child as examined. To increase the efficiency of the process, he suggested that these assessments be made in a small room near the classroom with two to four children waiting to be seen.

THE ANNUAL SURVEY

As described by Ainsworth, these procedures are to be accomplished during the first two or three weeks of school. Children from the following categories should be tested: 1) those in the active and inactive files of the speech therapy department, 2) all those dismissed as corrected the year before, 3) all new students in the school, including kindergarten and first grade children as well as transfer students, and finally 4) any other children that teachers may recommend. Drawing from Ainsworth's original plan, a number of elaborations can be presented to show in greater detail how certain types of speech survey techniques might be established in the schools.

The Survey Method

Screening Tests

A speech survey purports to assess the prevalence of speech problems as exactly as possible. The degree of exactness necessary in any particular survey is obviously dependent upon the ultimate use of the data gathered, the existence of adequate techniques for conducting the survey, and the efficiency required to make it practical. The speech clinician working in a school setting is probably interested in all these factors as he plans a speech survey of school children. In most cases the final decision concerning a survey plan and the choice of a survey technique is dependent upon these considerations. Commonly, an instrument for testing is chosen because it can be administered easily and quickly and yet "sorts out" those having speech problems from those who do not with a high degree of accuracy. A test of this type is usually called a screening test, since it sets parameters of performance at a fixed level and runs subjects against those predetermined standards. Subjects whose performances fall below the established standards of performance may receive more elaborate and intensive testing later in the form of the so-called diagnostic test.

Instruments

One of the frequently used speech screening devices consists of picture cards constructed so that each card allows the examiner to judge the correctness of a subject's response to naming the picture as a function of the position of the particular sound in the word. Sounds are tested as they occur in the initial, medial, and final positions in words. Representative tests are commercially available —Montgomery (1960), Bryngelson and Glaspey (1962), Hejna (1955). However, many speech clinicians have made their own tests. A set of thirty such cards allows a clinician to test a subject's performances on the ten most difficult consonant sounds: $s, z, s, ts,$ $l, dz, \theta, \int, v,$ and r—Roe and Milisen (1942), Templin (1953), Pendergast (1963). This screening test can be administered to most kindergarten, first, second, and third grade children in about five minutes per child if limited to these ten sounds. Phonetic analysis sheets are completed on subjects demonstrating misarticulations on any of the sounds tested; subjects found to have totally correct articulation are listed on a screening sheet which merely notes this fact. This type of spontaneous three-position screening is usually employed to survey the speech of primary-aged children or nonreading older ones. Although intended as a screening test for articulation, experienced clinicians usually listen for the voice and rhythmic qualities of speech as well and occasionally detect these problems.

Graded Reading Materials

Examples of reading material suitable for speech screening have been developed, such as the following:

My Grandfather

You wished to know all about my grandfather. Well, he is nearly ninety-three years old; he dresses himself in an ancient black frock coat, usually minus several buttons; yet he still thinks as swiftly as ever. A long, flowing beard clings to his chin, giving those who observe him a pronounced feeling of the utmost respect. When he speaks, his voice is just a bit cracked and quivers a trifle. Twice each day he plays skillfully and with zest upon our small organ. Except in the winter when the ooze or snow or ice prevents, he slowly takes a short walk in the open air each day. We have often urged him to walk more and smoke less, but he always answers, "Banana Oil!" Grandfather likes to be modern in his language.*

This and similar materials are usually "graded" in two ways: 1) they are developed so that the reading difficulty level is appropriate for use with upper elementary aged children or for junior and senior high school students and 2) they are also "graded" in the sense that almost all consonant and vowel sounds are represented as they occur in the initial, medial, and final positions in words. Most are one paragraph readings of approximately 120 words or less. Experience shows that a normal reader at the upper elementary level takes about three minutes to read such material; the normal reader at the high school level can read material such as "My Grandfather" in less than two minutes. Some enterprising speech clinicians have developed their own graded materials. The continuous flow of speech during oral reading allows the clinician to determine the normalcy of other attributes of speech besides articulation. For this reason, reading material is also valuable to some degree as a screening test for voice quality and rhythm problems. A recommended procedure for scoring responses which is efficient in terms of time and material is to complete a speech screening form of phonetic analysis on only those subjects evidencing misarticulations or other speech aberrances and merely recording the names and grades of others who show completely normal speech.

More Thorough Testing

Clinicians not comfortable utilizing the basic screening tests previously described may find additional ways of eliciting speech

*Van Riper, Charles: *Speech Correction: Principles and Methods.* Englewood Cliffs, Prentice-Hall, 1954, p. 178.

samples. Of real concern, even in screening testing, is a child's spontaneous speech production. Older or upper grade children, in particular, may show a disparity in the correctness of their speech productions from one mode (oral reading, conversational speech, picture card responses) to another. For example, some subjects may stutter in conversational speech but show no indications of this disorder when reading aloud. Others may only stutter when reading. Still others may appear to have only slightly defective voices in oral reading but show major voice problems when producing more relaxed conversational speech. Since an occasional child in the primary grades may misarticulate a sound other than the ten most difficult ones measured in the basic screening test or be inconsistent in his misarticulation of these sounds, some clinicians may prefer a slightly more intensive screening test. For these reasons and others, some clinicians may want to sample more speech. More intensive screening tests take many forms. Not infrequently the clinician may try to elicit an early sample of a child's speech by asking certain questions, How old are you? What's your dog's name? Where do you live? What do you like to watch on television? This questioning method obviously takes many forms. A further technique consists of asking the child to recite learned material such as counting from one to ten or saying the Pledge of Allegiance. Recitation of nursery rhymes or similar material may also be requested.

More elaborate spontaneous articulation testing can be undertaken to measure less commonly defective sounds such as $w, d, t, p, b,$ and j. In addition, pictures stimuli may be introduced to check the production of vowels and diphthongs.

The Templin-Darley screening test (1953) can be used to measure the production of commonly defective blends such as st or $bl,$ or a clinician can find suitable pictures to elicit these responses. A short version of McDonald's deep test of articulation (1964) can be used to determine the accuracy of articulation of selected consonants as a function of their interaction with about fourteen other sounds. Such a procedure takes ten to twelve minutes with most children from grades one to three. In summary, screening tests can be very simple and brief or more elaborate and time-consuming. None is really intensive or diagnostic, nor are the tests intended to be so, since the need is to identify speech problems so that further assessments can be made at a later time.

Procedures

According to returns from the nationwide study of speech and hearing services in the schools (Bingham *et al.,* 1961), most clinicians provide therapy to both elementary and secondary school children. Under such conditions, it often becomes necessary to establish a total testing plan if all children within an assigned school area are to be examined. Two considerations appear paramount in arriving at a workable and efficient survey plan. The first of these is the amount of time that can justifiably be spent screening children, and the second relates to the amount of support needed from school administrators and other professional staff to accomplish this task.

It would be impossible for a speech clinician to justify a screening program which continues during much of the school year and allows for little therapy time. This would also hardly be possible in some states since local school districts must show evidence of the number of children enrolled in clinical speech in order to receive state reimbursement for such services. It would appear expedient for the clinician to arrive at a compromise which would insure that most service would be in the form of therapy with a reasonable amount devoted to the survey. Many possibilities present themselves, and most of these are somewhat dependent upon the amount of screening that has been done in the particular school area.

Certain suggestions can be made concerning procedures to be followed regardless of the extent of the screening program. In a system where no speech screening has been completed, for example, the following procedures might be followed in order to complete the elementary grades:

1. As soon as possible after school begins in the fall, the clinician should begin to screen children. Some clinicians prefer screening kindergarten children; others prefer first grade children; while others prefer screening second and third grades (Templin and Darley, 1960), relying on teacher referral for all other grades.

2. After devoting the first week or two to accomplishing Step 1, the clinician should begin to organize some therapy classes for children meeting requirements for admission into such classes; however, one day per week should be set aside for screening.

3. The clinician should schedule time in particular school buildings for this additional screening and proceed to screen the sixth grades next since any undetected problems at this level may be difficult to schedule as they move into junior high the following year.

4. Screening should then proceed from the fifth grade down through the second grade.

5. An alternate, and perhaps preferred, procedure is to block out a four to six-week period of time at the beginning of the school year, before a therapy schedule is established, and complete all of the screening of elementary children or as much as possible; if this is not completed, the clinician can schedule the balance of the testing for his "coordination day" or therapy time, if desired.

In school areas where all of the elementary children enrolled have been screened by speech clinicians, two procedures should be undertaken yearly in order to safeguard the integrity of the survey. First, the clinician should screen all kindergarten classes, followed by all first grade classes, early in the school year. Secondly, all transfer or new students should be screened.

Although it may seem somewhat redundant to screen children in kindergartens one year and then rescreen them as first graders the following year, this may be necessary to some extent since a number of nonkindergarten children may enter first grades. A further point should be made about this practice as well: Steer and Drexler (1960) have indicated that changes in articulation of kindergarten children may have prognostic implications for case selection; therefore, a rescreening followed by additional testing may prove of real value to the clinician in this regard.

Some persons, as previously mentioned, prefer to screen at the second or third grade levels only, relying on teacher referrals at the kindergarten or first grade level. This involves basic philosophy regarding the development of speech and the effect on early-grade children who do receive speech help. Each clinician needs to carefully study the available evidence and develop a program consistent with his philosophy. Hopefully, future research will clarify this matter.

Screening in Secondary Schools

One Day Per Week

Evidence, previously presented, has indicated that the teacher referral method of case finding at the junior and senior high school level is rather ineffective. Assuming that these findings are valid, it behooves a clinician responsible for children at these grade levels to develop a screening procedure. It is particularly important that these children be examined if they were not screened as elementary students. High schools frequently include children from private and parochial elementary schools where speech help was not available. As before, a number of various plans can be developed. One of these will meet the clinician's and the school's requirements best. Two principal plans will be suggested. One is predicated on the fact that the speech clinician works by himself; the other is based upon a team approach in which a number of speech clinicians from one administrative organization, or several neighboring ones, work together to accomplish this task.

As an example, an individual clinician wished to screen a combined junior-senior high school by working one period daily. The choice was to try to use the homeroom or activity period. Unfortunately, many other activities occurred during this time, e.g. the teacher did guidance work, the chorus practiced, special clubs met, and there were multiple interruptions of various types. In general, it was difficult to coordinate the testing; interruptions were frequent, and the atmosphere was too informal for controlled screening. The clinician then reviewed the program of instructions for all the students and consulted the master schedule. It was subsequently determined that each student was scheduled for English every day (a common requirement for many states). The high school principal and speech clinician conferred and ultimately planned a schedule which allowed a screening of the entire school body of one thousand students in five working days. This plan had the following features: 1) there were eight fifty-five-minute periods of instruction each day with a minimum of four and a maximum of six English classes taught each period; 2) testing would be done in the English classes for an entire day, one day each week over a five-week period; 3) the English teachers would be alerted according to a schedule concerning when a particular class would be screened and prepare seat work accordingly; 4) the clinician would sit in the back of each classroom and indicate to each of the twenty-five or so students when he was to walk over and read the screening material—which would take approximately one-and-one-half minutes to read—; 5) a brief phonetic analysis was completed for students showing speech problems; all others were not listed, but the attendance in each class was carefully noted, and 6) between class periods the clinician moved to the next scheduled English class until the day's screening was completed.

During the conference with the principal, it was decided that all testing would be scheduled on Mondays, since this was more stable in the sense of fewer interruptions in school routine. It will be noted in the hypothetical example contained in Table IV that almost all testing could be accomplished over a five-week period except for three classes (periods one, two, and three). These were planned another time.

TABLE IV
HYPOTHETICAL SCHEDULE

Period	English Classes Scheduled on Mondays
1	Rooms: 210, 212, 214, 216, 217, 210
2	Rooms: 211, 212, 214, 109, 306, 307
3	Rooms: 209, 210, 212, 111, 214, 306
*4	Rooms: 212, 210, 208, 209
*5	Rooms: 207, 208, 210, 209
6	Rooms: 209, 211, 212, 306, 208
7	Rooms: 211, 210, 111, 306, 212
8	Rooms: 206, 209, 306, 111, 211

A hypothetical schedule of high school English classes.
*Lunch periods of ninety minutes each, forty-five for lunch and forty-five for a class.

A One-day Program

It can be seen quite readily that the plan for screening in English classes can be adapted so that an entire school can be completed in one day if a sufficiently large group of testers is available. Six speech clinicians working on a Monday, for example, could test the entire school of one thousand pupils. Although arrangements for such mass testing might appear to be formidable, experience shows that they really are not. The advantages of completing a school in one day are obvious. Testing plans are particularly simplified if all the participating speech clinicians are employed by one administrative unit, i.e. a county or city school program. In such instances, permission to leave assigned schools for a day is easier to obtain, since the screening service is part of a total program. Clinicians working by nature of being employed by an independent school district might find that other neighboring clinicians similarly employed would be willing to participate in screening their secondary schools if reciprocity were agreed upon.

A number of ways of screening secondary students for speech problems also may prove efficient. For example, a junior high school with an enrollment of 925 students was screened by a staff of seven speech clinicians in less than three hours. This was accomplished as a result of careful planning, a most cooperative principal, and the use of one of the facilities in schools, the Audion. This amphitheater-type room with multiple entrances and exits and seating accommodations for two hundred students was particularly suitable for organized, quiet reading. Clinicians were spaced four to six rows apart, and as many as fifteen students were seated adjacent to them. After each student was screened, he left the Audion by an exit and returned to his class. The principal and his assistant kept whole classes of students flowing into the Audion and to the testers without interruption and with excellent control over noise and extraneous movement. The sound proofing of the Audion was also of significant value. In this case, the disruption in junior high classes was minimized due to the rapid flow of students examined and their quick return to their assigned classes. The principal was willing to allow a major change in a morning's activities in order to complete this screening. The auditoriums of most junior and senior high schools are probably almost as ideal for this type of testing as the Audion proved to be in this case. In summary, a number of efficient ways can be developed for screening secondary schools. Each of these should probably be tailored to a particular school's program and can be developed jointly by key school personnel and the speech clinician.

Summary

It is suggested that the case-finding techniques utilized by the clinician working in the schools deserve study prior to their inception in terms of their relative efficiencies and effectiveness. Although probably more time-consuming, the survey method seems most defensible on the basis of known research findings and authoritative opinion. Perhaps the case-finding plan and its rationale set the tune for the subsequent actions of the clinician relative to selecting children for therapy and constituting a case load. Hopefully, future research concerning the needs of younger children for speech therapy and their abilities to benefit by these services will shed light upon the issues involved in choosing among these methods of locating children who may require correction. The next phase of the therapy program, case selection, seems dependent upon the case-finding one.

CASE SELECTION

The Importance of Careful Case Selection

At one time case selection was relatively simple. Any child with a speech deviation was considered as speech defective. However, Van Hattum (1954) called attention to the fact that methods of case selection were necessary to distinguish between those children in the process of speech development and those with real speech defects in need of speech therapy.

The most competent speech clinician in the schools cannot be considered effective if he is working with the wrong children. Said differently, all the best therapy techniques and skills in the world are of no consequence if wasted on those not needing it and denied those who do. These arbitrary statements might well apply to speech clinicians employed in settings other than the schools; however, it would appear that case selection must be considered a fundamental problem for those working in the schools, since as many as 50 per cent (Sommers *et al.,* 1961; Byrne, 1962) of first grade children, for example, display articulatory deviations. The clinician is therefore frequently faced with the task of selecting the bona fide speech problems from this large group of children. Although not nearly so great, the percentage of second grade children showing speech deviations also is reported to be high (Sommers *et al.,* 1962).

A further consideration rests upon the ratio of speech clinicians to total school population served. Although nationwide figures are not available, information from California (Coates *et al.,* 1963) indicated that 60 per cent of school clinicians were serving areas with from one thousand to five thousand students. These figures suggest that many clinicians may have as many as 150 speech problems to select from for therapy, and in addition, the usual number of speech deviant younger children who must be examined. Unless careful assessments are made by the clinician, a certain percentage of children with errors but not speech defects may be entered into therapy; conversely, a certain percentage of speech defective children may not be entered into therapy—unless the clinician decides to take everyone from both groups. This last practice would tend to be self-defeating in arriving at an effective clinical speech program.

Judgments Concerning Case Selection

One salient characteristic of a profession is that its members are responsible for making enlightened judgments. The implicit assumption is that the specialist has been trained to make decisions dealing with certain professional matters. A vital one to any speech clinician revolves around which ones to help. For the most part, information from the national study of speech services in the schools indicated that most clinicians in the schools make judgments about case selection without interference from others (Bingham *et al.,* 1961). These results tend to show that policy rather than specifics may be decided by certain school personnel such as principals and supervisors, but that the clinician most often assumes and maintains his professional prerogative about selection. It goes without saying that any other way of selecting children for therapy might be considered a breach of·professional ethics, since only the clinician is qualified to decide on the basis of his evaluation and experience.

Parent Permission

All of this is not to deny the basic right of a parent of a speech defective child to reject the offer of speech help. Interestingly, results from this same study (Bingham *et al.,* 1961) indicated that only about two out of five speech clinicians requested parental permission before enrolling a child in speech therapy. Apparently, common practice has been merely to notify a parent that his child is enrolled rather than request that he be entered into the program. In rare instances school boards have been known to insist that any child selected for therapy be entered into the program, regardless of the parental feeling about it. The basic question again is whether clinical speech is education like reading or more like medicine and dentistry. If the former, parents have little to say. However, if the latter, the parents do have a choice.

Classroom Teachers

Classroom teachers have influenced case selection in some indirect ways. Although speech clinicians reported that the classroom teacher influences the time that children are scheduled for therapy (Bingham *et al.,* 1961), it would appear that this type of judgment may bear heavily in some instances upon who is selected. For example:

> A clinician has a tentative schedule in a particular school building. The remainder of the weekly schedule is rather "fixed" in the sense that four other schools are scheduled on other days and all of these require as much or more time than the amount now alloted. By the middle of the school year, some children are "dismissed" as corrected, and children from the waiting list are retested to determine who should be added for therapy. Two children from one third grade seemed to deserve priority on the basis of degree of speech defectiveness. Further assessment indicated that one of the two was more deserving of help on the basis of total need, and, unfortunately, only one of the two could be scheduled. The particular therapy class for this child had been established from 9:00 to 9:45 A.M. The third grade teacher said, "Please don't take Charles if you have another choice, because he's doing poorly in reading and that's the time for his reading work." The clinician acquiesced and chose the other third grade child.

In effect, the classroom teacher had influenced case selection.

School Policy

Even more dramatic is the effect of junior or senior high school policy upon case selection as it is reflected in case scheduling. The principal may say, "We will allow you to work with our students, but they cannot miss classes for this." This means that only those in need of therapy who have study halls at a time suitable for scheduling can be helped. As before, restrictions on scheduling are directly related to a decision about who is to receive therapy, since some of the most severe problems may not have any study halls or these may occur at a time totally unsuitable for the clinician. The enterprising clinician, of course, tries to find other ways to schedule some of these problems (such as after school), but this is an increasingly difficult problem. Fortunately, most policy established in secondary schools allows students to miss a class each week, if necessary, in order to receive help.

Selection as a Function of the Total Program

The Ideal Program

Although there are few clinicians working in the schools who are without waiting lists, who are able to devote as much time as necessary for bona fide speech problems, and who have an active and adequate speech improvement program for kindergarten and first grade children to handle speech deviations, these utopian conditions do exist. One crucial aspect in case selection now seems predicated upon which of these programs (improvement or therapy) is indicated for some children. Fortunately, some suggested guidelines are available stemming from research into the relative effectiveness of these approaches.

Articulation Assessment

Careful and systematic assessment of articulation must, by its very nature, be considered the *sine qua non* for case selection. The characteristics of a child's articulatory behavior appear to offer some valid cues concerning his basic need for remedial assistance and suggest which type of assistance may be best for him. The qualities of articulation deserving attention and study include the specific sounds misarticulated, their positions in words, the number of misarticulated sounds, the consistency of misarticulation of these sounds, and the ability of the child to correct misarticulations as a function of stimulability testing. Some research evidence will be cited later to support the importance of all of these factors.

Defective Sounds

A clinician working in the "ideal" situation previously described may wish to determine which kindergarten and first grade children should receive speech therapy and which speech improvement. Perhaps this clinician is also interested in the advantages of providing both types of experiences to children with severe problems. A view of a particular child's articulatory behavior may help in arriving at a sound decision. Evidence to support the notion that the identity of the misarticulated sounds should be considered can be found in the Armstrong County studies (Sommers *et al.*, 1961 and 1962). In this project, more than 1500 first grade subjects were sampled to receive either speech therapy, speech improvement, or both. The sounds most amenable to correction in speech improvement as a result of an analytical ear-training method were studied. In the order of highest to lowest percentage of correction, they were as follows: v, 50 per cent; f, 41 per cent; r, 38 per cent; g, 37 per cent; k, 36 per cent; θ, 33 per cent; s, 26 per cent; $ş$, 22 per cent; $tş$, 20 per cent; and l, 18 per cent. The authors were of the opinion that an ear-training method was not capable of making significant improvements in misarticulations taking the form of lateral sigmatisms on s and z. Also, this was to hold for lateral emissions of $ş$, $tş$, and $dʒ$. They also felt that evidence indicated that second grade children showing errors on l, $ş$, and $tş$ should receive speech therapy rather than speech improvement.

Severity as a Factor

The severity dimension has not been studied at all levels to determine its importance in case selection. The clinician having an opportunity to arrange both speech therapy and speech improvement for severe articulation problems in first grade children may be interested in an additional finding from the Armstrong County studies (Sommers *et al.*, 1961). Twenty-five pairs of first grade children having six or more of the ten sounds tested defective and prognostic scores, based upon the Carter and Buck Test (1958), which indicated that they were "poor risks" were randomly assigned to speech improvement once weekly, or speech improvement once weekly plus speech therapy once weekly. Those who received both were significantly improved in articulation compared with those who received speech improvement only. These results, which also supported the predictive validity of the Carter and Buck Test, were interpreted to mean that speech improvement did not possess the "strength" to accomplish what a period of speech therapy plus improvement could do for subjects with severe problems and low prognostic scores. Although no evidence exists to demonstrate the combined effectiveness, the supposition is that there may be some relative degrees of combined effectiveness. Obviously, additional research information is needed.

Number of Defective Sounds

One tangential study of Steer and Drexler (1960) shed some additional light upon the effect of the number of defective sounds as it relates to ultimate improvement as a result of twelve weeks of speech improvement in kindergarten. These investigators noted that subjects showing greater degrees of defectiveness on the twelve sounds used in the speech improvement program tended to evidence more improvement in articulation when tested five years later. This finding, although difficult to interpret, may suggest that it is not necessarily the number of sounds that are defective which bears most attention in selecting subjects for speech improvement, but which sounds are misarticulated and the characteristics of their defectiveness. Interestingly, the two most predictive variables were errors in the medial positions and the combined number of errors for the phonemes *f* and *l*. Accordingly, subjects showing these types of errors might be poor candidates for kindergarten speech improvement programs of the type provided by the original investigator, Wilson (1954). A number of other factors of articulatory performance, e.g. inconsistency, responses to stimulability, and ability to discriminate errors, will be discussed in some detail in a following section.

Nonspeech Factors

Two nonspeech factors should be presented at this time, since they tend to show a relationship to the effectiveness of speech improvement activities. The first of these factors is the sex of the subjects. Some investigators who have studied the effectiveness of speech improvement activities have reported that boys tend to show significantly more improvement in articulation than girls (McWilliams, 1959; Byrne, 1962; Ruggieri, 1950; Wilcox 1959). There appears to be unanimity of findings for this factor among investigators who have isolated it from their data. No explanation for this finding is readily apparent, but it does commonly reoccur.

The second factor deals with socioeconomics. Studies by Byrne (1962) and Andersland (1961) have tended to show that children from lower socioeconomic levels receive the greatest improvement from speech improvement activities, particularly when the results are analyzed a year or more after the speech program. It would seem that further research is needed if we are to safely assume that children from lower socioeconomic levels will profit most from speech improvement, even though these studies suggest that this might be true. It may well be true that speech improvement activities provide for an important increase in language experiences for children from lower socioeconomic groups; which tends to negate the influences of language deprivation which, presumably, they have experienced.

Speech Therapy Only

The process of selecting children for speech therapy under the condition of not having an adequate speech improvement program is essentially the same as that used when this program is available, except that the task is made more difficult. The child with a speech problem is allowed to make his own degree of change as a function of time and experience. The accuracy of the judgment relative to defectiveness versus deviancy, important under any conditions, now becomes critical. Since many clinicians are faced with the task of making the right decision and cannot take all children of both types into therapy, it may be well to review some findings and principles which bear upon this type of case selection.

Prognostic Factors

Of the many factors explored which relate to articulatory defectiveness, one has become progressively better supported as a result of investigations. This finding appears predicated on the notion that a child's ability to correct misarticulations as a result of a change in the mode of their presentation to him is predicative of improvement. Snow and Milisen (1954) determined that the differences between articulatory performances of second grade children as a function of a picture and an imitative test were highly correlated to the degree of their improvement when no speech therapy was provided. Carter and Buck (1958) developed a test which incorporated this principle and found that even greater predictive validity resulted when a nonsense syllable imitation test was used for comparison with a spontaneous picture test. In this case, first grade children were studied. The validity of the Carter and Buck findings has been supported by studies by Farquhar (1961), Sommers (1961 and 1962), Irwin (1964), Stoia (1961), and Katinsky (1967). The degree to which stimulability performances, degree of articulatory defectiveness, and grade level contribute to the effectiveness were recently determined experimentally (Sommers *et al.,* 1967). The results indicated that children from kindergarten, first, and second grades having poor stimulability scores benefited significantly more from a year of speech therapy than did those having good scores. Other findings dealt with the interactions among these variables. The findings generally supported the effectiveness of group articulation therapy for children at these grade levels and suggested the conditions under which they tend to receive significant benefits from these services.

Two additional factors regarding articulatory behavior of primary grade children have been cited as being prognostically important. One of these deals with the rate of change towards correction of kindergarten children and the other with the degree of inconsistency of first grade children. The first of these factors was investigated by Steer and Drexler (1960). It was determined that the total number of errors in all positions in words has predictive value, and the authors suggested that kindergarten children showing little or no error reduction during this year's period probably require speech therapy in first grade. Essentially, the notion inherent in this reported finding is that a standard sample of articulatory change as a function of a school year will uncover a "natural" rate of change which will be predictive of what will occur during subsequent years. This idea appears reasonable and supports the view that careful assessment of the articulation of young children may be a most important aspect of sound case-selection procedures.

The second factor, inconsistency of misarticulation, has long been noted as a characteristic of younger children (Hale, 1948, and Nelson, 1945). The role of this factor in case selection has been virtually unexplored, except for one recent study. Brungard (1961) investigated the inconsistencies of misarticulation of *s*-defective first grade children using a version of McDonald's Deep Test of Articulation (1964). She reported that those subjects demonstrating 15 per cent or more errors on this instrument tended to achieve a minimal and nonsignificant improvement in production of this sound unless enrolled in speech therapy.

In summary, there is a limited body of experimental data to assist a speech clinician in case selection. However, available evidence indicates that stimulability testing should not be overlooked as part of the armamentarium of the clinician. Furthermore, both inconsistency of misarticulation and rate of change as a function of no corrective assistance may provide even more cues concerning which of the vast number of children in the primary grades should be enrolled in therapy.

Other Factors

Although case selection probably should be tied closely to speech needs, a number of other considerations are important and, in some instances, perhaps more important. A few principles would appear to apply to guide the clinician in weighing the values involved. Since, as Johnson (1956) has said, we are dealing not with *speech defects* but with *children having speech defects,* we cannot separate the child and his problem. To paraphrase Johnson, we probably cannot also separate the child's problem from the family. If this be so, parental anxiety and reactions to a child's defective speech ought to be considered and weighed in the case-selection proposition. A clinician, for example, had therapy space for an additional child in a group session. On the basis of careful assessment of all aspects of the articulatory defectiveness of two children on his waiting list, he chose one. The child who was chosen had a more severe problem and prognostic testing had indicated a lesser likelihood for improvement without therapy. On the other hand, his teacher reported that he had many friends, talked freely in class, and did above average work in academic subject areas. The child not chosen was reported to be, by his teacher, withdrawn and lonely, occasionally a behavior problem in the classroom, and obviously aware of his speech problem. Furthermore, his academic work was reported to be poor. Of interest was the fact that the mother of the unchosen child had called the clinician at least twice during the past year indicating concern about her child's speech and asking when therapy would be provided for him. Under these conditions, the concomitant factors would seem to militate for a decision to enter the second child into therapy.

A somewhat similar situation may involve two children of the type cited as "the selected one" above. Again space is currently available for only one in the therapy program. One difference emerged: the parents of one child were disturbed and apparently embarrassed about his defective speech. This factor might be considered the one that tipped the scales, since what is a problem for a parent may in fact be a problem for the child. In summary, careful case selection demands an intensive view of the children thought to be in need of assistance. The articulatory, social, and emotional adjustment and family-attitude factors may be weighed and decisions made accordingly. A few additional statements might also be presented relative to other principles of case selection.

Based on Need

Although it was found in the national study of public school speech and hearing services that three-fourths of a total of 1462 clinicians work primarily with children in the primary grades, a few clinicians have developed a policy of working with children from third grade through twelfth and not scheduling any others. It would appear that such a practice ignores the need for service of younger children, and it is probably not the age or grade level of the child that is most important, but it is his need for help. Conceivably, a kindergarten child may have more total need for speech therapy than a sixth grade child—if all aspects of the problem are viewed, i.e. the degree of communication disturbance, social and personality adjustment, educational impairment, and parental anxieties. It would appear difficult to defend such a practice also on the basis of information concerning the values of early correction and the major emphasis on early training of exceptional children. This is not to imply that the age of a child is not a worthy consideration in case selection. Assuming that all other factors of need are determined to be equal, older children should probably be given a preference in case selection, since they have fewer opportunities as they grow older to receive this service and it is unlikely that maturation will exert any influence on their speech performance.

Etiology

A further concern centers around etiology. What preference should be given to children who are cerebral palsied, have a cleft palate, or are speech defective due to hearing losses, for example? If a basic criterion for case selection is response to careful speech assessment, many of these children will demonstrate a resistance to change and a consistency of error in many of the aspects of speech, e.g. articulation, voice qualities, and rhythm. Secondly, the physical disability which accompanies many of these problems tends to increase the magnitude; therefore, an increase in problems related to social and emotional adjustments might be predicted in many instances. Finally, parental anxiety concerning total defectiveness often seems centered around the communication aspects of the total problem.

A further consideration rests upon the ability of the child to make improvements as a result of the therapy that can be provided in the school program. Assuming that further progress is indicated judging by stimulability testing, trial learning, past progress, and other prognostic indicators, the clinician might be well advised to continue scheduling the child. Other conditions which might tend to suggest further therapy might include the determination that past therapy was inadequate in terms of both intensity and method or that carry-over of newly learned speech patterns is incomplete. Obviously, the inexperienced clinician would do well on occasion to consult with more experienced clinicians who would see the child in question and help make the necessary professional judgments. These "consultants" might be qualified and more experienced clinicians from other schools, or programs in hospitals, universities, or private practice.

Tongue Thrust

Although studies tend to disagree (Fletcher *et al.*, 1961; Ward *et al.*, 1961), recent evidence appears to indicate that children with a so-called tongue thrust syndrome can be found in many kindergarten and first grades. This disorder also referred to as aberrant swallowing pattern often is reported to have a structural component, i.e. a dental malocclusion taking the form of an open bite. The articulatory defectiveness which seems to occur rather commonly under these conditions is often found to be unpromising as far as change to normalcy without correction is concerned. Under these conditions (in conjunction with other important aspects of case selection previously discussed), some persons have indicated that children with these conditions might be eligible candidates for clinical speech services. A related problem of case selection of such children has tended to emerge. Essentially, this deals with the correction of faulty tongue positioning and swallowing habits of children when speech is not defective. Is it the speech clinician's responsibility? If not, whose responsibility is it?

It would appear that the answer to the first question is decid-

edly no. This can be supported on two bases: 1) most state governments which assist in the financing of speech correction services
reimburse for speech therapy or diagnosis of speech problems only
and 2) speech clinicians generally do not receive clinical training
or practicum in the correction of this type of nonspeech disorder.
The answer to the second question is unknown. Perhaps the ortho-
dontist interested in the treatment of such children should provide
for this type of training, or perhaps a new specialist is needed.

Summary

Case selection presents a formidable problem for the clinician
working in the schools. Recent research findings tend to suggest
that children in kindergarten, first, and second grades may be
selected on the basis of certain articulatory behaviors, namely
stimulability performances, consistency of phonetic errors, and
specific defective phonemes. It is additionally suggested that nonspeech factors may continue to play a role in case selection. The
attitudes of parents, teachers, and others concerning the need for
speech therapy must be considered and all factors, measured
speech ones, and nonspeech ones, must enter into a final judgment
concerning the inclusion of a particular child into the case load. A
view of the case-load composition will reveal the case selection
procedures and rationale, along with those of the case-finding
phase, previously discussed.

CASE LOAD
The Number

A most perplexing question confronting clinicians is, What
size case load has maximum effectiveness and maximum efficiency?
To date we have no definite research findings which will aid us in
answering this question, although some authoritative opinion has
stated that the maximum case load for a school clinician should
not exceed one hundred students (Van Riper, 1954; Ainsworth,
1948, and Irwin, 1953). It is obvious that a particular determination about the size of a case load is dependent upon a number of
factors unique to the particular situation. What is advisable in one
program may not be in another. Since effectiveness and efficiency

are relative variables, it is conceivable that the size of the case load may not be a totally limiting factor in achieving these goals; it may be that the entire program of case finding, case selection, the techniques of therapy, the competencies and skills of the clinician, size of classes, and other factors such as socioeconomics may serve to nullify the influence of size of case load on these factors. When viewed as a function of the total program, this variable of case-load size may account for a relatively small percentage of overall effectiveness and efficiency. Since the type of large-scale investigations necessary to explore the various effects of all of these factors on effectiveness and efficiency have not been undertaken, it is not possible to do more than speculate about the specific degrees to which one such as case load size is, in itself, of importance in spite of all the reasonable inference that it "just has to be." An example may help illustrate the point that a factor such as case-load size per se may not characterize the effective and efficient program.

Dependency on Other Factors

Two speech clinicians in adjoining school districts each provided speech therapy services to total school populations of three thousand children. Both selected and provided correction to children from kindergarten through twelfth grade and neither had a speech improvement program. Each developed the comparable practice of entering all children from grades three through twelve into the therapy program so that they received at least one thirty-minute period of therapy each week. Both had twelve severe problems from these grades which received therapy twice weekly. Each clinician had completed a total screening of all children in the school district with the case-finding method. Each clinician depended upon the use of group as well as individual therapy with an average of four children seen in group sessions. Each found some time available to provide service to selected children from kindergarten through third grade. The procedures for case selection were the same and based heavily upon careful assessment of articulation, social, emotional, and educational considerations, and the presence of organicity. At this point we come to the difference between the two programs. One clinician rank-ordered children from these grades on the basis of total need for therapy and found room for twenty of thirty-five showing genuine need for therapy by arranging five forty-minute group articulation classes of four subjects each. The remaining fifteen were somewhat less severe and were placed on a waiting list. The second clinician also located thirty-five children with genuine speech problems and devised a way of scheduling all of them. How was this possible in view of the fact that both clinicians had the same amount of time available for these younger children? The answer lay in a difference in thinking between the two clinicians. The second clinician used the two-hundred minutes and varied both the number of minutes per session and the size of the membership per class according to a plan which allowed the smallest class size and membership for those with the most severe problems. The four children with the poorest prognoses and greatest total severity were scheduled for one forty-minute period weekly. The next six most needy problems were seen for one thirty-minute period in one class. Eight children with somewhat better prognostic scores were scheduled for a forty-minute class, and the final seventeen children were divided into two classes so that the first eight received one thirty-minute period of therapy and the last nine were grouped together for a like amount of time. These procedures allowed for more individualized attention for those with the poorest prognoses with more emphasis on ear training and less on production in the largest classes where the prognosis for improvement was found by testing to be greatest.

In comparing the hypothetical programs described, one finds it difficult to answer the question, Which one is more effective and efficient? Until we have a body of research information about the effectiveness of grouping, case selection, therapy techniques, and other factors, we probably cannot do more than offer an opinion. It might well be true that the second clinician's program, in spite of a slightly higher case load, was both more effective and efficient. The size of the case load per se may therefore be misleading when programs are evaluated against these criteria. It should be mentioned, however, that even a postulated curvilinear relationship between case load size and other factors related to program effectiveness and efficiency can demonstrate a powerful influence; therefore, it is difficult to conceive that large case loads (perhaps 125 or more children) would not have adverse effects upon the effectiveness and efficiency of service (under most conditions).

Rules and Regulations

Determining the size of case load is a simple matter for some clinicians. State or local arrangements often mandate what this should be for school programs. In this regard both minimum and maximum limits have been established as controls over case load size. Irwin (1956) reported that one half of the states set the maximum number of one hundred; recommended case loads in other states varied from thirty-five to one hundred. These "magical numbers" would tend to imply that case loads of these sizes allow for maximum effectiveness and efficiency and perhaps suggest that other factors contributing to these criteria (case-selection practices, scheduling, and therapy) ought to be developed around the size of the case load. Some might disagree with this type of thinking.

Case-load Determinations

The fact remains, however, that at least 45 per cent of the speech clinicians establish their own case-load size (Bingham *et al.*, 1961). As part of this same survey, it was found that 23 per cent of 705 responding clinicians establish their case-load size on the basis of the number of children presenting speech problems. It would appear that such a practice would allow a case load which is predicated on the existing speech needs of the population and could fluctuate from year to year. Since meeting needs hinges to a degree upon adjusting programs, such flexibility appears desirable. Although the flexibility principle would appear to be one of the most important ones in arriving at the size of the case load, a potential danger is inherent in enrolling all children into therapy who have speech needs. The size of the caseload, as Bingham and others have indicated, is conceivably unlimited if this practice is followed. This may be particularly true if the clinician serves total school populations of five thousand or above, since the predicated numbers of children with speech problems might range from one hundred to five hundred. Since the judgment of case-load size should be based upon the specific needs of children for therapy, the type of therapy to be provided, case-finding and case-selection procedures, and other factors, a clinician faced with this problem must consider all of these factors and their interactions, and plan a total program in which case-load size is one variable. Perhaps a case load of fifty of the most severe problems seen two or three times weekly is the most efficient and effective approach under certain conditions; perhaps a case load of one hundred carefully selected children is best; perhaps a case load of 150 children is most efficient and effective. This "total judgment" can only be determined by the clinician able to study the entire situation and establish a judgment about case-load size as one aspect of the entire clinical program. This is obviously the major reason why only those with full knowledge and technical skills should make a judgment about case-load size.

The California case-load study (Coates *et al.,* 1963) would tend to suggest that some speech clinicians have allowed other persons and agencies to affect case-load size in spite of the fact that 70 per cent of the 581 clinicians responding indicated that they made the final judgment. Paradoxically, 60 per cent of these same clinicians reported that case-load size was too high to provide effective service (the median case load was reported to be 151 children).*

Conditions created by persons and agencies which may have altered or affected clinical judgment included 1) not enough speech and hearing personnel in the district, 2) pressure from parents and teachers to provide therapy to more children than the clinician felt could be served effectively, 3) not enough speech and hearing personnel to fill available positions, and 4) a lack of district policy regarding professional criteria for deciding which children should receive therapy. It would appear that these outside influences were chiefly responsible for case-load sizes and that clinicians in California at that time were uncomfortable with the size of the case loads which they felt obligated to serve. A similar find-

---

*Since this report, the State of California has set the maximum case load for clinicians in the public schools at one hundred children per week.

ing appeared in the nationwide study of public school speech and hearing services (Bingham, *et al.*, 1961) .

National Study

Table V, based upon the national study of public school speech and hearing services, contains data concerning case-load size for various geographical areas of the United States. Inspection will show that the heaviest case loads were reported in the Northeast and on the West Coast, with the lightest in the Southwest-Mountain-Hawaii region and the Midwest. Although no information is available to account for these area differences in case-load sizes, it may reflect the tendency for neighboring states to be influenced by each other's practices and policies more than by those established in other areas of the country. Other factors such as the density of population, program philosophies, methods of financial support, and total pupil population served per clinician may also explain these differences.

TABLE V
CHILDREN ENROLLED IN SPEECH THERAPY

REGION	GROUP I N = 705	GROUP II N = 757
Northeast	166.91	186.10
Midwest	103.18	108.12
Southeast	121.98	118.63
Southwest-Mountain-Hawaii	89.13	104.56
West Coast	136.00	118.00
Total	125.78	132.07

Note: Reported numbers of children enrolled in speech therapy for various geographical areas of the United States.

In summary, it should be noted that many clinicians have options in deciding the size of their case loads even under the conditions of having maximum limits set by state or local regulations, since a maximum-minimum range is commonly permitted. It would appear that many clinicians are uncomfortable with the size of these case loads but maintain them because they feel obligated to do so. The lack of definitive research evidence about many aspects of program management, e.g. grouping, case selection, scheduling, and the lack of evidence for efficiency of therapy techniques contributes to our inability to state what case loads should be. In the final analysis, case-load-size determinations must reflect a carefully developed and well-supported plan for the total clinical speech program—and the clinician should make this determination.

Types of Disorders

It has been said that "Schooling selects intelligence." It might also be said that schooling selects speech disorders as well. Private schools, institutions, and out-of-school agencies often tend to "drain off" certain types and degrees of speech and hearing problems away from the public school setting. Communities not uncommonly have special schools or programs for physically handicapped children, emotionally disturbed, severely hard of hearing children, and aphasic children. Many of these children were never considered for regular public school placement; hence, the typical school clinician finds few of them. This is probably the chief reason for the reported results of Bingham and others (1961), presented in Table VI.

TABLE VI
VARIOUS TYPES OF DISORDERS

Type of Disorder	GROUP I N = 705	GROUP II N = 757
Articulation	102.63	108.62
Cerebral palsy	1.24	1.21
Cleft palate	2.18	1.95
Delayed speech	5.47	6.09
Hard of hearing	3.22	3.55
Stuttering	8.05	8.81
Voice problems	2.86	3.36
Aphasia	.26	.12
Mentally retarded	.25	.06
Bilingual	.66	.45

Mean number of children presenting various types of disorders composing average total case load reported by two representative groups of clinicians.

Analysis of the data from Table VI indicated that 81 per cent of the children served had articulation problems with the percentages of other disorders obviously very small. These findings also suggest that a clinician highly trained and competent in the techniques of articulation therapy would be able to function well in a school setting, since other disorders such as cerebral palsy, cleft palate, delayed speech, speech of the hard of hearing, and speech of the mentally retarded have significant components of defective articulation.

A View of Case Load

A different type of breakdown of case-load composition and a description of the types of children waiting for speech therapy services can be seen in Table VII. These data, based upon information from nineteen speech clinicians, are not presented as typical of what one might find nationwide; however, it should be noted that the average clinician reporting had a case-load size comparable to that reported as being average for the nation (115 children seen once weekly for a minimum of thirty minutes). These personnel were employed in a county program and assigned to school districts so that the per-pupil ratio to clinician was approximately 3000 to 1. The total of 4768 children found to have some degree of speech problem was based entirely upon clinician screening in the elementary grades (about one half of the secondary grades were screened by clinicians, and teacher referral was used for the remainder). It should also be mentioned that 5 per cent of the children received individual therapy and that group therapy classes contained on the average of four children.

Inspection of Table VII will indicate that the categories of types of problems are broad (under Articulation Problems, for example, are cleft palate, cerebral palsied, mentally retarded, and speech of the hard of hearing). The total number of articulation problems reported in therapy was 1977, and this was 94.3 per cent of the total number of children of all categories served. This breakdown for Rhythm Problems and Voice Problems respectively was 94 (4.5%) and 26 (1.2%). Of further interest is the fact that 95 per cent of the reported waiting list for therapy was comprised of children with mild or moderate degrees of articulatory defectiveness. A further analysis revealed that 83 per cent of this number were children from the lowest grade levels (grades K-3).

TABLE VII
Distribution and Waiting Lists by Grades for a Suburban County Clinical Speech Program (19 Clinicians)

GRADE	ARTICULATION PROBLEMS						RHYTHM PROBLEMS						VOICE PROBLEMS						TOTAL		
	MILD		MODERATE		SEVERE		MILD		MODERATE		SEVERE		MILD		MODERATE		SEVERE				
	T*	W**	T	W	T	W	T	W	T	W	T	W	T	W	T	W	T	W	T	W	TKP***
K	1	175	11	326	60	52	3	2	3	0	0	0	0	1	0	1	1	0	79	557	636
1	96	638	187	477	132	17	1	4	3	0	3	0	1	6	2	1	1	0	426	1143	1569
2	140	221	208	222	51	6	2	4	2	1	1	0	0	6	1	3	0	0	405	463	868
3	115	123	182	49	30	1	2	2	4	0	2	0	1	1	3	3	0	0	339	179	518
4	100	92	149	8	23	0	2	0	6	0	1	0	1	5	0	2	1	1	283	108	391
5	75	50	103	4	17	0	2	1	5	0	1	0	0	3	1	1	2	0	206	59	265
6	49	38	70	8	10	0	1	0	3	0	3	0	1	0	0	0	0	0	137	46	183
7	32	38	31	5	2	1	4	5	7	0	3	0	5	1	2	1	2	0	88	51	139
8	13	17	11	10	3	0	5	2	2	1	0	0	0	0	0	2	0	0	34	32	66
9	7	12	13	2	4	0	3	2	4	0	1	0	0	1	0	0	0	0	32	17	49
10	9	2	15	4	4	0	0	2	3	0	3	0	0	0	0	0	0	0	34	8	42
11	5	6	9	0	3	0	1	0	4	0	0	0	0	0	0	0	1	0	22	6	28
12	4	0	3	1	0	0	1	1	3	0	0	0	0	0	0	0	1	0	12	2	14
TOTALS	646	1412	992	1116	339	77	27	25	49	2	18	0	9	24	9	14	8	1	2097	2671	4768

* In Therapy
** Waiting List
*** Total Known Problems

Summary

Case loads of clinicians working in schools are uniquely tied to the types of problems which are encountered in schools. Depending upon the clinics, institutions, private programs, private practioners, and special schools for exceptional children which exist in the area, the clinician may find varying degrees of speech defectiveness and various types of organic speech problems in his case load. For the most part, however, present information tends to show that 80 per cent or more of the problems encountered and scheduled for therapy are articulation disorders. It is also probably true that most clinicians have waiting lists which consist to a large degree of children who are either "speech deviant" or only mildly speech defective, and these children tend to be from grades kindergarten through third. Finally, it should be observed that the case-load composition reflects all that has preceded it. If case finding and case selection have been done with diligence and thoughtfulness, the case load will be well constituted.

SUMMARY

The soundness of the judgments of the speech clinician is the prime determinant in the success of the program. The foundation for the therapy to be provided rests irrevocably upon the axes of case-finding, case-selection, and case-load practices. It follows logically that without well-supported and thoughtful judgments concerning the "what" and "how" of these pillars of the program, little meaningful success will be attained by even the most dedicated speech clinician.

It sometimes happens that a speech clinician will be presented with an opportunity to establish a new therapy program in a school area. At this time, the clinician is in the best position to develop his rationale and ultimate decisions about which procedures to incorporate as basic tenets of his total program. Many clinicians will be fortunate enough to be able to make these decisions themselves; others, less fortunate, will embark upon a road of trying to convince and cajole others that such measures are of vital concern to the overall success of the corrective program. In most instances, the persevering speech clinician will tend to achieve his purposes.

It frequently happens that a speech clinician enters a school system in which a history of practice has been developed concerning case finding, case selection, and case load. The logical next question then may become How do I manage to change these methods which appear ineffective and inefficient? The answers are not easily forthcoming, since they are highly dependent upon the uniqueness of every situation and the personalities of those involved. However, it probably holds true that all professionals are "selling" something during the time of their careers; the clinician in this setting must "sell" also if he is going to prevail. Data often speak louder than words. Data gathered from local programs may tend to be more impressive to some school administrators than published data from research reports. Both types of data can be obtained to bolster the arguments of the clinician concerning a need for a change in methods of case finding or case selection or case load. Under most conditions, the chief problem would appear to be one of being able to demonstrate and convince others that either or both effectiveness or efficiency of the services will improve as a result of the proposed changes in doing things.

Finally, it should be said that attempts to fractionate a corrective program and view case finding, for example, as a discrete factor may be misleading in judging the worth of the service. The inextricable nature of case finding, case selection, and case load makes it difficult to appraise the effectiveness and efficiencies of a school program unless all three of these factors are studied, one to another. Regardless of the quality of the therapy provided by the clinician, these basic ingredients of the program stand as basic and vital determinants of success in a school setting.

DISCUSSION TOPICS

1. What are some ways in which the teacher referral technique of case finding might be improved?
2. Are there some instances not presented in this chapter in which others besides the clinician should influence the choice of a case-finding technique?

3. What types of forms or records could be developed by a clinician as archives of his case-finding technique? Where should these records be stored?
4. What are some possible explanations for the finding that secondary school teachers have been inefficient in locating students with speech or voice problems?
5. What are some other ways of accomplishing case finding at the secondary school level? How could you evaluate the effectiveness of such methods?
6. Should elementary and secondary students be required to receive speech therapy?
7. What are other factors besides those mentioned which might be important in case selection?
8. What are some basically unanswered questions regarding case-selection techniques? What types of investigations might be necessary in order to answer these questions?
9. In your own opinion, what constitutes the most desirable type of case load for a school clinician? Who should be included and what should be the case-load size?
10. What are the implications of decisions about case finding, case selection, and case load upon actual therapy techniques used by the clinician?

REFERENCES

1. AINSWORTH, S.: *Speech Correction Methods.* Englewood Cliffs, N. J., Prentice-Hall, 1948.
2. ANDERSLAND, P. B.: Maternal and environmental factors related to success in speech improvement training. *J Speech Hearing Res, 4:*79-90, March, 1961.
3. BINGHAM, D.; VAN HATTUM, R.; FAULK, M., and TAUSSIG, E.: Public school speech and hearing services, IV. Program organization and management. *J Speech Hearing Dis, Monogr Suppl, 8:*33-49, June, 1961.
4. BRUNGARD, M.: Effect of Consistency of Articulation of *r* and *s* on Gains Made With and Without Therapy, Unpublished doctoral dissertation, Pennsylvania State University, University Park, 1961.
5. BYRNE, M.: *Development and Evaluation of a Speech Improvement Program for Kindergarten and First Grade Children.* U. S. Dept. HEW, 1962.

6. BRYNGELSON, B., and GLASPFY, E.: *Speech in the Classroom (With Speech Improvement Cards)*, 3rd ed. Chicago, Scott, 1962.

7. CARTER, E. T., and BUCK, M.: Prognostic testing for functional articulation disorders among children in the first grade. *J Speech Hearing Dis, 23:*124-133, March, 1958.

8. CHAPMAN, M.; HERBERT, E.; AVERY, C., and SELMAR, J.: Public school speech and hearing services, V. Clinical practice: Remedial procedures. *J Speech Hearing Dis, Monogr Suppl, 8:*58-78, June, 1961.

9. COATES, N.; GARBEE, F., and HERBERT, E.: California's public school programs for speech and hearing handicapped children: Dilemmas and horizons. *Voice, Monogr Suppl,* May, 1963.

10. DIEHL, C., and STINNETT, L.: Efficiency of teacher referrals in a school speech testing program. *J Speech Hearing Dis, 22:*113-117, March, 1956.

11. FARQUHAR, M. S.: Prognostic value of imitative and auditory discrimination tests. *J Speech Hearing Dis, 26:*342-347, November, 1961.

12. FLETCHER, S. G.; CASTEEL R. L., and BRADLEY, D. P.: Tongue-thrust swallow, speech articulation, and age. *J Speech Hearing Dis, 26:* 201-208, August, 1961.

13. HALE, A. R.: *A Study of the Misarticulation of 1 in Children from Kindergarten Through Third Grade.* Unpublished master's thesis, *University of Iowa,* Iowa City, 1948.

14. HEJNA, R.: *Hejna Developmental Articulation Test.* Madison, Wisconsin College Typing, 1955.

15. IRWIN, R. B.: *Speech and Hearing Therapy.* Englewood Cliffs, N. J., Prentice-Hall, 1953.

16. IRWIN, R. B.: State programs in speech and hearing therapy III; Organization and administration. *Speech Teacher, 5:*125-131, March, 1956.

17. IRWIN, R. B.; WEST, J., and TROMBETTA, M.: Effectiveness of speech therapy for second grade children with misarticulation: Predictive factors, *ASHA, 10:*415, September, 1964.

18. JOHNSON, W., *et al.: Speech Handicapped School Children.* New York, Harper, 1956.

19. MONTGOMERY, J.: *Look and Say Cards.* Chicago, King Co., 1960.

20. McDONALD, E. T.: *Articulation Testing and Treatment: A Sensory Motor Approach.* Pittsburgh, Stanwix House, 1964.

21. McWILLIAMS, B. J.: *The effect of Speech Improvement Activities Upon Consonant Articulation in Four Pittsburgh Kindergartens.* Unpublished master's thesis, U. of Pittsburgh, 1959.

22. NELSON, J. T.: *A Study of Misarticulation of s in Combination with Selected Vowels and Consonants.* Unpublished master's thesis, State University of Iowa, Iowa City, 1945.

23. PENDERGAST, K.: Speech improvement and speech therapy in the elementary school. *ASHA, 5:*548-549, December, 1963.

24. ROE, V.; HANLEY, C.; CROTTY, C., and MAYPER, L.: Public school speech and hearing services, clinical practice: Diagnosis and measurement. *J Speech Hearing Dis, Monogr Suppl, 8:*50-58, June, 1961.

25. ROE, V., and MILISEN, R.: The effect of maturation upon defective articulation in elementary grades. *J Speech Hearing Dis, 7:*37-50, February, 1942.

26. RUGGIERI, M. K.: The Effect of a Speech Improvement Project on Consonant Articulation in Four Pittsburgh Kindergartens. Unpublished master's thesis, University of Pittsburgh, Pennsylvania, 1950.

27. SOMMERS, R. K., *et al.*: Effects of speech therapy and speech improvement upon articulation and reading. *J Speech Hearing Dis, 26:*27-39, February, 1961.

28. SOMMERS, R. K., *et al.*: Effects of various durations of speech improvement upon articulation and reading. *J Speech Hearing Dis, 27:*54-62, February, 1962.

29. SOMMERS, R. K., *et al.*: Factors in the effectiveness of articulation therapy for kindergarten, first, and second grade children. *J Speech Hearing Res, 10:*428-437, September, 1967.

30. SNOW, K., and MILISEN, R.: The influence of oral versus pictoral presentation upon articulation testing results. *J Speech Hearing Dis, Monogr Suppl, 4:*29-36, 1954.

31. STOIA, L.: An Investigation of Improvement in Articulation in a Therapy Group and Non-Therapy Group of First Grade Children Having Functional Articulatory Speech Disorders. Ed.D. dissertation, Columbia University, New York, 1961.

32. STEER, M. D., and DREXLER, H. G.: Predicting later articulation ability from kindergarten results. *J Speech Hearing Dis, 25:*391-397, November, 1960.

33. TEMPLIN, M.: Norms on a screening test of articulation for ages 3-8. *J Speech Hearing Dis, 18:*323-331, November, 1953.

34. TEMPLIN, M., and DARLEY, F. L.: *The Templin-Darley Tests of Articulation.* Iowa City, University of Iowa Bureau of Educational Research and Service, 1960.

35. VAN HATTUM, R. J.: Speech grows too. *New York State Education, 43:*184-186, December, 1955.

36. VAN HATTUM, R. J.: Evaluating elementary school speech therapy: Preliminary findings and research needs. *Exceptional Child, 25:*411-414, May, 1959.

37. VAN RIPER, C.: *Speech Correction, Principles and Methods.* Englewood Cliffs, N. J., Prentice-Hall, 1954.

38. WARD, M., *et al.*: Articulation variations associated with visceral swallowing and malocclusion. *J Speech Hearing Dis, 26:*334-341, November, 1961.

39. WILSON, B. A.: The development and evaluation of a speech improvement program for kindergarten children. *J Speech Hearing Dis, 19:* 4-13, February, 1954.
40. WILCOX, E. M.: The Effect of Speech Improvement Activities Conducted by the Classroom Teacher Upon Consonant Articulation of Children in Grades One, Two, and Three. Unpublished master's thesis, University of Pittsburgh, 1959.

Chapter 10

THE THERAPY PROGRAM
RONALD K. SOMMERS

T HIS CHAPTER IS NOT INTENDED to be a detailed description of
therapy techniques and a repository of methods for correcting
speech disorders. Rather, it is designed to highlight certain
unique problems which face the clinician in the schools and to
show how these affect the therapy program. In a sense it also suggests that therapy in a school setting is both like and unlike therapy in any setting; the principles undergirding the therapy program may be similar, but there may be some specific procedures
which tend to be unique, since most environments operate to
influence both the efficiencies and effectiveness of services.

The hour is now; it is time for the clinician to do his chosen
work. All the diligence and thoughtfulness about how to find
children for the therapy program, how to select those most critically in need of help, and organizing and scheduling a case load
are behind him, and he is ready to begin the correctional work for
which he is trained. Many decisions await him; many questions
will arise, and each day brings new challenges into sharper focus.
Although resources will be available to help him forge his mettle,
he will be chiefly responsible for the honing of his own skills on
the wheel of experience. The crux of the contest may hang heavily
upon his ability to learn from his mistakes, observe critically the
efficacy of his techniques, develop increasingly finer degrees of
perceptual abilities, apply problem-solving methods to daily activities, and stay encompassed within the sphere of his chosen profession by talking, reading, and otherwise interacting with his colleagues.

THE NATURE OF THE THERAPY PROGRAM
Its Clinical Nature
Clinical Orientation

How do you define "clinical work"? What is a "clinician"?
These questions appear to be worthy of thoughtful consideration,

for they are basic to an understanding of the therapy program. For purposes of discussion, we might maintain that a clinician is a professionally trained worker seeking to alleviate, mitigate, or correct a problem of an individual. Further, he bases his procedures upon his diagnosis and can defend these on the basis of a rationale. He has no "one technique"; he has many, and he uses these in a discriminating manner so as to afford the greatest opportunities for improvement. In this regard, he observes and alters his techniques during the therapy process. He works purposefully, systematically, and is fully able to identify the markers along the way. These behaviors describe the so-called clinical approach; these behaviors should characterize the therapy program as well.

Games

It is conceivable that a "clinical approach" could consist of the use of numerous, highly specific, goal-directed games which the clinician uses as a primary or exclusive therapy method. However, it appears unlikely that even the most skillful clinician could adapt games which would be capable of great precision in advancing children from one step in therapy to the next. It would also appear that the use of a few games with all children having articulation problems, for example, would militate against a systematic therapy approach (in spite of the fact that many children would be well entertained). In a paper presented to the American Speech and Hearing Association in 1957, Van Hattum (1959) reported upon the relative effectiveness of thirteen speech clinicians working in the schools as a function of the degree to which they utilized the "games approach." When he compared the measured changes in articulation and the percentage of dismissal rates for the top six clinicians (few, if any, games used) with the bottom six (heavy use of games), he found the top six clearly superior in improving articulation and in achieving higher percentages of dismissal from therapy.

Since a dearth of research information exists which has explored the efficacy of therapy techniques, it is difficult to attest confidently to the ineffectiveness of the games approach. However, experience tends to show that clinicians who rely upon a few game activities and apply these to group after group of children having articulation problems fail to advance children rapidly and, in some instances, fail to improve them at all. There is often a strong suggestion that children who improve under these conditions are merely children with speech errors and not speech defects; therefore, improvement may be expected regardless of the techniques used or even whether or not therapy is provided.

We lack information concerning how the speech clinician in the schools and his therapy program are perceived by others. We do not know, for example, how parents of speech defective children conceive the role of the clinician or how they understand the functions of the techniques employed. Of interest would be an investigation of these ideas in parents of children receiving therapy in school compared with parents of normal speaking children from the same schools. An additional one might then deal with parental concepts about the clinician and his therapy program as a function of the degree to which (among other things) he utilized the game technique. We might hypothesize that those relying exclusively upon this technique would be found to have less professionally acceptable images among parents of children receiving therapy.

Medical Approval

The clinician working in a school setting usually does not function as a member of a medical team. He must, however, establish a system of referral to medical agencies and medical personnel both within and without a school system. It is imperative that medical opinion be sought *prior to* the inclusion of some children into the therapy program. The rather surprisingly high number of young children demonstrating vocal nodules (Anderson, 1965; Wilson, 1961) and other pathologies, for example, makes it mandatory that all children requiring voice therapy be examined by a physician before they are entered into therapy. The implications are obvious: misdirected therapy may aggravate some problems, and the clinician may be guilty of malpractice. Similarly, children having recently experienced cleft palate surgery or those showing an active oral pathology of almost any type should not be entered into therapy without gaining authoritative medical permission. Three other types of conditions would appear to be important enough to warrant noninclusion until medical permission has been gained. One of these is active ear pathology; the second consists of cardiovascular conditions, and the third comprises active seizures or controlled ones due to medication. In all instances, the problems and their implications are ongoing ones, and it behooves the speech clinician to take the precaution of securing proper medical permission prior to providing speech therapy. Generally, this permission should have been medically evaluated, or can be referred for such, but this does not appear to be necessary before therapy is undertaken by the speech clinician. This probably holds true also for children demonstrating speech and language disorders of possible central nervous system origin. It would appear that the great bulk of the clinician's articulatory defective children are exempt from approval by a medical practitioner either prior to or during the therapy experience. This would also include the nonfluent or stuttering children as well.

THE PARAMETERS OF THE THERAPY PROGRAM

The Therapy Session

In a large sense therapy is a nebulous thing. We find it difficult to limit; we find it difficult to define. It is obviously multifaceted and, like the child involved in it, is dynamic, not static. It must, by its active and organismic nature, extend beyond the walls of the speech therapy room. If it does not do so, the child may never carry over his new skills into his daily speaking activities. Since maximum learning appears to occur under the conditions of having both stimulus and response, opportunities for expanding the sphere of influence, of providing for maximum reinforcement, and of increasing motivation must be provided by the clinician who guides the "therapy process." This, then, implies that therapy, in a real sense must extend beyond the four walls of the speech room. Unfortunately, some beginning clinicians find themselves so engrossed with the mechanics of speech that they fail to develop a broad-based therapy program. For the most part, they "go it alone" by going to their assigned spaces, meeting with their children on schedule, providing direct speech therapy to them, and courteously saying Good-bye to the school secretary as they leave the building. In many instances there is no contact with parents and virtually none with classroom teachers or other personnel except in written form. The "therapy program" under these conditions is restricted to the once or twice a week sessions conducted by the clinician. The clinician must provide all the motivation and all the reinforcement.

Lesson Planning

Since the correction of defective speech also constitutes a type of daily problem-solving activity for the clinician, it might be argued that reflection, identifying the problem, developing hypotheses, testing hypotheses, and reviewing the results should be conducted many times each day if maximum results are to be achieved. For the first and second year clinician, it would appear most important to develop lesson plans for many or most sessions. The most experienced clinician may not rely upon this particular technique for planning and viewing therapy; however, some persons of great experience might maintain careful daily notes or logs which are referred to from session to session and used to guide the therapy process. Frequently, clinicians working in the schools will utilize teacher plan books to record therapy activities for groups of children as well as for individuals. Since children are seen in most instances once or twice a week in most school programs (Bingham *et al.*, 1961), many clinicians are not comfortable relying upon memory and tend to use devices which will allow for recording of events, techniques used, estimates of the effectiveness of particular techniques with particular children, and a place to list future activities and goals. The time spent in doing so apparently is felt worthwhile in terms of systematizing therapy.

Van Hattum (1964) has recently reviewed the therapy process. He maintained that each therapy session should consist of five parts. The first of these dealt with *preplanning*. This initial step included a review of the child's past performances based on former techniques, goals to be attained next, and the activities used to incorporate the technique along with some idea concerning the success realized. The second step he labeled *preparation*. As expected, this included reading materials and equipment for the impending task. The third step consisted of the *therapy session,* i.e. the face-to-face meeting between the children and the clinician. *Evaluation* comprised the fourth step. During this time, the clinician evaluated the relative success or failure of the planned activities and also the relative effectiveness of the materials and equipment which were used. The final step he termed *clean-up* which obviously referred to the returning of appropriate materials, supplies, and equipment to their proper places and setting the room in order. It was his opinion that many clinicians (particularly beginning ones) focused on step three (the therapy session) to the exclusion of the four other aspects of therapy. It follows rather logically that a clinician viewing the therapy process in this fashion would not be guilty of using the same techniques and activities during each session.

Assessing Progress

Since as many as 80 per cent of the children served in school therapy programs have articulation problems (Bingham *et al.,* 1961) and in view of the fact that many other speech disorders have articulatory components in their total defectiveness, a carefully completed phonetic analysis would appear to be a vital assessment. A minimal assessment of annual change, therefore, for many speech problems might consist of a measurement of articulation at the beginning of the school year (or when treatment commenced), followed by one at the end of the school year (or when treatment stopped). Frequently, however, this appraisal should be considered inadequate. There are two reasons why this may be the case. Firstly, as McDonald has suggested (1964), the articulation of children under therapy becomes more inconsistent particularly for some speech sounds. A clinician who looks carefully at inconsistencies as a function of phonetic context may gain some valuable insights into ways of making more rapid improvements.

Secondly, the entire pattern of articulatory defectiveness (particularly in primary grade children) should be viewed carefully during the therapy process. A clinician who focuses his attention upon the behavior of the sound in question to the exclusion of other defective sounds yet to be handled may fail to note important patterns of change which have inplications for the selection of the next sound to be introduced. Furthermore, there is a strong suggestion from experience that certain patterns of articulatory defectiveness commonly reoccur in younger children and the further suggestion that these are most amenable to a multisound approach in which a primary sound is selected and a secondary sound from a different "sound family" (e.g. sibilants and glides) is introduced at an appropriate time. The observant clinician may or may not detect certain changes in other defective sounds unless some additional measurements are made during the therapy period. It follows, therefore, that the clinician may not be aware of changes of importance, and this lack of information may impede his decision-making.

The phonetic analysis may constitute a primary way of recording change or status for many clinicians, but it is often not capable in and of itself in allowing careful judgments to be made about a child's progression in speech. For example, the total number of misarticulations has been demonstrated by Jordan (1960) and Barker (1961) to correlate highly with ratings of intelligibility of speech, but it may not be a good predictor of his improvement with or without correction. We may have a good measure of prediction in terms of intelligibility but we may have a poor measure of improvement and perhaps of defectiveness. For this reason and others, many clinicians have developed rating scales which tend to be based upon levels of defectiveness. An example of a rating scale of this type developed by the author and a former associate can be seen on following page.

Scales of this type may be reasonably reliable. These authors rated twenty children from grades one, two, and three on this scale independently and found that their ratings agreed 80 per cent of the time. The use of scales of this type allows the clinician to attend to other items of empirical importance that deal with improvement, and many such factors cannot now be measured on most articulation tests.

Ratings	*Item Criteria*
1	One defective consonant sound. This sound only occasionally misarticulated in spontaneous speech.
2	One consonant sound is misarticulated. It is correctly produced in articulation testing[1] but usually misarticulated in spontaneous speech.
3	One defective consonant sound which is not correctly produced in articulation testing but can be produced correctly under stimulation[2] by a speech clinician. The sound is not correctly articulated in spontaneous speech.
4	Two or more defective consonant sounds correctly produced during articulation testing but usually misarticulated in spontaneous speech.
5	One or more consonant sounds are defective. One sound is not articulated correctly in articulation testing, under stimulation by a clinician, or in spontaneous speech. If other sounds are defective, they must be inconsistently faulty in articulation testing and/or spontaneous speech.
6	Two or more sounds consistently misarticulated in articulation testing, under stimulation by a clinician, and in spontaneous speech.

FIGURE 17. THE SOMMERS/FURLONG ARTICULATION RATING SCALE.

---

[1]Based upon a three-position articulation test in which each sound is measured.
[3]Based upon a one session period of time with the subject.
once in the initial, medial, and final positions in words.
[2]Based on procedures followed in the Carter/Buck Prognostic Test.

Of real value for the clinician in the schools also is the recording of speech before, during, and after therapy. Many articulation problems do not require this type of elaborate assessment in order to appraise progress; however, many more severe articulation problems in children, voice problems, stuttering problems, speech problems of the cerebral palsied and others deserve this type of documentation. Furthermore, such tapes are valuable for in-service teaching of school personnel, with other clinicians, with parents of speech defective children, and for purposes of motivating the children to want better speech. It is suggested that this type of record be retained and safeguarded. Small reels of tape are available and particularly suitable for recording a child's speech periodically.

A RATIONALE FOR THERAPY TECHNIQUES AND METHODS

Evaluating Techniques

In the evaluation of a clinical speech program the *experimentum crucis* tends to be the degree to which the clinician has a rationale for the use of his techniques and methods. A rationale is a collection of logically deduced reasons for using particular techniques or methods. Basically, the rationale should seek to answer the following question, Why is this technique needed at this time? What does it accomplish? How does it contribute to the total therapy plan for this child?

The answer to the first question is heavily dependent upon the experiences of the clinician in providing therapy to children with similar disorders. It rests upon an overview of the total therapy required in order to gain correction, and it follows logically from the last step. A clinician posing this question might benefit by asking himself, Is this technique really necessary? In the case of ear training in articulation therapy, for example, the clinician might normally have advanced to teaching a child to identify the sound in the initial, medial, and final positions in words. After reviewing the need for this procedure, he decides to forego this step since the child appears not to be confused about the nature of the sound and shows no indication of needing training in accomplishing this task. The clinician advances rapidly to the next step and omits this one entirely as "not required." Inextricably involved with this decision is the question, What does this technique accomplish? Perhaps it must be done in order to gain the proficiency in articulation required before the child is able to advance to the next step. For example, when the *r* phonemes are defective, must a child first gain total correct production in all possible nonsense syllable productions prior to his working on words? Or for the *s* phoneme must a child gain perfect production

of the sound in isolation prior to his moving into nonsense syllables, or can further "shaping" of this sound occur when the unit
of speech is the syllable rather than the sound in isolation? What
does this technique accomplish for this child under the unique
conditions which exist? The answer may be that it is a total necessity, it does little of real worth, or that it does nothing of any
consequence.

As the clinician gains experience and constantly questions the
need for a technique or a method, he finds himself filling in the
outline of a therapy program for a particular type of problem.
As a function of intuitive reasoning (and a dose of trial and error
now and again), the sequence of therapy steps comes into focus —
the blueprint is drawn and a morphological concept has emerged.
Each of the techniques now relates to every other; the logic of the
therapy regimen becomes clear, and the clinician finds to his
satisfaction that he is better able to judge the worth of each
technique and procedure in terms of the total therapy required
for the problem at hand. Now that the concept has ben developed,
improvements in techniques and methods can be made by the
clinician.

New Techniques

The business of developing new techniques is a simple task
for some clinicians and a not-so-simple task for others. Outstanding originality and creativity, like superior intelligence, appear
to be sprinkled lightly among the population. The need for new
techniques is obvious, for even the clinician becomes tired of
doing the same thing the same way. The lack of enthusiasm for
the use of a technique or activity on the part of the clinician is
probably reflected in the children — who really find it easy to
become bored on their own. Even a tiresome technique, however,
may be vital in a clinician's total therapy program for a problem.
Inherently, it may prove very effective and comprise a corner-
stone in the overall program. How can the valuable ingredients
of this technique be presented in a different and interesting way?
How many additional ways can be developed and added to the
clinician's repertoire? Depending upon the uniqueness of the orig-

inal technique the answer may be none, or one, or many. Fortunately, others are often available to offer suggestions about new ways of doing things.

Professional Consultation

The single best source for this information is a professional colleague. The probabilities of gaining a fresh idea concerning another way that this important technique or procedure can be presented are probably dependent upon either having another clinician observe the original technique being used or having a lucid description of it presented to him along with an account of why it is used, what it accomplishes, and a notion of the total therapy program for this type of speech problem. When speech clinicians are employed by one school agency, opportunities for interaction obviously increase, and both informal and formal training sessions can be devoted to the development of new techniques and procedures or in devising new ways to teach old techniques of importance. Under the conditions of being employed by different school districts, the clinician must actively seek this type of assistance from nearby professional workers employed elsewhere. Usually the camaraderie of speech clinicians is such that ideas are exchanged socially. The supervisor of speech therapy services may also be an important source for new techniques and procedures. This is particularly true if the supervisor is an experienced clinician and has opportunities to observe the clinician doing therapy. Ideas can be gleaned from professional publications such as speech pathology texts and from published and unpublished manuscripts, pamphlets, and term papers. Frequently, the clinician surveying material of this type will uncover new ideas and, having received stimulation and experienced "Gestalten" discovers a number of additional ways of doing things.

Learning From Others

Other types of professional workers in school settings may stimulate new ideas. The experience of observing a regular or a special class teacher may suggest a way in which a commonly used teaching method may be amenable to change to make it effective with a particular type of speech defective child. For example, the phonovisual method may be used to teach reading in a particular school system. The clinician observing this teaching may feel that it could serve well, with some degree of modification, in teaching a brain-injured child speech and language. Or the clinician may note its usefulness as an ear training method with a group of articulatory-impaired retarded children. Or the clinician may observe that one and only one stage in the phonovisual method has value in the total therapy program for a particular articula-tory-defective child who has difficulty, shifting his production of speech from one sound to another. Similarly, the clinician may be stimulated to develop additional techniques by observing a read-ing specialist work with selected children. Techniques of improv-ing word attack skills or in reinforcing associations between letters and phonemes may suggest numerous ways of expanding tech-nique for the enterprising clinician. Perhaps techniques of teach-ing respiration to cerebral palsied children can be developed by observing the music teacher or methods of gaining better carry-over of improved speech sounds can be developed by observing a physical education class. This broadening of horizons can fre-quently result in the development of unique and possibly very effective ways of doing speech therapy. Some speech clinicians have learned some new techniques from parents of children re-ceiving therapy. It would appear that the environment of the speech clinician in the schools would allow for an infinite number of stimuli to impinge upon his nerve endings and provide the food for thought which ultimately results in the development of new and improved techniques and methods.

GROUP THERAPY

Common Weaknesses

Training

In many training centers opportunities for clinically super-vised practicum of group therapy are very limited. Some clinicians entering the schools have never been instructed in techniques of meeting the speech needs of children under the conditions of having four or five working as a group, yet, according to information obtained from the national study of speech and hearing in the schools (Bingham *et al.*, 1961), most therapy in schools is done on a group basis. Although most clinicians working in schools utilized a combination of group or individual therapy, the latter tended to be provided to less than 10 per cent of the children comprising the case load. The reasons for their decision making in this regard are not known; however, we might speculate that case-load size might influence this judgment, since many more children can be served if group therapy is selected as the primary organizational unit. It also deserves to be mentioned that clinicians in schools may have found that group therapy is both an efficient and an effective way of handling most of the speech problems they encounter. The latter suggestion has recently been supported in an investigation of the relative effectiveness of individual and group therapy in a school setting.

Comparison with Individual

The relative effectiveness of group and individual speech therapy has been studied by Pfeifer (1958) with retarded children, Sokoloff (1959) with cerebral palsied children, and Sommers (1964) with articulatory-impaired school children attending a special summer program. All three investigators found group therapy to be as effective or even more so than individual therapy. In the latter study (Sommers *et al.*, 1964), it was determined that fifty minutes of group articulation therapy was generally as effective as thirty minutes of individual therapy in an intensive program, i.e. therapy was provided four times weekly for four weeks. However, it was difficult to generalize these findings to children receiving speech therapy during the course of a regular school year, because of the major differences in program management and the selectivity of the subjects who attended the special summer program. Therefore, a new study was conducted which investigated the relative effectiveness of these factors during a regular school year (Sommers *et al.*, 1966). The investigators were interested in determining the relative effectiveness of group and individual therapy for articulatory impaired school children when two factors were varied: 1) the grade levels of the subjects and 2) the severity of the speech problems. They hypothesized that older children (grades four and six) having more severe articulatory problems would benefit more from individual therapy than from group therapy, and further, that younger children (grade two) would benefit equally from either group or individual therapy. A total of 240 children served as subjects, allowing for twelve experimental groups of twenty children each. These twelve groups provided for the investigation of the following sources of variation: 1) therapy — half of each group of forty received group therapy and half individual therapy; 2) severity — half of each group had "mild" articulation problems and half "moderate" articulation problems; 3) grade — four of the groups were from grade two; four from grade four, and four from grade six.

Group articulation therapy consisted of one forty-five-minute session weekly; individual articulation therapy was provided once weekly for a thirty-minute period. Seventeen experienced clinicians provided therapy as part of a large county-operated speech correction program. Articulation was assessed by experienced clinicians before and after the eight-and-one-half-months treatment period (the school year).

When the results were analyzed, the investigators concluded that group and individual therapy were equally effective, independent of either grade level or the degree of articulatory defect (Sommer *et al.*, 1966). The results agreed with other studies dealing with group and individual therapy and strongly supported the notion that the procedure of providing speech therapy to groups of children is characterized by effectiveness as well as by efficiency.

Some Views

Nature of Groups

Because group therapy is practiced so widely by speech clinicians working in the schools, its nature and functioning deserve attention if a clinician is apt to be successful in this setting. Few training institutions highlight the body of knowledge about group behavior and group dynamics or relate this information to the methodologies of the speech clinician working with groups of individuals. This is in spite of the fact that this other body of knowledge exists and expands each year. This is particularly true in the case of children grouped for articulation therapy. A group is conceived to be more than a number of persons joining together in physical space; it is a process in which persons are joined together in such a manner that interaction, goal seeking, and goal striving occur, and it becomes a whole which is greater than the sum of its parts. A group in this sense takes on purpose and character. Members of groups motivate each other and, judging by studies in social psychology, the resultant motivation within members tends to be higher than if each person operated outside the group. Some of these studies suggest that persons learn better in a group situation than when alone because of an increase in cues and reinforcement. Further, it has been demonstrated that the strongest incentive for improvement in a group situation is the desire to be accepted and approved by the group. Children in articulation therapy, for example, are no different and very quickly take on the behaviors which typify members of groups. In this regard, the clinician has the responsibility for setting clear goals for the children to strive for if group drive is to be intensified and maintained.

A premise herein presented concerning group articulation therapy in the schools is that methods used in group therapy should be closely akin to those used in individual therapy. Although it is commonly held to be true that group therapy implies that children work on the same misarticulated sound, that similar ear training and production needs exist, and that therapy techniques are homogenous, this notion is essentially a sterile one and overlooks some important aspects of group therapy.

When we speak about "group therapy," in effect we mean group interaction. By "group interaction" we mean that members of a group relate to each other, develop group cohesiveness, common and specific goals, and most of all, common and specific motivations. The value of group articulation therapy probably hinges tightly to these so-called group dynamics.* These devel-

---

*Speech clinicians will find a large body of information and research in the area of group dynamics. In particular, see Cartwright, D., and Zander, A.: *Group Dynamics, Research and Theory*. Evanston, Illinois, Row-Peterson, 1958.

opments, which tend to occur in groups, are probably the essential features that cause group articulation therapy to differ from individual therapy. Fostering innocuous competition among the members of a group tends to increase motivation and goal striving. This fact implies that group therapy has the unique advantage of stimulating children to better speech by increasing the element of friendly group competition. Of course, not all children benefit from competition, and for some it may be undesirable. This requires the expert judgment of the clinician. Assuming that goal-directed activities are used by a speech clinician in group therapy, increasing group drive toward these goals may result in excellent improvements in speech for some children.

Establishment of group speech therapy classes currently appears to depend more upon the types of defective sounds and the ages of the children than upon the considerations of adaptability of the children into group situations, aspirations for better speech, and personal life adjustment. These factors of possible importance for children for articulation therapy have never been studied experimentally concerning their effects upon the improvement that children make in articulation. It is conceivable that some salient factors have essentially been ignored by school speech clinicians in establishing group classes. The principles of human learning certainly apply to the successfulness of articulation therapy, and many of these "psychological factors" may be found to be more significant in the amount of improvement made by the children than grouping them conveniently on the sounds that are defective. There are obvious research needs related to this issue.

Inadequacies

The following is a general look at a typical group articulation class followed by some specific recommendations for effective group articulation therapy. The typical group class contains four or five children of similar age or grade level who are working on one defective sound. Generally, one sound is approached at a time, and, hopefully, each child is defective somehow in his production or use of this sound. A minimum of individual therapy is provided to each child in the group, and, basically, little or no differentiation of production or ear training or carry-over techniques are observed. Some members of the group receive discrimination training on this defective sound who essentially have no problem with this auditory skill; some members receive additional stimulation on the defective sound and their need is for carry-over training; some members play speech games for some purpose and this activity does not fit into their articulation therapy paradigm. For the most part, all members work on the same activity, on the same sound, for the same purpose. Finally, the home assignment in the speech notebook (if any) is the same for all members of the therapy group. Frequently, speech correctional activities center around ear training or simple storytelling, oral reading, and game activities for development of the misarticulated sound with little or no specific improvement of a given child's defective sound. The articulatory proficiency of any child is rarely explored in depth, and in this regard, other related factors in articulatory production such as stress, rhythm, inflection, and speech rarely emphasized in therapy.

In the typical group therapy situation in the public schools, parents are notified of ways to assist the speech clinician via notes written often in the speech notebook. Occasionally, a telephone call is made or an appointment is arranged to see a parent of a child who is troublesome or not showing good improvement. When asked, most school clinicians feel that group therapy is effective, but they remain uncertain about who should be placed in group therapy and who should be helped individually.

A Plan

The first important consideration for selecting children for individual and group articulation therapy should be a careful evaluation of the articulatory status of the child. Tests such as McDonald's Deep Test and an assessment of a child's self-correction of his defective sounds (such as stimulability) are helpful. An evaluation of his spontaneous speech is important. Finally, a review of his speech therapy progress in the past may assist the clinician in making this judgment. These factors are important, since it is suggested that some group therapy classes should consist of children who require more work in learning to produce their defective sounds correctly, and other classes should be established for children who have sufficient articulatory proficiency to be working on carry-over.

A second consideration consists of a total impression of the child based upon his motivation to improve his speech, his life adjustment, and his willingness to work along with other children who have similar speech problems. Some negative, rebelling, and poorly motivated children with articulation problems may require a period of individual therapy prior to being admitted into group classes. Other children who appear disinterested in speech correction are occasionally found to respond well to the group situation without any prior individual therapy.

Deemphasizing the role of the types of defective sounds is an important third consideration. Obviously, it is often convenient for a clinician to group young lateral lispers together (especially if they all are in a production stage or all in a carry-over stage). Similarly, it is often helpful to group all children of certain ages together for group therapy if the *r* sound, for example, is their only defective one. However, this consideration is most often given the highest priority; whereas the articulatory proficiency and other before-mentioned factors may be more significant in terms of efficient scheduling for therapy services and rapid improvement. It is desirable, in this respect, to think about arranging some group therapy classes for young children who need an intensive period of ear training. These children should be entered into these classes for this treatment on the basis of an auditory discrimination test. After improvement has been accomplished, they can be considered for classes where production techniques are stressed. Later they can be transferred by the speech clinician into classes where carry-over activities are stressed. This plan has many real advantages for the speech clinician.

The alternate to the plan of having different types of group therapy classes (ear training, production, and carry-over) is the fourth consideration. This proposal may be used frequently in small schools having few children in therapy and where speech clinicians cover many schools and have high case loads. All of the previously mentioned considerations probably apply to the selection of children for these classes. The first step in arranging group articulation classes is careful evaluation of the defective sounds. Stimulability testing should be employed as a primary tool for the selection of the sounds to be worked on in therapy (a child who has previously worked on another sound generally should probably not change until he has reached an appropriate place in therapy). After all of the children have been tested and selections have been made concerning which children require individual therapy, the remaining children should be grouped. This grouping should be based primarily on proficiency of articulation; secondarily, by some consideration for age; and lastly, grouping on the basis of similarly defective sounds.

This practice may mean that a speech clinician may have five children in a class, three of whom need work on s, θ, and r, and two who need work on l and $t\varsigma$. Although this appears to be a difficult task, it can be done well as follows: The clinician initially works on s and l, since they were found to have the highest degree of improvement under stimulability testing and showed the least resistance to change. Ear training is begun; however, this is accomplished concurrently with production. Identification is used so that each child knows the sound that he is trying to improve; stimulation is used to acquaint him with the phonetic qualities of the "good sound"; discrimination training is used to get all of the class members skilled at hearing the differences between s and l and finally between the "good s" and the "poor s," and between the "good l" and the "poor l" and between all gradients of these extremes. This is one activity in which all class members participate. Each child learns to listen for these sounds and their phonetic qualities when correctly and incorrectly produced, and ear-training activities change as a function of the improvements in production which are attained. All of these activities result in good listening for speech sounds and develop speech awareness. After a few weeks or a month, the other defective sounds (r and $t\varsigma$) are entered into the discrimination game activities that all the children participate in so that future work in therapy on these sounds is made without recourse to long periods of ear training.

Each child does work on one defective sound at a time under this plan. At every session the clinician provides about five minutes (or less depending upon the needs for careful production training) working with every child individually in front of a large mirror. During this production training, nonsense syllables and finally words, phrases, and sentences are used to improve the proficiency of production and appropriate individualized discrimination is provided by the clinician. Accent, stress, speed, and inflection patterns are systematically used by the clinician. Recording devices are used to improve "self-hearing." This individual work to increase articulatory proficiency for each child is most important because it increases each child's articulatory skills and his awareness, and allows the clinician to motivate the child individually to continue improving the quality of the defective sound. The mirror reflects his image and integrates body imagery, self-concept, and speech goals to the child, thus making group therapy more intensive. Production work can follow a total group ear-training exercise or game.

While children receive this individual assistance on production, the clinician can arrange for appropriate small group work. Two children now in production on *l*, for example, can work on getting it into nonsense syllables or words on the chalkboard by "climbing up the ladder." Highly specific sound games can be used for a carry-over activity for these children. Recording devices can be used with the other two *s* problems on materials that the clinician provides (many young children can learn to use this machine under supervision). Generally, the speech clinician must be adept at preparing a variety of speech activities designed to meet the needs of the subgroups in the group therapy class.

After the individual production work, more total group activities can be undertaken. The children can listen for errors on *l* and *s* in the clinician's speech and play a team game of catching and correcting for points (Some children with good production can do this in the clinician's place if suitable materials are provided for them to use). Each child can demonstrate his old "poor" way of saying his sound and his new "good" way. As the members of the class improve in articulatory proficiency on these sounds, class activities can shift to more carry-over techniques. When some degree of carry-over is achieved for the *s* defectives, they begin to work on *r* (if stimulability and other signs indicate that it is more promising than θ. The *l* defectives can now begin to work on *ts*. As before, periods of individual production are conducted at each session. These are followed by specific ear training designed to get the children to hear the difference between the "poor" and "good" sounds. By this time, most children are speech conscious and well ear-trained, and improvement with these sounds comes more rapidly than it did when therapy classes first began.

Throughout the group articulation therapy, most speech notebook assignments are different for each child. All work is tailored to the speech needs of the individual child. Grouping for therapy may allow for increased motivation and the increasing of personal aspirations and desires for better speech. The combination of specific speech activities, intermittent reinforcement of improved or correct responses, and group goals, as well as individual ones, may culminate in a highly satisfactory degree of improvement for all members of the group therapy class. These suggestions do not or should not exclude the basic considerations, previously noted, concerning goal setting in groups and group aspirations — which are vital to gaining the advantages of grouping and thusly creating a new and unified structure in which better speech may emerge.

LENGTH OF SESSIONS

In the absence of well-supported evidence, decision making takes the form of being based upon empiricism and experience as the guide. Since we currently cannot be guided by research findings to shed light on the variables involved in deciding about how much therapy should be administered and for what period of time, we must look to the impressions of clinicians. The national study of speech and hearing in the schools (Bingham, *et al.*, 1961) revealed that most clinicians provided therapy twice weekly to school children and the great bulk of the remainder provided it once weekly. Implicit in this finding is the statement that less than once weekly is not felt to be adequate under most conditions. Further, it was reported that most group sessions lasted twenty-five to thirty-four minutes and individual sessions fifteen to twenty-four minutes. Again the assumption is that most experienced clinicians deemed periods of fifteen minutes or less inadequate. A majority of the clinicians sampled in this national study reported a dissatisfaction with the number of weekly sessions they were able to provide in their schools (Bingham *et al.,* 1961).

FREQUENCY OF SESSIONS

In order to intensify speech therapy in the schools, a number of clinicians have turned to intensive scheduling methods. Research evidence related to the relative effectiveness of block versus traditional scheduling, i.e. once or twice weekly all year or until correction is achieved, is reported in Chapter 7. As mentioned, the relative effectiveness of any method is dependent upon some other factors such as the severity of speech defectiveness, the ages of the subjects, motivational variables, the level or stage of improvement, and other things. Unfortunately, we know little about the relevancies of such variables or their strengths. In spite of this major limitation, however, we might address ourselves to a view of some factors of importance which might bear upon decision making regarding the length and frequency of therapy sessions.

McDonald and Frick (1960) have expressed opinions concerning the importance of some factors which might affect some choices. These authors maintained that scheduling practices have commonly been influenced by convenience rather than careful clinical judgment. Four conditions were specified by them as having relevance for judgments concerning the length and frequency of therapy sessions. The first of these conditions consisted of the evaluation and program-planning stage, the second dealt with periods in which new skills and attitudes were being taught, the third with periods of emotional upset on the patient's part, and the fourth condition specified related to periods in which the patient was unable to assume a high degree of responsibility for his own progress in therapy. In effect, all of the above four conditions are ones in which McDonald and Frick recommend more frequent therapy. The essence of their thinking about the principle involved can probably be seen in their statement that follows.

> Ideally, perhaps, all patients should receive intensive therapy initially and, as they develop more ability to become responsible for their own treatment and become more independent, they can be seen less frequently. Therapists should be aware of this dependence-independence continuum and should use it as a guide to help determine the frequency of therapy.

Generally, these authors suggested that both the frequency and duration of sessions might be reduced during periods in which new speech skills are being habituated. Presumably, during this time the subject's newly acquired skills are being strengthened by him as he works alone and sees the clinician for shorter periods of time and less frequently. Finally, McDonald and Frick remind the readers that all such recommendations concerning the length and frequency of therapy sessions will vary according to the nature of the problem, the age of the subject, and other factors. The principle of flexibility is lauded; the practice of being schedule-dominated is abhorred by these authors.

Limitations

As presently constituted, the work-a-day world of many clinicians in the schools tends to militate against the application of the praiseworthy principles cited by McDonald and Frick. This seems particularly true for the many clinicians who serve more widely spread school areas, since they must spend a considerable portion of their time traveling from one school to another. Under the conditions of having six or more school buildings to serve, most of which have fewer than a few hundred children enrolled, the clinician finds it difficult to provide service more than twice weekly, and in some instances, it becomes difficult to see them more than once weekly. Assuming that conditions do impose major barriers to alternating the duration and frequency of therapy sessions for some clinicians, how can some portion of this dilemma be resolved? Two possibilities may be worth considering.

Twice a Day

The first possibility consists of seeing some children more than once on the same day. McDonald and Frick suggested that more frequent sessions seem commonly warranted during the intake and evaluation stages; they further suggested that this is true also during the stages in which the clinician must teach certain new speech skills. It may be feasible for some clinicians to schedule a child early in the morning on a particular day and then see him later on the same day for an additional period of time which may be either shorter or longer than the original session. Perhaps this same child (or children) can then be seen on another day for two more sessions or one more, if desired. This system obviously provides for four sessions weekly for a child rather than two; furthermore, two of the four sessions can be discontinued as the child improves and enters into carry-over or otherwise assumes more of the responsibility for working independently. Therefore, a program originally designed so that children can be seen twice weekly becomes one in which some of them can be seen four times weekly.

Summer Programs

The second proposition takes the form of providing intensified services to selected children who require this assistance in order to achieve a substantial amount of improvement in speech. The most likely provision for this is a summer clinical program. Programs of this type have been operated successfully by school clinicians for more than ten years. One such program, the terminal speech program, has served more than one thousand speech handicapped children during the past ten years. Essentially, this intensified service operates in the manner described below.

PROCEDURES

Selected clinicians from the schools are employed with extra pay for an additional month's service. Early in the spring of the year, the clinicians prepare form letters which are mailed directly to the parents of speech defective children. These letters are sent to the parents of all diagnosed speech defective school children in the clinicians' areas who appear to need intensified therapy. Parents respond by returning a detachable form from the bottom of the letter indicating whether they desire their children to attend the program. Appointments for speech evaluations for each child are then made by the clinicians and recorded on post cards. These post cards are sent later during the month of May and indicate final directions for attending the program.

Normally two separate clinics are maintained during the month of July. Each clinic operates four days weekly. Each is located geographically so that all members of the county have relatively easy access to one clinic or the other. Three or more speech clinicians staff each clinic. School buildings are usually provided during this time by local school boards without rentals and usually many different buildings are offered by local school administrators for this purpose. Parents are responsible for transporting their children to and from the clinics.

Children who attend are seen in small groups and also individually, if this is desirable. Groups usually meet for one hour. Some select cases are seen for longer periods or shorter periods if required depending upon their speech defects, severity of the problem, their ability to tolerate longer sessions, and scheduling convenience. While two or more clinicians work with small groups or with individual children, their parents are instructed by the third clinician concerning how to help them at home.* A rotational system is used so that all clinicians are provided with opportunities to counsel parents. After the discussion period during the parent training sessions, the parents are allowed to observe the therapy for the remainder of the hour. Usually they are requested to observe the specific happenings in therapy such as a technique used in ear training on a particular sound.

This intensified clinical program is an adjunct to the regular public school program. It operates so that children and their parents receive help four days weekly for almost four weeks. The

---

*Experience shows that more than 95 per cent of the parents who are trained to help their children are mothers.

average child enrolled in the terminal speech program receives about fourteen hours of speech therapy during the period of this clinical program. Some children may receive as much as fifteen hours of therapy, while others may receive as little as ten hours.

EVALUATION

A terminal speech program is not a panacea and certainly does not fully compensate for the lack of intensified speech therapy during the course of the school year. In addition to the intensified therapy this program permits, experience shows that such a program offers the following important advantages:

1. Because of the smaller speech therapy classes that this type of terminal speech program allows, each speech clinician has more flexibility in utilizing a variety of therapy techniques. Since no travel or moving of equipment is involved, clinical devices and apparatus can be used in therapy with convenience and relative ease.

2. Such a program allows the clinician working in the schools an opportunity to work with parents of speech defective children who are interested in their children's speech .This may be a morale building factor, for many clinicians often have little time to interact professionally with genuinely interested parents. It is an excellent way for such a clinician to end his working year.

3. Although children with speech problems often go on throughout the year with these problems, many well-trained and talented clinicians working in the schools terminate their working year after about nine months and provide no further professional service to these children even though the need is always present. Furthermore, many clinicians are hampered in their school therapy by a school day which may be as short as six hours of actual time that they can devote to therapy. When travel time is accounted for, actual therapy time may be well below this figure. Extending the working year of a clinician beyond ten months allows for greater service with little additional cost. It therefore is more efficient from an economic standpoint.

4. Two or more clinicians working together in a terminal clinical program have a free exchange of therapy techniques, thereby fostering professional growth. Such working together clinically helps satisfy the need of clinicians for professional interaction and exchange which may be difficult to realize on many school programs. If the therapy is supervised, a terminal speech program provides an excellent opportunity for the supervisor to work closely with his staff on improvement of therapy techniques and for the development of successful therapy materials. Ideas, materials, and techniques are easily shared under these conditions.

5. A well-integrated terminal speech program provides opportunities for clinicians in schools to do research. Those clinicians who have

indicated desire to do research but who have maintained that insufficient time is available during the school year for this endeavor may find that a greater amount of freedom, time, and opportunity is available when a terminal speech program is established. The possibility of research involving parents of speech defective school children exists under such a program and needs to be done. This may be less easily managed during the regular school year. Many types of clinical speech experiments can be conducted. Under these conditions, controls in research may be more stringently enforced than is often possible when similar research is accomplished on the typical school scene.

Other Considerations

There is a suggestion that a few other factors should be considered when deciding upon the length and frequency of therapy sessions. One of these concerns methodology. According to data gathered in the national study of speech and hearing services in the schools (Bingham *et al.,* 1961), most clinicians working in schools employ a combination of therapy methods which tend to be "direct" rather than "indirect" in nature. This finding may restrict judgments about the suitability of certain prescribed durations and/or frequencies of therapy sessions, since it may well be that many of the techniques utilized as part of one therapy approach or the other necessitates shorter or longer sessions or more or less frequent ones. For example, clinicians relying upon a highly direct therapy method, e.g. the motokinesthetic one for articulation problems, may tend to find that results are better under conditions of having frequent sessions of relatively short duration; whereas one using highly indirect methodology might find the converse to be the case. Although the validity of this idea has not been determined experimentally, it seems logical to expect that the choice of methodology may also affect decision making in this regard.

Nature of the Problems

A second consideration, mentioned briefly by McDonald and Frick (1960), may also prove to be a potent one. This revolves around the nature of the problem. It is suggested, for example, that children working for production of correct sounds might well be seen twice weekly (or more if possible) for periods of twenty-five to thirty minutes (in many cases this can take the form of group therapy) . Similar children who have advanced to a carry-over stage in sound production might possibly gain more improvement by being seen more often than this for even shorter periods of time (however, less than fifteen-minute sessions seem ineffectual) . Children having the following problems under specified conditions may require more frequent sessions in order to gain the proficiency needed to advance to the next stages: 1) those having voice disorders, particularly those for whom a change in optimum pitch level is indicated; 2) advanced or secondary stuttering children who are working to develop skill and use in alerting the "moment of stuttering" by the use of appropriate controls, and 3) primary or transitional stuttering children who require a maximum number of sessions of various durations in order for them to develop relationships and gain support from the clinician. In summary, it would appear that children manifesting difficulties in the development of certain critical skills in sound production, voice production, or speech control may require more frequent therapy and that the duration of these sessions should depend upon the techniques employed by the clinician as well as the subject's ability to benefit by more prolonged instruction.

Motivational Factors

Although we know virtually nothing about the effects of motivation upon the correction of defective speech, we suspect that both a general motivational factor and some specific motivational ones are operative. Occasionally poorly motivated children are discontinued in speech therapy by some clinicians who feel that their time is better spent with children who desire to improve and will make sincere efforts to do so. Perhaps increased motivation for improvement can be achieved by varying the length and frequency of sessions for these children. It seems probable that some poorly motivated children might respond best to frequent sessions (three or four weekly) of short duration (twenty minutes), particularly if more efforts were made to specify therapy goals from session to session which were capable of being realized by the children.

Poor Progress

A related consideration concerns children who have a history of poor progress in speech therapy. Many of these children may be motivated towards a desire to succeed in correction but have failed due to other reasons, e.g. lack of continuity in therapy, inappropriate therapy techniques, or poor attendance. It is suggested that children of this type be considered for more frequent therapy sessions, which may or may not be shorter in duration. This intensification of therapy may provide the impetus for the establishment of some basic speech skills required before the child can advance to another stage. Conversely, children showing good progress in therapy may be able to achieve a satisfactory resolution of their problems by remaining on essentially the same program of scheduling.

Parental Cooperation

A final consideration dealing with the choice of length and frequency of therapy sessions relates to the degree of parental cooperation and assistance that the clinician has engineered into the program. It is conceivable, for example, that well-directed parental help might allow for satisfactory degrees of improvement without an increase in either the length of sessions or their frequency and, in some instances may allow for some decrease of these factors. An hypothesis to be formulated might specify that children of disinterested and uncooperative parents should be seen more often and that children of interested and participating parents might be seen less often in order to obtain comparable levels of improvement. Such an untested hypothesis would seem particularly probable with elementary aged children; it might not hold with children from the secondary school levels.

Summary

None of the factors related to the length and frequency of therapy sessions has stood the test of adequate experimentation. All are in a sense intuitive ones. However, experience would tend to indicate (and common sense dictates) that many factors bear upon the decision concerning an increase or reduction of one or both or a combination of the two. Among these are the four conditions cited by McDonald and Frick and the so-called "other factors" such as the type of speech disorder, the techniques and methodologies of therapy, the motivation of the children for better speech, and the history of past progress in speech correction. In addition, the age of the children and their abilities to respond intellectually may be important considerations. Each decision is unique and probably should be made on the basis of these factors and others.

PROBLEMS IN THERAPY

Dismissals

Speech clinicians tend to be busy, active, and dynamic persons. There are as many problems as there are children to be served, and this describes one of the major difficulties of the clinician in the schools: the clinician must be able to generate sufficient enthusiasm and have an efficient expenditure of energy in order to face the task at hand. However, unlike a classroom teacher, for example, the clinician must motivate and develop interest in different groups of children from one therapy session to another. In some instances, there is little or no time for a cessation of therapy activities except for a brief lunch period. The challenge is to be able to accomplish this in such a way that the clinician and the children are eager to engage in the corrective process. A flexible and clinically oriented therapy program in which parents, teachers, administrators, and others are inextricably involved tends to reduce the boredom and fatigue often seen in the schedule-dominated program. A problem-solving approach to therapy in which data are gathered and investigative or experimental research is accomplished also may tend to make and maintain interest within the clinician. The important interest and motivational factor for the clinician, however, is the constantly emerging evidence that the children are improving and the final satisfaction of dismissing a child as "corrected."

Carry-over

Among the specific problems faced by any speech clinician, one looms as most troublesome: how to get the subjects to put into habituated spontaneous speech what they have mastered in the clinical situation. This so-called carry-over problem has received little study and has generally been overlooked in most standard texts and publications dealing with speech correction. In this regard, few techniques have been enumerated for achieving carry-over, and many authorities have glossed over the problem in their writings as though it is nonexistent. Experienced clinicians, however, have reported it to be their most perplexing problem. Table VIII shows the results of a study completed by the author dealing with the difficulties of speech correction (1960).

TABLE VIII
AREA OF DIFFICULTY IN SPEECH THERAPY

Area of Difficulty	Rank Order						
	1	2	2.5	3	4	4.5	5
Teaching production of defective sounds	7	8	1	42	61	3	54
Teaching ear training on defective sounds	5	27		28	60	3	53
Carry-over of new sounds by patients into spontaneous speech	134	19	1	15	5		2
Gaining parental cooperation in the therapy process	14	46	2	48	31		35
Motivating speech defective children to want better speech	15	74	2	39	16		30

Note: Number of clinicians assigning various ranks to five areas of difficulty in speech therapy. A rank of 1 represents greatest difficulty and a rank of 5 indicates least difficulty. N = 176.

Further analysis of the questionnaire data revealed the following: The seven clinicians who ranked teaching production of defective sounds as most difficult, ranked the following areas as least difficult:

Teaching ear training on defective sounds	2
Carry-over of new sounds by patients into spontaneous speech	1
Gaining parental cooperation in the therapy process	4

The five clinicians who ranked teaching ear training on defective sounds as most difficult, ranked the following areas as least difficult:

Teaching production of defective sounds	1
Gaining parental cooperation in the therapy process	2
Motivating speech defective children to want better speech	2

The 134 clinicians who ranked carry-over of new sounds by patients into spontaneous speech as most difficult, ranked the following areas as least difficult:

Teaching production of defective sounds	40
Teaching ear training on defective sounds	38
Teaching production of defective sounds, and teaching ear training on defective sounds—equal rank	3
Gaining parental cooperation in the therapy process	28
Motivating speech defective children to want better speech	25

The fourteen clinicians who ranked Gaining parental cooperation in the therapy process as most difficult, ranked the following as least difficult:

Teaching production of defective sounds	5
Teaching ear training on defective sounds	6
Carry-over on new sounds by patients into spontaneous speech	1
Motivating speech defective children to want better speech	2

The fifteen clinicians who ranked Motivating speech defective children to want better speech as most difficult, ranked the following as least difficult:

Teaching production of defective sounds	6
Teaching ear training on defective sounds	7
Gaining parental cooperation in the therapy process	2

Assuming that the "carry-over problem" is not uniquely one experienced by clinicians in Pennsylvania, we might find it of sufficient importance to speculate concerning why it exists and perhaps develop some notions for how to reduce its effects. Perhaps a number of factors might be cited which bear upon the lack of carry-over on the part of some subjects. Six such possibilities are 1) insufficient therapy, 2) superficial therapy, 3) nature of the defect, 4) lack of flexibility in the therapy program, 5) poorly motivated children, and 6) no "spread of effect" in the therapy program. Perhaps each of these possibilities merits some discussion. It would appear that the first three causes are related to the skills of the clinician.

Insufficient Therapy

How much therapy is required to achieve the totally successful carryover of new speech patterns? This is a question worthy of investigation, but unfortunately, we lack evidence in this regard. The level of proficiency in the use of new speech skills required to gain total carry-over, therefore, cannot be accurately specified and unquestionably varies considerably with a host of unknown factors. It becomes difficult to know when to dismiss a subject from therapy. The premature dismissal of individuals having inadequately established and nonfunctional speech patterns obviously dooms some persons to fail in this regard. The clinician who is impatient or who closes his eyes and hopes for carry-over is probably most often misleading himself if he allows a subject to be dismissed without recourse to careful evaluation concerning the adequacy of the skills required on the subject's part. Since assimilation of newly acquired speech patterns takes time and must be developed in all situations (in the speech room, in the classroom, in the hall, at home, at the store), many persons require additional support and assistance from the clinician in order to gain total carry-over (which is the only kind of importance in most cases). Furthermore, a basic tenet of the therapy program is rechecking and reevaluation. A clinician doing this diligently probably learns not to make premature judgments about readiness for dismissal.

Superficial Therapy

A clinician desiring immediate recognition for his efforts might be influenced to dismiss children as "corrected" on the basis of a certain criterion of successful performance. For example, a beginning clinician working in the schools might dismiss a child from therapy because he showed the ability to retract his tongue on *s* and *z* and correct his interdental sigmatism. Furthermore, this child was able to use this form of correction in reading and in spontaneous speech in the therapy room. However, a careful view of the situation might reveal that the child in question was actually being asked to put a distorted and unstable "corrected" form of these sounds into his spontaneous speech. The sound was inadequately perfected in isolation; it was not well developed in the sense of being articulated almost the same way every time it was produced and, in spite of the fact that the child was well motivated to use it, it was not acceptable to him as a "correction." The contrast auditorily, visually, and tactually between the incorrect forms of production and the correct forms was made very difficult for the child to perceive, since the "correct form" was not really remarkably different. In this sense, therapy was insufficient, i.e. it should have been conducted more thoroughly in the isolation stage before any attempt at carry-over was made by the clinician.

Nature of the Problem

In the above discussion an example of lack of carry-over on interdental sigmatisms was presented. An investigation completed by the author as part of a procedure to identify subjects for another project revealed that these types of errors in articulation were particularly susceptible to regression. The results of this study on the effectiveness of carry-over in articulation therapy can be seen in Table IX. The procedure used in obtaining these data was based upon a recheck by the author of 177 school children dismissed during a six-month period by clinicians. All children were from elementary grades and most were from the third, fourth, fifth, and sixth grades. Each was interviewed individually for periods of time varying from ten to fifteen minutes. In most instances the children were engaged in conversations about television programs, hobbies, pets, or families. A child who misarticulated a sound more than once in spontaneous speech was deemed not to have carried over, and only the sounds worked on in speech

therapy were studied. The highly significant percentage of interdental sigmatisms which failed to carry-over and presumably re-
gressed would tend to indicate that these forms of misarticulations
require careful study by the clinician before it is decided that a
child will be successful in using them in everyday speaking
activities.

TABLE IX
UNCORRECTED MISARTICULATIONS FOUND AFTER DISMISSAL

Sounds Considered Corrected by Clinicians	Number of Subjects Examined	Number Found Corrected	Number Found Not Corrected	Percentage Not Corrected
s and *z* Interdentalized	74	31	43	46.0
s and *z* Lateralized	22	19	3	13.6
$ʂ$, $tʂ$, and $dʒ$ Lateralized	16	13	3	18.7
r phonemes	48	45	3	6.3
$θ$	17	16	1	5.9
Total	177	124	53	

Types of misarticulations found uncorrected after "dismissal" by clinicians in schools.

On the other hand, it appeared from these results that elementary age children having had therapy for defects of *r* phonemes
were highly successful in carry-over. Of course it is difficult to
determine whether this finding reflected a fundamental difficulty
in maintaining correct production of *s* and *z* interdental sigmatisms as compared to *r* problems and others or was evidencing
some differences relative to the therapy process per se for these
various sound errors.

Inflexible Program

It is conceivable that carry-over problems for the clinician in
the schools might also be created or perpetuated by a schedule-
dominated program which failed to supply more or lesser degrees
of "treatment" as the needs of the children indicated. A child
attempting to establish a new optimum pitch range, for example,
might require periods of brief yet intensive assistance from the
clinician prior to his dismissal in order to gain the proficiency

necessary for total usage of his "new voice" in all situations. The period of skill development might be one in which more intensive treatment for other disorders is needed so that later carry-over activities develop easily and quickly, thus allowing the process to be consummated.

Poorly Motivated Children

We might inquire about the possibility that some children resist the usage of new speech patterns outside the therapy room. Perhaps they find this change to another way of speaking somewhat threatening. Perhaps they will work effectively for the speech clinician under the conditions of having the person present as a motivator but will not make efforts to utilize what they have learned. The poorly motivated child in this regard may be one for whom carry-over is nearly impossible unless the clinician has managed to make correct usage an automatic process. This type of child may require different and more intensive treatment in the therapy sessions themselves if he is to gain correct production outside the therapy room, since he may not monitor his own speech and alter its form without assistance and reminders to do so.

No Spread of Effect

Finally, it appears likely that a major contributing factor to a lack of carry-over is the "no spread of effect" phenomenon. The clinician in the schools who fails to seek the assistance of parents, teachers, and other persons to "set the stage" for carry-over may have a disappointing record. A number of the suggestions listed earlier in this chapter pertain to how and why these types of experiences become important as basic pillars of the therapy program. It might be said that therapy in isolation is therapy with limitation and for some children this may mean a failure to carry-over the use of correct patterns.

The carry-over problem has been found to be a critical one for the speech clinician. Clinicians working in schools have resources available to them which may tend to mitigate this problem to a degree. Many reasons probably exist for the existence of this lack of carry-over condition; those presented here are some suggested ones.

ASSISTANTS IN THERAPY

Teachers

Although it has frequently been said that classroom teachers are capable of correcting speech defects, no research other than that gathered as a result of improvements in articulation based upon speech improvement attests to the validity of this statement. In the experiments conducted by Byrne (1962), in which classroom teachers administered speech improvement exercises, all teachers were willing volunteers drawn from a much larger population and all were carefully trained and supervised. Whether they are capable of correcting some types of speech defects is part of the issue. An important related issue is whether they are generally willing to undertake this task. In spite of the numerous statements indicating that they should do so, experienced clinicians find that few classroom teachers feel that this is their responsibility and a paltry few will attempt any type of correction on their own. Experienced clinicians often report that most classroom teachers will not and do not become involved in helping to correct a child's speech problem unless they are formally asked to do so and then not until someone identifies the problem and makes specific recommendations about how to achieve improvement. This then suggests that the clinician should actively seek to develop interest among teachers in the correction of defective speech, work vigorously with the most cooperative and interested ones, and evolve a systematic and concrete program for their inclusion in the total therapy program.

What then should be the role of the classroom teacher in the therapy program? To teach the production of defective speech sounds, develop and improve listening skills in her classroom, do ear-training activities on commonly defective speech sounds, work individually with each child who attends speech therapy to practice specific assignments given by the clinician, promote a healthy climate of acceptance for the speech handicapped child, or try to integrate a child's improved speech pattern into other language media such as oral reading? Ideally and with professional help from the clinician, the classroom teacher might be successful in accomplishing any or all of these—and all may have real value for the children enrolled in therapy. Practically speaking, most classroom teachers would not be able or willing to become that involved in the therapy program. Those familiar with the modern educational scene can probably cite many reasons for the limited involvement of teachers in this program. Chief among these may be that classroom teachers are busy professional workers whose task is primarily outlined by directives charging them with advancing the learning skills of children in certain prescribed areas so far each year, and typically, speech constitutes a very minor portion of this charge. Secondly, modern schools are replete with educational specialists, many of whom want the teachers' support and cooperation on a variety of tasks whether it be art, music, physical education, foreign languages, or school health programs. The speech clinician is only one more.

The alert speech clinician occasionally may be fortunate in locating a primary grade teacher who wants an active role in the therapy program for children with problems from her classroom. Perhaps she is interested in trying a program of speech improvement. Since she has little or no prior experience or training to do this, she calls upon the speech clinician. After gaining the permission of the school administration, the two develop a series of lesson plans suitable for the grade level of the children and designed to correct certain phonemic errors prevalent in the classroom. The clinician begins the program by providing the teacher with information concerning who has defective speech and specifically what each child's phonemic errors are at the time. The clinician introduces the speech improvement program by teaching the first lesson. The teacher proceeds to teach a similar lesson, with slight modification, daily for the particular week in question. The following week these activities continue; finally, the classroom teacher begins to develop confidence in technique and ultimately is doing all the instructional work with the clinician serving as the consultant. The teacher's interest and willingness has helped to insure the success of the efforts.

Many classroom teachers may make a significant contribution to the therapy program without recourse to participation in a speech improvement program. Although in some instances teachers may be successful in teaching the correct form of a defective phoneme, this particular type of activity is generally contraindicated for most teachers and belongs at the level of the clinician. Apparently, many children who are truly speech defective are not capable of altering a defective phonemic structure without the application of special techniques patiently provided by a skilled clinician. As in the case of parents of speech defective school children, the inclusion of the classroom teacher as an active co-worker in the therapy program should probably most often occur after the correct form of the phoneme has been learned. However, it may prove of real value to have the classroom teacher aware of attempts that the child is making to learn to produce the correct phonemic form, since the teacher can serve to encourage him and perhaps develop some degree of understanding concerning the difficulty of achieving this aspect of correction. This can be accomplished in a variety of ways, including having the teacher spend a few minutes in the therapy room at the time that production efforts are being directed towards this problem, demonstrating some degree of change in sound production outside her classroom door as the child returns from therapy, or perhaps playing a tape for the teacher after school showing a shift towards correct production of the phoneme.

The second suggestion has proved rather effective in many instances, particularly if the degree of improvement is capable of being perceived by the teacher. Frequently this results in "How nice, John, you are getting it better," and this from many teachers provides extra impetus on the part of the child to continue to try to improve what may be a difficult task. After the sound is in totally correct production, this procedure may seem even more effective. This is outstandingly true if the child can then demonstrate his "old way" or "bad way" followed immediately by his "new way" or "good way." Few teachers will fail to commend the child for this success. Furthermore and most importantly, the speech clinician may have set the stage for the carry-over of the new speech sound into reading and speech in the classroom, since, in effect, the child has acknowledged his ability to correct his speech before an important adult in his life—his teacher.

Other School Personnel

A number of other school personnel are useful in getting children motivated to improve in speech. At the elementary level, for example, the elementary supervisor or building principal is often in an excellent position to influence the behavior of children. He is probably viewed as the supreme authority figure on the scene, and, as such, he may be perceived with awe by some children. In most instances both the children and the teachers look to him for approval. Unfortunately, the elementary supervisor or principal frequently plays a passive role in the therapy program. He may confer with the clinician about a problem, occasionally ask about a particular child, and assist in locating room space and otherwise help to coordinate the service, yet he rarely really becomes meaningfully involved in the dynamics of therapy. The reasons for this are generally not clear at this time; however, this type of professional person has a myriad of responsibilities and frequently has countless details of school administration to handle daily. Two other reasons seem plausible: 1) the clinician has never sought the assistance of the elementary principal in ways other than those described and 2) the principal realizes that this type of "instructional service" is completely alien to his training and experiences; therefore, he elects to support it but he makes no commitment to understand or become actively involved in it.

Experienced clinicians tend to find that interest and identification with the therapy program rises dramatically among professional personnel who observe therapy sessions. Many have also found that few such persons will observe sessions unless they are provided with specific times to observe. The elementary principal may never observe unless such arrangements are made and the clinician takes the initiative. The importance of his observing therapy revolves around the continuous need for the clinician to increase the acceptance of her program, provide the principal opportunities to see the goals and techniques outlined for the attainment of these goals, and, hopefully, to recognize that many of the children enrolled in therapy classes are showing important improvements. The importance of his being involved in the therapy which he observes can be seen in a number of incidents in which enterprising clinicians capitalized upon his uniqueness both as a person and as an authority figure. He now not only sees the degree of improvement made by each child, but he also works to increase it.

A first-year speech clinician, working in ideal working space in a large, modern elementary school was experiencing grave difficulties in motivating and controlling a group of four sixth-grade girls, all of whom had correct productions of *s* and *z* in isolation but were not progressing to other stages. Unfortunately, because of an extremely high turnover rate among clinicians, these girls had a new clinician almost every year, and they obviously began to take speech therapy less than seriously. Two ways of improving this situation were developed. Firstly, the beginning clinician was instructed in detail concerning how to work with each girl in the group individually during the group session for purposes of showing progress on subgoals, motivating her as an individual, and thereby increasing her level of aspiration for ultimate total correction. Secondly, the youthful, male elementary-building principal was apprised of the fact that these four girls required additional motivation and encouragement and, in effect, an endorsement from other authority that "this was important." The principal was asked to observe during the entire therapy period; the girls worked cooperatively with the clinician who occasionally said things such as "Mr. Charles, you can probably see how well Sandra has mastered this *s* sound when she says it alone. Now she is trying to put it with other sounds and still say it correctly." At the end of the forty-five-minute session, Mr. Charles remarked to all of the girls that he saw improvement and that each of them would no doubt improve more, and furthermore, he would visit them again the following week for a few minutes in order to see the additional improvement which they obviously were going to achieve. During the week's time between sessions, the clinician and the principal conferred about the class. The principal entered the subsequent session and observed about fifteen minutes of the therapy. Before leaving, he spoke to each of the four girls about specific efforts and successes on their part to achieve further improvements. He indicated that he would return in a week or so and see how much additional improvement had been accomplished. The brief encounters with the class of girls continued for two or three months; however, later contacts became more random. The beginning clinician was amazed to find that three of the four girls advanced to a final carry-over stage in three months. The principal appeared pleased about being involved.

Motivation problems among junior and senior high students plague many speech clinicians. Frequently, many such students will not do home assignments, and appear completely disinterested about speech therapy. The high school principal may be of help in much the same way in which the elementary one was of value with the sixth-grade girls. The guidance counsellor can be useful in this regard as well, since his unique role is stressing to the student the need for preparation and training in achieving life goals. The importance of correct speech is most often highly regarded by guidance personnel, and they frequently will undertake special counselling with students for purposes of giving them insights into vocational and personal needs. Obviously, it becomes rather simple for them to interweave a theme around "total preparation" which includes statements such as "It is very important for you to gain correct speech and we are so pleased to see that you are working at it."

Although little is known about the particular types of persons who are usually regarded as the "failures" in speech therapy, clinicians working in secondary schools occasionally locate such individuals. Frequently, these "failures" are disillusioned, complaining, and apparently almost totally defeated persons. Commonly, they appear rather incapable of competing either in school or in society in general. They present a picture of little confidence and low levels of aspiration toward many tasks—one important one being their ability to correct defective speech. This may be the same type of youngster that some clinicians find it "difficult to schedule." The success ratio with such individuals is apparently quite low; there are many reasons for this—some of which relate to the students and some of which relate to the therapy program implemented by the clinician.

Some prescription consisting of more specific, goal-directed therapy along with a significant increase in motivation toward the task seems indicated if such students are to be helped. Not unlike therapy for most individuals, these appear to stem from some degree of success with the task at hand. Subgoals in the corrective process therefore need particular specificity, and the students require motivation from one level of performance to the other. Furthermore, the therapy or corrective process should be outlined for the student, who needs a total concept of what it involves in order to see where he now resides in light of where he must progress. Motivation comes from success in accomplishing some aspect of the problem at hand. Coupled with this in such instances, however, is a long-standing defeatism and rejection of the need for help—a denial, if you will. Who will reinforce the need for correction? Not the high school principal, for this student has also been a behavior problem in school and may tend to feel (rightly or wrongly) rejected by him personally or rejected by the authority of the school. The guidance counsellor may have had limited success in dealing with this student, since he is obviously not "college bound" and, again, the student feels no kinship with him. The speech clinician now pins his hopes upon another faculty member. Is there one teacher that this student admires and respects? Does he show any inclination to want to become better acquainted with even one teacher? Can this teacher assist in trying to motivate him to want better speech, to accept the help that is being provided him, to understand that he can do it if he will cooperate with those who have a genuine interest in helping him? The answer is frequently Yes. Many such students will indicate that they feel this way about a teacher who may be the basketball coach, the band leader, or the one teaching biology. The clinician has found a new direction for movement. The horizons have brightened to a degree.

The clinician now embarks upon a joint task: therapy is *within* the working space and *without* it. The accepted teacher and the clinician develop a plan to increase both general and specific motivations. The teacher speaks to the student privately but briefly about his classroom performances and attempts to identify promising aspects of his work; he shows real interest in him as a person, and soon introduces in a casual way statements such as "Improving your speech is important, Karl. You seem to be getting somewhere with it." Hopefully, the clinician has been successful in showing the student that he can learn to produce the sound or alter his speech during the time in which the teacher is reinforcing the need for this and commenting favorably upon any improvements that he detects in the student's speech. Contacts between the clinician and the teacher continue during the school year. Although obviously no panacea, such an approach is organismic and meaningful, and affords a promise of some success with some students of the type described. Most importantly, the therapy process has been expanded to encompass both the *within* and the *without* effects, and in a sense, it deserves to be called "clinical."

The speech clinician working in the schools may not enjoy the same benefits that his colleagues in other settings have, especially in regard to parents being fully desirous of speech correction and well motivated towards it. However, it can be demonstrated that an important percentage of parents of school children will show interest, and if a systematic approach is made toward demonstrating the problems and showing how they can assist in correction, some of these parents will become valuable adjuncts in the therapy process. On the other hand, the speech clinician working in the schools often has recourse to other professionally interested personnel who can assist rather effectively at times and may act to supplement and complement the efforts of the clinician. It seems improvident not to utilize such resources as problems and conditions dictate. It deserves to be mentioned also that a more integrated speech therapy program gives greater import to the work and allows it to become a part of a greater effort to help children.

Parents

One of the salient differences between speech therapy programs in clinics and hospitals and those in schools has been the degree of parental involvement in the therapy process. By their very nature most so-called outpatient services in other types of settings deal with parents, since parents usually transport their children to and from therapy sessions. It becomes rather simple under these conditions to ask the parent to "step in here a minute and see what John has learned to do." This frequent exposure to the child's speech improvement status lends itself well to utilization of the parent in the therapy process. Furthermore, parents who refer their children to other agencies for therapy are usually concerned and well motivated; consequently, they frequently prove cooperative and quite willing to undertake some responsibility providing that the clinician sets the pace and instructs them in how to help in the corrective process. In this regard, the clinician working in a school setting is disadvantaged. If he is going to get the parent into the therapy process, he must put forth special efforts. The success ratio of getting parents involved in the therapy program during the regular school year has been disappointing to some clinicians. Although some report that as many as 75 per cent of their parents are working actively with them by attending special parent classes or by making regularly scheduled visits to school and to confer with them, the experiences of a number of clinicians over a period of years of trying to accomplish this would tend to show that perhaps 25 per cent might be a more accurate estimate. Again, experience would tend to suggest that a clinician having twenty-five out of the one hundred families involved in the therapy process would be doing a creditable job.

Of the many techniques which have been used to get parent understanding and assistance, providing each child's parents with a written appointment during school hours appears most effective. This approach seems to be effective because most parents will come for the first appointment. Most importantly, this first appointment should be established at the time that the particular child's speech class is conducted. This allows the parents an opportunity to observe part of the therapy and then receive directions concerning how they can assist and the importance of their being actively involved in the therapy activities. The value of this approach seems enhanced in many instances also if more than one parent is scheduled into group therapy sessions, probably due to the combined effects of knowing that others have children with speech problems and the innocuous and unapparent competition which develops among the parents concerning correction. In effect, this mysterious unknown called "speech therapy in the schools" takes on form, substance, personal, and interpersonal meaning. Under the conditions of having scheduled two or more parents into a particular group therapy session, the clinician can develop a number of interest-building and positive ways of gaining cooperation. For example, the first fifteen minutes of a forty-five-minute group session can consist of providing direct therapy to the entire group of children. The parents serve as observers. Those children whose parents are not in attendance are dismissed from this particular session and allowed to return to their regular school classes. The remaining children whose parents are in attendance are engaged in individual therapy activities by the clinician. At an appropriate point in this therapy, the clinician stops work and begins to explain the nature of the problem to the parent and demonstrates the proficiency level of the child at the moment. He may, for example, ask the child to say his "snake sound" the "old way" or the "bad way" and, after this, ask him to say it the "new way" or the "good way." The clinician may then ask the parent if he detected the difference between these two sounds. Assuming that the parent was successful in perceiving the differences between the incorrect and correct productions, the clinician can demonstrate the degree to which the child can combine the correct sound into nonsense syllables and indicate where more practice at home is needed to help him achieve competency in accomplishing this "next step." Finally the clinician can explain the subsequent steps in the therapy program for the child if he proves successful in mastering the nonsense syllables stages. In effect, the technique utilized by the clinician is geared to demonstrate some success, show the need for and the promise of success at the next step, and generally raise the parental expectancy concerning ultimate total correction of the problem. Experience tends to show that most parents exposed to these experiences will try to assist the clinician with home assignments and many of these will return, if scheduled, for further information and instruction.

Extent of Parental Involvement

The extent to which speech clinicians in schools rely upon speech notebooks as a vehicle for involving parents in the therapy process has not been determined. However, it seems likely that many clinicians utilize these devices, or similar ones, as ways of gaining better understanding on the part of the parents of the goals and progress of the therapy and as a means of reinforcing improved speech through home practice. This type of written information may constitute a very minimal type of parental involvement and participation. The efficacy of this practice of providing supplemental home assignments to children enrolled in school therapy programs was studied by Shea (1955). He found that children whose parents received this type of written form of instruction were not significantly improved in articulation compared with a control group whose parents were not in receipt of this information. Shea's procedures, however, did not include even minimal training sessions for parents or demonstrations of their children's articulatory skills; rather, they were based upon additional home assignments and special instructional sheets which were sent home via the child's speech notebook. On the other hand, Egbert (1957) found that children with articulation problems improved well in speech therapy when their mothers were informed about therapy practices and goals. Again, experimental evidence from one study does not resolve a problem, but one possible implication from a comparison of these two studies might be that parents must be involved on a face-to-face basis before important undertakings occur in the therapy program. This is not to suggest that written home assignments have no value or that all parents will fail to assist in therapy unless the clinician meets with them. It does suggest that such practices are limited in value and that further efforts to gain parental cooperation and assistance must come by utilizing other approaches. Clearly, most school clinicians would probably attest to the fact that both teachers and parents are interested in speech notebooks and that they are generally of sufficient value to continue their usage.

Is it worthwhile for a speech clinician to train parents to assist in speech correction? When viewed in terms of articulation problems, research findings to date clearly say Yes. This appears to be true for preschool articulatory defective children (Tufts and Holliday, 1959) and for school-aged ones as well (Sommers *et al.*, 1959; Sommers, 1962; Sommers *et al.*, 1964). The evidence on school age children was based upon three related experiments in which intensive training was provided to parents of children having articulatory problems during a period in which their children received daily speech therapy. In all three studies, the children whose mothers were trained to assist in correction made significantly greater improvements. The first study in this series demonstrated that this held more for certain types of speech errors than for others; the second study demonstrated that this was the case regardless of the intelligence of the children and generally irrespective of whether or not they received individual or group therapy; and findings from the third study revealed that this was true regardless of the attitudes of the mothers trained concerning child rearing practices. All three experiments were conducted during special summer programs operated by clinicians working in the schools. In each case the mothers trained and their children attended these programs daily for periods of one hour for four weeks.

A small study was conducted to determine the efficacy of training mothers of articulatory defective school children during the course of a regular school year (Sommers, 1960). This study will be described in a general way, since its procedures and findings appear generally applicable to many school therapy programs. The purpose of the study was to determine the effects of minimal amounts of parent training upon improvements in articulation of second and third grade school children who were waiting for inclusion into speech therapy classes. Six clinicians randomly selected forty-eight of such children to serve as subjects because they met the two criteria of evidencing mild degrees of misarticulation and showing good stimulability scores on the Carter and Buck Prognostic Speech Test (1958). All forty-eight subjects were found to have inconsistent misarticulations and moderate to high prognostic scores. Sixteen of this number were randomly selected to serve as controls and receive no therapy; sixteen were randomly selected to be entered into group articulation therapy; and sixteen were selected so that their treatment consisted of having their mothers trained to assist in therapy. The sixteen subjects in the latter group were not enrolled in speech therapy classes. All subjects were found to have IQ's within normal ranges and have normal hearing.

The experiment was conducted over a three-month period. Comparisons were based upon prearticulation and postarticulation testing for all three groups. An analysis of variance of articulation-difference scores, based upon methods, subjects, and trials revealed that the children who received group therapy and those whose mothers were trained achieved significantly greater improvements in articulation than did the control group subjects. Further analyses revealed that there was not significant difference in the amount of improvement made by subjects who received therapy compared with those whose mothers received a minimal amount of training by clinicians.

In view of the findings of this small study it might be worth-while to examine the extent to which these sixteen mothers were trained by the six clinicians and how this was accomplished in the schools. These trained mothers were seen individually for thirty-minute periods twice monthly, and a maximum of six training sessions was provided for each.

On the occasion of the first visit, each mother who was trained was acquainted with her child's articulation errors. This was accomplished by having the child present and administering portions of articulation tests. Clinicians emphasized the fact that each child was able to correct a portion of his misarticulations, and every effort was expended to show mothers that children could possibly be helped at home. All positive aspects of each child's speech problem were presented to mothers in order to develop enthusiasm for the task at hand. At this point, mothers were encouraged to ask questions, and brief discussions concerning specific types of speech activities which could be accomplished at home were commonly conducted. Clinicians demonstrated a few simple placement and/or carry-over exercises which mothers could use at home with their children. Each mother received an appointment to return in approximately two weeks for the second visit.

All subsequent training sessions followed the pattern of providing encouragement to mothers in their efforts to work with their children at home, answering specific questions about ways of using techniques, and showing mothers additional techniques designed to advance the child closer to the goal of fully corrected articulation. If a child had more than one defective sound, the speech clinician selected a sound for the mother to work on and advanced to another sound if correction was achieved. It should be emphasized that mothers did not receive detailed explanations of causes of articulation problems, nor were they provided with details of speech disorders per se. All training was brief and tailored to a particular child's speech needs.

This study provides experimental evidence of the effectiveness of trained mothers as clinicians. Children in second and third grades with mild articulation problems may be helped to improve if school clinicians supply their mothers with a minimal amount of training. The average mother in the present study received only two hours instruction over a twelve-week period.

Because of the small number of subjects used by these investigators and other limiting factors, these results must be considered as suggestive rather than conclusive evidence to show that this type of training of mothers is effective in achieving correction of some types of misarticulations.

Additional ways of getting parents involved in assisting in the correction of their children's articulatory errors have been explored by speech clinicians. One clinician reasoned that the degree of regression or the lack of further improvement in children receiving therapy via an intensive scheduling plan could be overcome by training parents to assist the clinician. She was able to secure the cooperation of more than thirty mothers of children in her program. These mothers attended bimonthly individual or group training sessions conducted by the clinician during the period in which she was seeing their children three or more times weekly. Mothers were informed about the plan of services and specifically were requested to "take over" during the period in which no therapy from the clinician was available (six-week periods of therapy and six-week periods of no therapy). Reports from the clinician were encouraging, although no research data were gathered to determine the measured effectiveness of this type of procedure.

Less direct methods have been employed by some clinicians. Classes for parents have been conducted late in the school day, either weekly or bimonthly. A discussion of normal speech and language development often constituted the first topic presented by the clinician. Sessions were initially lecture-discussion and gradually evolved into discussions only. A major aim of such classes was to establish standards of normalcy in the minds of parents for many aspects of human development. Concurrently, discussions of child-rearing practices and related topics of good mental hygiene were included as the desires of the group dictated. Invariably, questions and discussions also centered around the correction of some of their children's speech errors. The permissive and indirect nature of this type of parent training program did not allow for demonstrations of therapy techniques or stressing of the mechanics of speech correction. Although research information has been gathered to explore the efficacy of this type of training program in the schools, an early study by Wood (1946) demonstrated that children of mothers of articulatory defective children in a clinical setting who received periods of nondirect group therapy improved significantly in articulation compared to children of similar mothers who did not receive this treatment.

It is conceivable that trained parents may prove helpful in more than one stage of articulation therapy. Most often, authoritative opinion has suggested that parents can be useful in the carryover stages (Powers, 1957). Logically, it follows that parents aware of a child's new skills can remind him to use them, provide opportunities for him to do so, and reward him for this by praise or otherwise. No special skills are required on the parent's part and intensive training of the parent may not be indicated. In many instances, a few nonpressuring techniques used by parents may assist dramatically in helping the child to establish the correct speech pattern. Because gaining carry-over of new speech patterns constitutes one, if not the most important, problem for many clinicians, the use of parents to assist and set the stage for carry-over would appear to be most timely at this point in therapy.

This is not to imply that the parent cannot or should not assist in the production stages; research findings to date point to the fact that this may be an effective procedure and an important part of the therapy paradigm. This appears to require a more systematic and more frequent contact between the clinician and the parent. In some cases it may be most effective to let the clinician teach the correct sound in isolation and work concomitantly to improve the child's auditory perceptual skills and abilities prior to the introduction of the parent on the therapy scene. Once the frequently most difficult part of the therapy is completed, the parent can be used well to assist in the development and nurturing of the newly learned sound.

It is also conceivable that parents can be trained by speech clinicians working in schools to assist in improving the speech of children having other problems besides articulation errors. Although, with the exception of articulatory defects, research is lacking to support the notion, it is possible that trained parents may prove of real value in the improvement of all types of speech and language disorders. If studied carefully, we might uncover evidence to show that the frequency or duration or both of contacts with parents tends to be greater for nonarticulatory disorders. The fourth-grade child with the hoarse voice, for example, may be referred to his parents by the clinician for a laryngoscopic examination. The diagnosis of vocal nodules is confirmed by the examining physician who also recommends speech therapy and indicates that vocal abuse is responsible for the condition. The clinician, armed with information about the child's pitch level, his breathing, his oral resonance, his articulation, and a study of his vocal habits at school, asks the parents to come to school for a conference. A therapy plan is presented by the clinician who explains that daily practice is a "must" if results are to be forthcoming. The clinician demonstrates how to work to expand the vocal range by using a piano and lets the parent work with his child doing this exercise under his supervision during this session. The parent is instructed to do *this* and *only this* for two weeks and asked to do it daily for five to ten minutes. He is given an appointment to return to see the clinician in two weeks to review the problem and help further with the voice improvement program.

Training the parents of nonfluent or stuttering children may take a different form but it has essentially the same purposes, i.e. setting the stage for the extinction of poor speaking habits, finding desirable ways of rewarding good speech performances, and generally seeking valuable ways of fostering good speaking situations. Parents may be "trained" differently in that, depending upon the nature of the stuttering behavior and other factors, their specific activities and role may vary more than in other speech disorders. Training may, for example, consist of rather frequent meetings to study together written evidence that the parent has helped to gather showing the variance of nonfluent speech as a function of time of day, events in the home, television shows, interruptions by siblings, and other factors. Training may be based almost singularly upon the development of insights concerning the relevance of these environmental factors upon the child's difficulties. On the other hand, the transitional stutterer or advanced stutterer's parents may be asked to get involved in any number of relatively simple yet promising techniques. It goes without saying, of course, that experienced clinicians study each child and his parent carefully before allowing the parents to embark upon a program of direct activities for a particular child, and it is probably true that this type of parental assistance may be contraindicated in many stuttering problems.

There does not appear to be any obvious reason why parents of children with cleft palate or cerebral palsy cannot be "trained" to assist with the therapy for their children when these children are enrolled in the schools. Because of the difficulties often inherent in improving the speech of such children, parents need understanding concerning the goals of therapy so that frustration and disappointments do not work adversely upon them or the child. However, the clinician can select the most promising areas of endeavor and seek the parents' assistance, perhaps particularly in carry-over of new speech patterns. Similarly, children demonstrating language disorders who are scheduled by the speech clinician seem to require frequent reinforcement and some degree of over-learning in order to improve. The parent trained to understand and assist can serve well to strengthen auditory-visual associations, learn how to develop better listening skills, increase visual or auditory sequencing abilities, and other similar tasks. This may be accomplished efficiently by simple explanations, accompanied by a brief but lucid demonstration, and followed by a question-answer period. Again, the clinician might establish classes for parents of children with delayed speech problems or other types of language learning difficulties, perhaps in conjunction with other specialized school personnel, e.g. the director of instruction, the elementary supervisor, a teacher of remedial reading, or a school psychologist. The degree of overlapping and the common denominators in speech and language problems appear to militate for further inclusion and the spread of influence of the clinician into this area of professional work.

SUMMARY

It has been suggested that flexibility is the earmark of the successful therapy program. The implementation of many desirable features into the therapy program within the schools would appear to depend upon the clinician's establishment and maintenance of a climate of change towards betterment. Further, it has been suggested that there are a variety of unique opportunities for providing a clinical service such as speech correction within a school system. The utilization of key school personnel such as the classroom teacher and building principal should operate to enhance both the effectiveness of the service and its acceptance as a valuable part of school services to children. Perhaps a criterion for success in this environment is the degree to which the clinician is able to mold speech correction into the total school program.

Similarly, it was suggested that clinicians in schools may be able to develop some procedures and methods for acquainting parents with the program and of training some of them to assist in therapy at appropriate times and thus gain some of the advantages of clinicians working in settings where parents refer their children for therapy. Hopefully, university and college training centers will expand opportunities for clinicians in training to gain the skills and the assurances which they need in order to manage this most important part of clinical functioning.

Although few specific therapy techniques were described in this chapter, the author did choose to speak in some detail about some ways of conducting group articulation therapy. The need for more elaboration and carefully defined procedures for the effective administration of therapy within groups cannot be over emphasized, since almost all beginning clinicians lack both an understanding of the dynamics of group therapy and knowledge concerning the way to meet individual needs within a group.

Finally, the carry-over problem was cited and some evidence was presented to indicate that this problem may well be the singularly most troublesome one for speech clinicians. Some suggested reasons for its existence and its extinction were also presented with the knowledge that other factors, probably more significant, may be operating to defeat the efforts of the clinician in gaining full and final correction of speech problems.

DISCUSSION TOPICS

1. What are some additional ways in which, typically speaking, speech therapy in the schools differs from speech therapy in clinics, hospitals, or other settings? What are the implications of these additional differences?

2. What principles should serve to guide the speech clinician in the schools as he refers children to other agencies for evaluations?

3. What roles should the school nurse and school doctor play in the speech therapy program?

4. Assuming that an elementary teacher has a legitimate speech defect and two children from her class are enrolled for therapy for similar speech problems, what procedures would you recommend to the speech clinician for dealing with the situation, e.g. treat the children and forget the teacher, suggest therapy for the teacher simultaneously, or what?

5. What are some effective procedures for explaining the therapy program to different groups of people, e.g. teachers, administrators, service clubs in the community, P.T.A. groups?
6. What principles should guide the clinician in his discussions with classroom teachers and other school personnel concerning children enrolled for therapy?
7. What evidence do we have that speech therapy in the schools is effective in correcting a significant portion of those enrolled?
8. Describe some additional ways in which a number of speech clinicians working in the schools on the same staff can improve their technical skills.
9. Outline an experiment which might be conducted in the schools for the purpose of determining the efficacy of two or more methods of obtaining carry-over of newly learned speech patterns.
10. What other factors would appear essential in the development of both efficient and effective group articulation therapy?

REFERENCES

1. ANDERSON, M.: Voice therapy pilot project. Hinsdale Public Schools, Illinois Speech and Hearing Association, *Newsletter, V:*4-6, 1965.
2. BARKER, J. O.: Numerical measure of articulation. *J Speech Hearing Dis,* 25:79-88, February, 1961.
3. BINGHAM, D. S.; VAN HATTUM, R. J.; FAULK, M. E., and TAUSSIG, E.: Public school speech and hearing services, IV. Program organization and management. *J Speech Hearing Dis, Monogr Suppl, 8:*33-50, June, 1961.
4. BYRNE, M. C.: *Development and Evaluation of a Speech Improvement Program for Kindergarten and First Grade Children.* Cooperative Research Project No. 620, U.S. Dep HEW, August, 1962.
5. CARTER, E. T., and BUCK, M. W.: Prognostic testing for functional articulation disorders among children in the first grade. *J Speech Hearing Dis, 23:*124-133, May, 1958.
6. CHAPMAN, M. E.; HERBERT, E. L.; AVERY, C. B., and SELMAR, J. W.: Public school speech and hearing services, V, Clinical practice: Remedial procedures. *J Speech Hearing Dis, Mongr Suppl, 8:*58-78, June, 1961.
7. EGBERT, J. H.: The Effect of Certain Home Influences on the Progress of Children in a Speech Therapy Program." Ph.D. dissertation, Stanford University, California, 1957.

8. JORDAN, E. P.: Articulation test measures and listener ratings of articulation defectiveness. *J Speech Hearing Res, 3:*303-319, November, 1960.

9. LILLYWHITE, H.: Make mother a clinician. *J Speech Hearing Dis, 13:* 61-66, February, 1948.

10. McDONALD, E. T.: *Articulation Testing and Treatment: A Sensory Motor Approach.* Pittsburgh, Stanwix House, 1964.

11. McDONALD, E. T., and FRICK, J.: Some factors which influence the frequency and duration of treatment sessions. *J Speech Hearing Dis, 22:* 724-728, December, 1957.

12. PFEIFER, R. C.: An Experimental Analysis of Individual and Group Speech Therapy with Educable Institutionalized Mentally Retarded Children. Ed.D. dissertation, Boston University, Massachusetts, 1958.

13. POWERS, M. H.: Clinical and educational procedures in functional disorders of articulation. In *Handbook of Speech Pathology,* L. Travis, Ed. New York, Appleton, 1957.

14. SHEA, W. L.: The Effect of Supplemental Parental Procedures on Public School Articulatory Cases. Ph.D. dissertation, University of Florida, Gainesville, 1955.

15. SOKOLOFF, M. A.: A Comparison of Gains in Communicative Skills, Resulting from Group Play Therapy and Individual Speech Therapy, among a Group of Non-Severly Dysarthric, Speech Handicapped Cerebral Palsied Children. Ph.D. dissertation, New York University, New York, 1959.

16. SOMMERS, R. K., *et al.*: Training parents of children with functional misarticulation. *J Speech Hearing Res, 3:*258-265, September, 1959.

17. SOMMERS, R. K.: Areas of Difficulty in Speech Correction. Unpublished study, 1960.

18. SOMMERS, R. K.: Factors in the effectiveness of mothers trained to aid in speech correction. *J Speech Hearing Dis, 27:*178-186, May, 1962.

19. SOMMERS, R. K., *et al.*: Effects of maternal attitudes upon improvement in articulation when mothers are trained to assist in speech correction. *J Speech Hearing Dis, 29:*126-133, May, 1964.

20. SOMMERS, R. K., *et al.*: Factors in the effectiveness of group and individual articulation therapy. *J Speech Hearing Res, 9:*144-152, May, 1966.

21. SOMMERS, R. K.: The Effectiveness of Mothers in the Correction of Articulatory Problems of Children on School Waiting Lists. Unpublished study, 1960.

22. TUFTS, L. C. and HOLLIDAY, A. R.: Effectiveness of trained parents as speech therapists. *J Speech Hearing Dis, 24:*395-401, November, 1959.

23. VAN HATTUM, R. J.: The Effectiveness of Clinicians in Schools as Related to the Use of Games as Therapy. Paper presented to the American Speech and Hearing Association, 1959.

24. Van Hattum, R. J.: Personal communication, 1964.
25. Weaver, J., and Wollersheim, J.: A comparison of the block system and the intermittent system of scheduling speech classes in the public schools. *ASHA, 6:*392, October, 1964.
26. Wilson, K. D.: Children with vocal nodules. *J Speech Hearing Dis, 26:* 19-26, February, 1961.
27. Wood, K. S.: Parental maladjustment and functional articulatory defects in children. *J Speech Hearing Dis, 11:*255-275, August, 1946.

Chapter 11

REPORTING: IN THE SCHOOLS, TO THE COMMUNITY

LEE I. FISHER

RECORDS AND REPORTS

Records and reports play a significant role in public school speech and hearing programs. As specialists in communication, we must communicate with others, keep others informed, and prepare descriptive records of our work. One should have a good perspective of the need to develop and use efficient and effective records and reports. A healthy attitude for fulfilling this responsibility is essential for quality records and reports. Clinicians should accept the challenge of this task with enthusiasm and a desire to do a professional job of record keeping and reporting.

> Keeping adequate records and making effective reports are thus basic and extremely important responsibilities of the speech clinician. The systematic recording of selected basic information about each child with a diagnosed speech or hearing problem facilitates the development of a meaningful sequence of services for the child regardless of the time involved or the number of people who are involved in the provision of those services. Reporting activities of the clinician can aid in providing optimal conditions for a child's growth in speech, language, or listening skills by affecting changes in the attitudes of school personnel, parents, and others in his environment. Record keeping and reporting are also essential to program development and justification.*

Definition

Records and reports are written accounts of the speech clinician's work in the schools. They are a means of communication which provide for dissemination and preservation of important information between a clinician and anyone who may be con-

---

*Iowa Committee for the Development of Speech and Hearing Record and Report Forms to be Recommended for Use in Public School Programs. *Basic Records and Reports For Public School Speech and Hearing Programs.* Des Moines, Iowa, Department of Public Instruction, p. x, 1963.

cerned with various aspects of the clinician's services. Written reports are records which may be kept for various reasons and for various periods of time.

The definition of a record may be considered to be a detailed discussion of diagnosis, therapy, or any other related factor that is pertinent to the problem or service that has been provided. The characteristics of good records are as follows: They should be brief, clear, descriptive, and easy to prepare. All of the information should be germane to the purpose of the record or report. The information should not be unnecessarily duplicated on other forms. They should not be so complicated that information becomes "buried" in them. The basic set of records and reports should be designed so as to permit one to review all of the varied aspects of a particular case in a short period of time.

Purposes

Records and reports serve many purposes if they are designed properly and prepared carefully. The primary purpose for preparing reports is to inform, while the primary purpose for keeping records is to preserve an account of the clinician's services which may serve as a reference for the future.

Some records and reports may be designed for a single purpose, while others need to be designed for multipurpose use. Records and reports may serve many different purposes. Some of these purposes are 1) to inform with language which is understandable to the reader, 2) to describe, to explain, and to provide details regarding diagnostic testing, attitudes, progress in therapy, and interrelationships, 3) to coordinate a child's speech therapy with the child's school work, 4) to caution if cautions need to be made, 5) to seek cooperation, 6) to offer general suggestions, and 7) to offer specific recommendations for future management.

Significance of Continuity

A coordinated set of records and reports is an asset to the provision of continuity of service. It is important to keep an accurate and cumulative account of each child's problem and the changes he makes regardless of whether one or more clinicians are involved in providing service to the child. Problems change as therapy continues from week to week and month to month, and thus it is important to have a continuous record of each changing problem.

Clinicians working in the schools work with many children. As such, it is sometimes difficult to remember some of the specific details of each child's problem. Unless good records are kept, these details are easily forgotten or confused. Effective records and reports serve as the primary tool of continuity of service to a given child. Consider the fact that a child makes long-range changes as a result of therapy in addition to changes which occur from week to week. The continuity which records and reports provide takes on greater significance as each child continues to change and improve. This continuity takes on even greater significance when either a child or the clinician moves, because the child's records then become the primary source of information about his problem. This continuity is extremely important as this occurs with increasing frequency.

A clinician entering the public schools for the first time or one who moves to a new position is indeed fortunate if a coordinated set of records and reports is available. A uniform record and report keeping system has merit when one considers that such a system can be easily interpreted by various clinicians.

A Study of Records and Reports

In 1961 this writer envisioned a nationwide need for the development of a "basic set" of coordinated speech and hearing records and reports to promote continuity of services and to provide for the sharing of essential information with administrators, parents, teachers, and others for clinicians employed in public schools.

A total of 107 Iowa clinicians in public school speech and hearing programs were invited to submit currently used forms. Ninety-three specialists (87.8%) submitted 708 different forms which were classified into 98 different categories.

A representative eight-member state committee was organized with the advisement, cooperation, and participation of the Iowa Department of Public Instruction State Consultants for Speech

Therapy and Hearing Conservation Services. The committee was charged to identify the essential records and reports, to study the problem of developing a basic set of forms, to design sample forms, to conduct a survey of the proposed forms, to correlate the evaluations, and to construct record and report forms for use in public school speech and hearing programs.

The committee studied the data and identified the basic purposes for which records and reports need to be kept. Proposed form titles, descriptions, and purposes were identified in a questionnaire of proposed speech and hearing record and report forms. A total of 107 specialists rated this questionnaire on a five-point scale and commented on the proposals.

As the forms were designed, items were selected and formats were constructed, based on the seven hundred and eight forms submitted, the purposes identified by the committee, and the ratings and comments on the questionnaire.

The Iowa committee (1963) designed nineteen coordinated record and report forms and arranged for their availability to all Iowa public school speech and hearing personnel. A description of the entire project, which included illustrations of the forms, was published in a manual by the Iowa State Department of Public Instruction, Division of Special Education. The committee spent three years developing the material contained in this manual. The forms which have been developed illustrate a major concentrated effort in developing records and reports for use in the public schools.

The Need for a Core of Information

It is necessary to have a core of information for each child who receives therapy. Certain basic information is essential to the effective management of every child in the speech and hearing program. In fact, one cannot provide meaningful services to speech handicapped school children without this basic core of information.

Clearly, considerable thought needs to be given to the contents of this basic core of information. One might begin this thinking by asking what kind of information is needed to provide therapy to a child? Indeed, it is quite important to give some thought to this question before therapy is initiated. The basic core of information contains items of importance about the child with a speech problem and items about the speech problem itself. Many of the items contained in these two aspects are interrelated and are frequently inseparable. Any information which has a direct bearing on a child's speech problem should be recorded.

The information contained in this core of information needs to be written down rather than left to memory and should be recorded in one record which is easily accessible so that additional information can be added or placed in the folder. As such, the record becomes a cumulative, continuous account of a child's problem. If core information is not contained in one central location, it becomes difficult to manage a child's problem as the pertinent facts of the problem may not be readily accessible.

The Cumulative Speech and Hearing Record

The Iowa committee on records and reports for the public schools gave considerable thought to what should be included in this core of information. After considerable discussion, the committee developed a Cumulative Speech and Hearing Record, which contains a minimum core of information that is felt to be necessary in the management of a child's speech problem. This record is composed of five major areas: Speech and Hearing, Behavioral, Environmental, Physiological—Development, and Educational. The information which is accumulated in completing these five major areas is of primary importance to the establishment of meaningful and significant service to the child. It is important to obtain the information which is outlined in each of these five areas for each child who is scheduled for therapy. The significant factor about the items contained in this record is that they are factors which contribute vital details about the child and the child's specific problem.

As designed, the most essential items are contained in the boxed sections. These sections should be completed for every child who is regularly scheduled for therapy. Additional information should be collected and recorded as needed. The purposes of this form

Name (Ink) ______ Last ______ First ______ Middle ______ Sex ______ School ______ (Pencil) Address ______ (Pencil) Phone ______ (Pencil) Pupil No. ______

CUMULATIVE SPEECH AND HEARING RECORD

Birthdate ______ month ______ day ______ year ______ Form Initiated by ______ Name ______ Title ______ Date Original Diagnosis ______ Completion Date Initial History ______

INSTRUCTIONS FOR ENTRY: Enter information in boxed sections for every child regularly scheduled. Collect and record additional information in each area as needed.

SPEECH AND HEARING — INITIAL HISTORY — ENVIRONMENTAL

Problem ______

Date of Original Examination ______ Examiner ______ Title ______

Previous Speech or Hearing Evaluations ______

Problem First Noticed ______ Action Taken ______

Language Readiness ______ Auditory and pre-speech behavior

Meaningful Language Usage ______ Age - first word, ______ two & three word combinations, ______ sentences

Amount of Verbalization ______

Examination Results

AUDIOLOGIC: ______

ARTICULATION: ______

CONVERSATIONAL SPEECH: ______

FLUENCY: ______

VERBAL OUTPUT: ______

ABILITY TO COMMUNICATE: ______

VOICE: ______ Pitch, quality, rate, loudness

Peripheral Speech Mechanism Deviations ______

Father or Guardian ______ Age ______ Occupation ______ Education

Mother ______ Age ______ Occupation ______ Education

Brother(s) ______ Age(s) ______ Sister(s) ______ Age(s)

Influence of Other Individuals Living in the Home ______

Influence of Paternal and Maternal Relatives ______

Marital Status of Parents ______ Separated, divorced, dissension

Family Problems ______ Speech problems, deafness, alcoholism, mental health, etc.

Siblings ______ Interaction, parental preference, total family relationships

Methods of Discipline Used ______ Parental agreement on method

Socio-Economic Status ______ Size of house, ownership, play space, neighborhood, church membership, leisure time activities, etc.

PHYSIOLOGICAL - DEVELOPMENT

Physical Anomalies ______ Mouth, ears, nose, eyes, teeth, etc.

Chronic or Acute Conditions ______ Discharging ears, head noises, earache, mouth breathing

Neuromuscular Condition ______ Coordination

Age (months) at: first tooth ______, sitting ______, standing ______, walking ______, feeding self ______, dressing self ______, bowel control ______, bladder control ______.

Pregnancy ______ Duration and mother's health

Birth ______ Normal, instrumental, premature, etc.

Feeding ______ Breast, bottle, problems, etc.

Diseases: Age ______ Injuries: Age ______ Operations: Age ______

Sequale ______

Health Habits ______ Diet, exercise, sleep, etc.

Physical and Dental Examinations

Date	Doctor's Name	Address	Findings	Recommendations

FIGURE 18. Cumulative speech and hearing record.

EDUCATIONAL

Language Arts _____ Strengths and weaknesses _____

Attendance Record _____ Reason(s) for Frequent Absences _____

Test Results

Date Administered	Grade Level	Tests of Mental Ability	C. A.	Verbal M. A.	Non-Verbal M. A.	M. A.	IQ	Grade Place

Date Administered	Grade Level	Tests of Achievement, Aptitude, Interest, etc.	Form	Findings

Age at entering School _____ Level at which entered (preschool, kindergarten, etc.) _____

Grades Repeated _____ Reason(s) _____

Likes _____ Dislikes _____

Most Difficult Subject(s) _____

Least Difficult Subject(s) _____

Teacher(s) Evaluation of Progress _____

Extra-curricular Activities _____

Work Experience _____ Outside School _____

Post-High School Plans _____ Complete for students in grade 9 or above

BEHAVIORAL

Pupil Attitude Toward Problem _____

Parent Attitude Toward Problem _____

Social Behavior _____ Peers (classroom, playground) siblings, adults _____

Teacher Description of Behavior _____

Observations of Behavior _____ Observations made by _____

Fears _____

Withdrawal _____

Habits _____ Thumbsucking, etc. _____

Tantrums _____

Attention Span _____

Distractibility _____

Perseveration _____

Awareness of Environment _____

Consistency of Behavior Pattern _____

Psychologist Interpretation _____

Personality and Projective Tests	Date and Examiner	Results

are to provide a method of organizing data prior to scheduling a child for service, to provide a record of service, to provide guidelines to insure continuity of service to the child, and to provide a file in which to place other individual records and reports. All of the items may not need to be completed for every child who receives therapy; however, if all items are not completed, the items are structured so as to make the clinician wonder if the uncompleted items are of importance. This concept implies that the items contained in this core of information suggest the type of information which should be obtained for each child who receives therapy. Furthermore, this concept implies that the information which is obtained on each child tends to outline and predict the type of service a child will receive as a result of this background of information.

As designed, the Cumulative Speech and Hearing Record is printed on the inside of a standard-sized heavy manila folder (see Fig. 18). In addition to the five major areas included on the inside of the folder a service record is included on the outside of the folder. This service record is designed to show the dates when the child has received therapy and a note regarding the disposition of his problem at the end of each period of therapy.

This folder has been designed with recognition of its limitations for accumulating case history information of a unique nature. This record is planned so that only brief notations are entered in the cumulative record itself. These entries are meant to be supported by more detailed records and reports which are inserted into the folder. For example, for many public school children with a functional speech problem a brief notation regarding the child's attitudes towards the problem may be sufficient and could be noted on the cumulative record. However, this particular item may be of greater importance for a child with a more severe problem. In this event a summary notation should be made on the folder which refers to a detailed account of a child's attitudes towards his problem. The detailed account should be filed in the folder so that it is readily available whenever a review of the problem is desired.

Specific diagnostic articulation and other diagnostic examination forms are not included as a part of the format of this cumulative record. These diagnostic formats were omitted, as there are so many different diagnostic tests in use today and many new evaluation techniques are yet to be revealed. Therefore, only brief notations should be made on the folder regarding the results of the diagnostic tests, and the completed diagnostic forms should be inserted into the folder.

The case history as elaborated in Chapter Two of *Diagnostic Methods in Speech Pathology* (Johnson, 1963) is another systematic example of a major attempt to gather information which is pertinent and necessary to have in working with speech handicapped school children. There are many excellent suggestions for obtaining and recording case history information in this reference.

It is doubtful that one could develop a satisfactory checklist which would contain all of the basic core of information because the term "core of information" implies that certain items must be described in detail. A written account is the only way that certain contributing factors can be included in an effective record. Another reason why an adequate checklist form for the basic core of information would be difficult to design is that some items would be omitted, as many questions cannot accurately be answered with Yes, No, or a check mark in a small box.

Terminology

The school speech clinician prepares records and reports for school administrators, teachers, parents, and for the clinician's own use. The clinician may also prepare records and reports for special education personnel, psychologists, guidance counsellors, nurses, physicians, dentists, specialists, and other professionals.

It is important to consider for whom a report is being prepared, as this factor gives the clinician an indication of the type of professional language that should be used in preparing the report. For example, it may be desirable to use different professional terminology in describing a voice problem to a physician than it would be to describe the same problem to the child's teacher. Likewise, consider the difference in describing a child's progress in therapy to the child's teacher and to his parents. Classroom teachers are generally better informed than parents with regard to professional terminology.

Written reports should be reviewed by the clinician before they are distributed. During this review the clinician should consider the appropriateness of the language and terminology in each report. This suggestion is particularly important for the beginning clinician, as it is sometimes difficult to describe a child's speech problem accurately without using a great deal of professional terminology to which the clinician became accustomed during his training. This suggestion is also important as one continues to work in the public schools and becomes better acquainted with the teachers, school administrators, and parents. The language and terminology used to describe a problem to one administrator, teacher, or parent may differ from that of another administrator, teacher, or parent.

Types of Records and Reports Which are Needed

One might think that it is a simple matter to determine the types of records and reports that are really needed. Unfortunately, too many clinicians in the schools have not given this topic sufficient thought, and thus, only the most obvious records and reports are designed and used. It is not practical to begin listing titles to various records and reports that might be needed, because these titles may be misleading and may not accomplish the desired communication.

To determine the specific types of records and reports which are needed, it is important to identify all of the major and minor tasks in the entire program. This can be done by preparing an outline of all of the responsibilities of the clinician in the schools. Keep in mind that this particular occupational setting creates a need for unique types of records and reports. Preparing a detailed outline of all of the responsibilities of the speech clinician in the schools is not easy and cannot be accomplished in a few minutes. As this outline is being prepared, it will be obvious that many of the responsibilities point out the need for various types of records and reports. After the outline is completed, select all of the tasks which indicate the need for any kind of record or report. You can then proceed to design a coordinated set of records and reports.

This procedure was followed by the Iowa committee on records and reports for the public schools during the development of a coordinated set of records and reports. The minimum tasks of program management were listed in the areas of organization of the program, examination and diagnosis, education, and professional, public, and lay organization relations (Iowa committee, 1963). If this outline is used, it may be necessary to add other tasks which are unique to a given situation. As a result of following such a procedure, the need for various types of records and reports is obvious. The following list contains some specific types of records and reports which have been identified by this procedure.

For Administrators
  Conference guide
  Referral form
  Evaluation roster
  Master schedule
  Statistical summary
  Daily therapy schedule
  Progress report
  End-of-the-year disposition report
  End-of-the-year narrative report

For Parent
  Evaluation report
  Therapy schedule letter
  Progress report
  Medical referral

For Clinician
  Registration card
  Cumulative speech and hearing record
  Anecdotal record
  Conference record
  Expense record
  Release of information
  Itinerary

For Teacher
  Referral form
  Evaluation report
  Evaluation roster
  Therapy schedule
  Progress report

The cumulative Speech and Hearing Record that was designed as a result of this procedure by the Iowa committee has already been illustrated. Some of the other coordinated records and reports that have been designed by this committee follow. Additional forms which have been developed by the Iowa committee (1963) can be viewed in the manual *Basic Records and Reports for Public School Speech and Hearing Programs*. Additional copies of these forms may be obtained from the Klipto Printing Company, Mason City, Iowa.

SPECIAL EDUCATION UNIT
Printed Here

SPEECH OR HEARING REFERRAL

REFERRAL

Name of Child _____ Grade _____
                last   first

Date of Referral _____ School _____ Room No. _____

Reason (s) for Referral _____

_____

_____

_____

_____

_____

Referred by _____
                signature   title

EVALUATION

Name of Child _____ Grade _____
                last   first

Date of Evaluation _____ School _____ Room No._____

Referred by _____ Date of Referral _____

Reason (s) for Referral _____

_____

Findings _____

_____

_____

_____

Disposition _____

Evaluated by _____
                signature   title

FIGURE 19. SPEECH OR HEARING REFERRAL

PURPOSES: To provide a means by which school personnel and others can refer a child for a speech or hearing examination and evaluation.

To provide a means of securing information about the referral from the referral source.

To inform the referrant of the results of the speech or hearing examination and evaluation.

To be used as a means of interprofessional referral.

ENTRIES: When the evaluation is made, the form is folded on the dotted line and a carbon is inserted. When completed, the bottom section is detached and sent to referrant.

USES: This form should be readily available to school administrators, teachers, parents, and other professional colleagues.

The referral section should be completed by the referrant and sent through proper channels.

A carbon of the evaluation should be sent to the referrant by the evaluator through proper channels.

One copy should be retained by the clinician for future reference.

School_____

Specialist_____

SPECIAL EDUCATION UNIT
Printed Here

Teacher_____

Grade _____ Room No. _____

SPEECH OR HEARING EVALUATION ROSTER

_____ Speech _____ Hearing   Screening Date _____Diagnostic Test Date _____

Name of Child		Screening Results		Diagnostic Test Results				
last	first	Adequate	Retest	Adequate	Referral	Service	Other	Remark
Totals		___	___	___	___	___	___	

FIGURE 20. SPEECH OR HEARING EVALUATION ROSTER

PURPOSES: To provide the clinician with a means of reporting information to the school administrator (s) or interested personnel following a speech or hearing evaluation survey.

To provide the clinician with a means of keeping a record for the administration of subsequent evaluations for those children in need of further evaluation.

To provide the clinician with a record necessary for gathering recapitulation statistics for the identification phase of his special education program.

ENTRIES: The clinician may request the school administrator (s) to have the following items completed prior to the use of the form. The items which should be completed are the school, teacher, grade, room number, and alphabetical listing of the children in each class to be evaluated.

At the time of the screening evaluation, the clinician completes the screening data area and places a check mark in the appropriate screening column following the name of the each child evaluated. Names of children who are absent should be recorded appropriately.

Totals for the first three columns may be tallied following screening.
At the time of retesting, the evaluator makes use of the last four columns, making a check mark or comment in the appropriate column.

Following retesting for each classroom, totals for the last four columns may be tallied.

USES: When made in duplicate or triplicate following screening, a copy may be left with the school administrator (s) and/or teacher (s) as a partial report.

The copy (ies) are collected at the time of retesting and appropriate entries made. They are left with the school personnel as a permanent record of findings following the identification phase of the program.

Information concerning the children discovered should be readily available to special education personnel to help in the planning of meaningful special education services.

A copy of each completed roster should be kept as a permanent record in the clinician's files. These forms may be used for gathering statistics, providing continuity of service, and providing information with respect to children in need of reevaluation.

SPECIAL EDUCATION UNIT
Printed Here

Date_____

Dear Parent (s) or Guardian:

Your child, _____, has received a speech evaluation at school. At this time your child's speech is considered to be:

☐ adequate.

☐ in need of reevaluation at a later date.

☐ in need of speech services.

Your child is enrolled for speech class at _____

_____ on _____

and _____ from _____

to _____. This service is a part of your school's educational program provided at no extra cost to you.

I may contact you at a later date for a conference appointment. At that time we will discuss your child's speech and how your child may be helped at home.

Feel welcome to attend speech class on any day when your child is scheduled to receive therapy. Please contact me if you have any questions regarding your child's speech. I shall appreciate your cooperation.

Sincerely,

FIGURE 21. REPORT OF SPEECH EVALUATION TO PARENTS

PURPOSES: To report a child's performance on speech screening and diagnostic tests.

To inform parents of enrollment for therapy.

To invite the parents to therapy.

ENTRIES: Self-explanatory.

USES: This form should be distributed to parents following the initial diagnostic speech testing.

When the form is used to inform parents that their child is considered to have "adequate" speech as a result of screening, the form should not be distributed until the children in need of speech services receive their form.

The completed forms may be distributed to the children to take home through the classroom teacher or they may be mailed.

SPEECH OR HEARING DAILY PROGRAM SCHEDULE

School _____ Specialist _____

Schedule to apply from _____, 19___ To _____, 19___

Day (s)	Time	Child	Grade	Room No.	Teacher

FIGURE 22. SPEECH OR HEARING DAILY PROGRAM SCHEDULE

PURPOSES: To provide a schedule of educational services offered in a particular school.

To provide scheduling information for school administrators and classroom teachers.

To provide a scheduling guide for the speech clinician.

ENTRIES: Self-explanatory.

USES: This form should be prepared each time therapy is initiated in each school.

A copy of this schedule should be distributed to the school administrator (s) and to the teachers who have children receiving therapy.

One copy should be retained for the clinician's use.

SPECIAL EDUCATION UNIT
Printed Here

OBJECTIVES AND OBSERVATIONS

School _____ Specialist _____

Name (s) _____ _____

CODE

Ultimate Objective	(UO)	Therapy Session	(T)
Intermediate Goal (s)	(IG)	Observation	(O)
Proposed Therapy	(PT)	Assignment	(A)

Dates
and
Code

FIGURE 23. OBJECTIVES AND OBSERVATIONS

PURPOSES: To record ultimate objective (s) of therapy.
To record intermediate goals attained during therapy.
To describe proposed therapy.
To record a periodic description of therapy used.
To record the behavioral changes which take place.
To record assignments given.

ENTRIES: The narrow margin on the left is designed for recording the date of the entry and the appropriate code item shown at the top of the form.

The large recording area on the right is designed to permit the clinician to write intermittent accounts for any of the above purposes.

USES: This form may be used for each individual or group session and a form may be prepared for each child receiving therapy.

All of the current objectives and observations for any particular school (s) should be kept in a notebook which is taken to therapy.

The information contained on these forms should be utilized when preparing progress reports.

Periodically these forms should be placed in the Cumulative Speech and Hearing Record for the children concerned.

SPECIAL EDUCATION UNIT
Printed Here

PROGRESS REPORT

Name of Child _____ Grade _____

School _____ Report To _____

Type of Service _____

Date of Report _____ Period Covered _____

OBJECTIVES:

OBSERVED CHANGES:

CURRENT DIAGNOSIS:

RECOMMENDATIONS:

CONTINUE SERVICE: __ Yes   __ No   __ Recheck   __ Other

_____
Specialist

FIGURE 24. PROGRESS REPORT

Purposes: To report to others regarding the objectives of therapy, observed changes during therapy, recommendations, and diagnosis.

To provide a basis for considering whether service is to be continued.

To serve as a guide for teachers between periods of service.

To serve as a guide for parents and others for summer and/or additional service.

Entries: List the specific objectives set forth at the beginning of therapy and during therapy.

List a summary of the observed changes in addition to the long-range and intermediate goals attained during the therapy period.

Describe the diagnosis of the child's problem at the termination of the therapy period reported in this report.

List the specific recommendations which should be carried out by the person receiving the report. Recommendations of a general nature or recommendations which should be carried out by someone other than the person receiving the report should be labeled as such.

Uses: This form provides a means for the systematic reporting of services and may be used as a periodic, annual, or final report. The extent of detail depends on the specific problem reported.

If the report is made to the classroom teacher, the report may be placed in the child's pupil cumulative record, and a duplicate copy should be kept in the child's Cumulative Speech and Hearing Record.

This form may be used for continuity of service and will be valuable information for new personnel.

This form may also be used for supplying information to other agencies.

STATISTICAL SUMMARY

Area Served _____

Period from _____ to _____ 19____

Total School Enrollment in Areas Served _____

	SPEECH	HEARING
Total Number of Students Evaluated	_____	_____
Number Evaluated as a Result of Previously Known Problems	_____	_____
Number Evaluated as a Result of Referral	_____	_____
Number Evaluated as a Result of Screening	_____	_____
Identify Grades Screened	_____	_____
Total Number of Students Receiving Service	_____	_____
Regularly Scheduled Service	_____	_____
Intermittently Scheduled Service	_____	_____
Indirect Service	_____	_____
Other	_____	_____
Total Number of Students on Waiting List	_____	_____
Total Number of Conferences	_____	_____
Total Number of Observations	_____	_____

Disposition of Students Receiving Service

	SPEECH	HEARING
Continue	_____	_____
Dismissed as Satisfactory	_____	_____
Dismissed for Other Reasons _____	_____	_____
Other _____	_____	_____

Distribution of Students

Receiving Speech Services	Grades 1-6	Grades 7-12	Ungraded
Articulation	_____	_____	_____
Cleft Palate	_____	_____	_____
Cerebral Palsy	_____	_____	_____
Hearing	_____	_____	_____
Stuttering	_____	_____	_____
Voice	_____	_____	_____
Other	_____	_____	_____

Summary Submitted by _____ Date _____

FIGURE 25. STATISTICAL SUMMARY

PURPOSES: To serve as a means of reporting information of a statistical nature which is pertinent to a particular school, or center, served.

To serve as a means for reporting statistical information which is pertinent to the area served.

ENTRIES: The statistical summary may pertain to all of the schools in the area served or to a particular school. Enter the appropriate statistics for speech and/or hearing services in the blanks on the right-hand side of the form.

In the "Receiving Service" section of the statistical summary, each child should only be listed once.

USES: A copy of this form will provide the school administrator with a general picture of the scope of the services offered.

The statistical summary should be prepared periodically at the discretion of the person providing the services.

A copy of this form should be posted in the schools to provide school personnel with statistical information.

A carbon copy should be filed in the clinician's files.

At the end of the year, the Statistical Summary should be used as the initial portion of the Annual Report.

SPECIAL EDUCATION UNIT
Printed Here

END OF YEAR DISPOSITION
FOR CHILDREN RECEIVING SPEECH OR HEARING SERVICE

School _____ Date _____ Specialist _____

| Name of Child | Grade | HEARING | | | SPEECH | | | | | |
		Continue	Other	Remark	Continue	Dismissed Satisfactory	Dismissed Other	Recheck	Disorder (See Code)	Remark
last first										
Totals										

Disorder Code: Hearing Handicapped (HH); Articulation (A); Cleft Palate (CL.P.); Cerebral Palsy (CP); Stuttering (S); Voice (V); Other (O).

FIGURE 26. END OF YEAR DISPOSITION FOR CHILDREN RECEIVING SPEECH AND HEARING SERVICES AND ANNUAL REPORT

PURPOSES: To provide administrators with a statistical summary of services provided during the year.

To provide administrators with an end-of-year disposition of children who received speech or hearing services throughout the year.

To provide the administrators with an annual narrative report pertaining to various aspects of the program.

ENTRIES: Statistical Summary—Prepare as previously illustrated.

End-of-Year Disposition—Entries self-explanatory.

Narrative Report—This report is designed as a current summary of the speech and hearing programs. The following areas of the program will be discussed briefly in this report: nature and purposes of the program as conducted; discussion of current and projected needs; school and community relations; evaluation of physical facilities; present and projected budgetary needs; recommendations for improving the program; and additional comments.

USES: The Annual Report, which was designed in three sections, should be prepared at the end of each school year for each school district in the area served. One copy should be sent to each school administrator concerned and a copy should be filed in the clinician's files.

A composite Annual Report consisting of the statistical summary and the narrative report should be prepared for the entire area served and should be distributed to the employing administrator and the employing board of education. A copy of this report should also be filed in the clinician's files.

Interrelationships of Records and Reports

Record and report design in program management may vary slightly from specialist to specialist, from locality to locality, and from one work setting to another, but the items found in this coordinated set of forms solicit and convey information which is considered minimal and essential to the effective provision of speech and hearing services.

Records and reports must be coordinated when they are designed. One cannot meaningfully describe the interrelationships of a set of forms unless they are coordinated as they are designed. A truly coordinated set of forms accomplishes many purposes. For example, one form might be designed specifically to inform the parents of the results of hearing screening. These results could also be recorded on a roster as a record for the clinician, teacher, and the administrator. The results may also be noted on the child's registration card if he is enrolled for therapy, and on his cumulative folder. This information is important as it is related to the child's speech problem, but if this notation is not recorded on interrelated and coordinated records and reports, then this test result may not be considered when the clinician reviews the child's record.

Taking Time

Since record keeping and reporting are two of the clinician's most important responsibilities, he should expect to spend some time and effort preparing and disseminating information. The big question is how much time should one use for record keeping and reporting? In planning the overall program the clinician should budget time to work on records and reports. When planning this budget, one should keep in mind that record keeping and reporting will take more time during the first few weeks and the last few weeks of the school year than during the intervening period of time. This is true as a great deal of diagnostic work is done at the beginning of the year, and if one is to record this information accurately, it will naturally take a considerable amount of the clinician's time. The same is true for the end of the school year when progress reports are prepared for the parents and teachers and when the end of the year reports are prepared for the school administrators and the board of education.

Even though one sets aside a given amount of time for records and reports, it is necessary to make brief notations of your activities as each day progresses. A specific amount of time, on a weekly basis, should be set aside for record keeping and reporting activities during the major part of the school year when the clinician provides therapy in the schools. The amount of time budgeted for record keeping and reporting practices may depend, in part, upon the employment setting. This responsibility is of sufficient importance to warrant setting aside work time for these activities.

Public school speech clinicians should utilize at least one half day each week for record keeping and reporting. In reality, one day each week is much better than one half day especially when one considers that this coordination time will also be utilized for other activities such as staff meetings, parent conferences, and other numerous functions. Even if one day each week is set aside for coordination purposes, the clinician will in reality not have over four to five hours or approximately only 10 per cent of his time for records and reports.

It is important to use the time which is reserved for records and reports regularly and effectively each week. As with other matters, it becomes easy to postpone the recording of some vital information and thus this valuable information is left to the memory of only one person. The clinician should not permit himself to get behind with recording and reporting as it becomes extremely difficult to catch up on these activities. Unfortunately, if one does get behind, the essential information may not be transmitted and recorded. Therefore, the clinician should accept the responsibility of record keeping and reporting as a challenge and prepare the best possible records and reports.

Secretarial Help

Preparing records and reports is very time consuming. Clinicians working in the schools really do not have as much time as it takes to prepare and type all of the many different kinds of records and reports which should be kept. Stated otherwise, clinicians need to spend the majority of their time working with children rather than typing. Consequently, every clinician should have secretarial services whenever needed. In school districts where several clinicians are employed, two or three clinicians can share the services of one secretary.

The availability of secretarial services makes a definite difference in the amount of record keeping and reporting that a clinician is able to do. In many cases when sufficient secretarial help is not available, the clinician is not able to keep up with his correspondence, keep his own files up to date, and keep his administrators, parents, and teachers well informed. Unfortunately in many school districts adequate records and reports are not kept because of a lack of secretarial services. Secretarial help and the use of a dictaphone make a tremendous difference in the total volume of work one is able to accomplish. It is most important to find out if this service is available when one interviews for a given position, as there is no substitute for good secretarial help.

A Filing System

Almost every public school speech clinician has a central office. This office serves as the record and report headquarters for the clinician. In the central office the clinician needs, in addition to other items, at least one four-drawer filing cabinet for keeping his records and reports. A clinician's filing system must be functional and is set up on a long-range basis. The clinician who is just starting a new program will need to spend some time organizing a filing system. There are many ways that a filing system can be organized. The following suggestions may be used as guidelines for setting up and maintaining an effective filing system.

The clinician should set up and maintain a registration card file for every child who is enrolled in the clinical speech program. The registration card should be prepared when the child is initially evaluated by the clinician. Each child's card is then filed alphabetically by school in an active registration card file. In addition to the active file, an inactive file should be developed. Whenever children are dismissed or move, their cards should be transferred to the inactive file. If this registration card file is properly prepared and kept up to date, it can be extremely helpful to the clinician. It is a good suggestion to inform other professional staff members in the central office as to the whereabouts of the registration file and the type of information that is maintained in this file. The colored tab system for filing may be used to identify the service the child is currently receiving, the major problem, and the school of each child who is registered.

One major section of the filing system should be designated for active cumulative therapy records set up and maintained alphabetically by school. Another major section should be designated for filing. This section may be subdivided into several sections. One section of this file drawer should be set up for correspondence. Folders for correspondence with the employer, special education director, school administrators, parents, teachers, training programs, state department of public instruction, and miscellaneous correspondence should be prepared. The clinician should always keep a copy of all correspondence, and it should be filed in the appropriate folder. Another section of this file drawer should contain copies of all reports prepared by the clinician. Folders should be prepared for screening reports, diagnostic reports, progress reports, statistical reports, medical referral reports, annual reports, and miscellaneous reports. Another section of this file drawer should be prepared for professional association correspondence and material. A fourth section of this drawer may be used for brochures which pertain to speech therapy materials and professional books.

The third major section should be designated for filing worksheets arranged by phonetic sound, therapy books, and activities. The fourth major section should be designated for filing pamphlets, literature, blank record and report forms, and inactive records and reports.

The policies of school districts vary according to the length of time which records and reports need to be kept. If this policy has not been determined by the time you enter the employment situation, it would be wise to develop such a policy with the employer and the special education director. Most records and reports

Speech-Hearing Registration

Name _____
last _____ first _____

School (in pencil) _____

Birthdate _____ Phone _____
month   day   year

Address _____

Date of Initial Diagnosis _____

Copyright 1963 Iowa State Department
of Public Instruction – D. P. I. 3348

_____ School
_____ Voice
_____ Stuttering
_____ C. Palsy
_____ C. Palate
_____ Articulation
_____ _____
_____ Hrg. Loss
_____ W. List
_____ Ind. Service
_____ Dir. Service

Parent(s) or Guardian _____

Family Physician _____

SERVICE RECEIVED

Grade	Type of Service	Date Init.	Date Term.	Comment	Teacher	Specialist

Special Education Cumulative Folder? Yes_____ No_____ Location: _____

Dismissal Date: _____ Reason for Dismissal:

FIGURE 27. SPEECH-HEARING REGISTRATION

This registration card was developed by the Iowa committee on speech and hearing records and reports for the public schools. This form was designed to serve as a means of identifying each child with a known speech or hearing problem, to provide information on the type of service each child is receiving, to coordinate diagnostic impressions for speech and hearing, and is coordinated with several of the other forms which have been illustrated from the basic set of records and reports as designed by the Iowa committee (1963).

MEDICAL TREATMENT: YES____ NO____ DATE____

By: _____

Diagnosis:

Findings:

Treatment:

Recommendations:

NOTES:

Date:

Date	HEARING SCREENING Results	Circle One	Date	THRESHOLD Specialist	Ear	Enter decibels below					
						500	1000	2000	3000	4000	6000
		ASA ISO			R						
					L						
		ASA ISO			R						
					L						
		ASA ISO			R						
					L						
		ASA ISO			R						
					L						
		ASA ISO			R						
					L						

should be kept for a period of five inactive years. Certain information such as the annual reports are permanent records and should be kept indefinitely.

Coordinating Speech Records with Cumulative Records

The clinician should strive to coordinate his records and reports with the school cumulative records. In many cases, school districts have set policy on the contents of the pupil cumulative folders. If such a policy has been determined, the policy should be studied by the clinician. If a policy has not been developed, this need should be thoroughly explored with the special education director and superintendent. It may be advisable to meet with the administrators regarding what information should be filed, where it should be filed, and who should be responsible for filing or recording the information.

Screening results, a summary of speech and hearing diagnosis, copies of medical referrals, and progress reports pertaining to speech therapy may be filed in or recorded on the children's cumulative folders. The important thing is that this essential information should be inserted into the folders whenever policy permits, for cumulative records are frequently used by administrators, classroom teachers, psychologists, reading specialists, and other professionals in the school environment. It is important to have this information readily available when others review a child's educational history, since speech problems are often related to other aspects of a child's history. For example, many children with speech problems also have reading problems. If a child has received speech therapy, the reading consultant is interested in knowing about the child's attitudes, motivation, and rapidity of progress in therapy.

The speech clinician should always be interested in the contents of the cumulative folders of the children who are receiving speech help. Unfortunately, some school clinicians very seldom, if ever, read a child's cumulative folder before or after diagnosing a child's speech problem. The information contained in the child's educational history can be most beneficial to the clinician as cumulative records include some very important observations which have been made by the classroom teachers, some significant information about grades, invaluable information about test results, psychological reports, and other recommendations.

Transfer of Records and Reports

Consideration should be given to the transfer of a child's records when the child moves from one school to another. A most interesting aspect of our educational program in this country is the fact that many school districts and states have not developed a uniform policy for the transfer of pupil cumulative folders. Some schools forward the records when a child moves, some send the records with the child, some send the records only on request, and unfortunately, some schools refuse to forward cumulative records. It is not unusual to have an elementary or a high school pupil move into a new school district and be there for several weeks before any of the child's educational history is acquired by his new school. At any rate, the clinician has an obligation to recommend that certain information pertaining to diagnosis, prognosis, and notations regarding therapy progress be inserted into the child's cumulative folder so that when the child moves, this information will hopefully be transferred with his cumulative records.

Whenever a child who is receiving therapy moves, the clinician should take the immediate initiative to forward all of his therapy records to the clinician in charge in the child's new school district. If the child moves to a large school system, the therapy records may be forwarded to the supervising clinician or to the special education director so that the child can be located and service resumed as soon as possible.

PUBLIC RELATIONS

All public school clinicians perform public relations directly and indirectly. The manner in which these relationships are built and maintained is of vital importance to the clinician and his program. The most valuable public relations asset is the clinician himself. The personality of the clinician as discussed in Chapter Two of this book greatly contributes to the manner in which he performs public relations. A mature clinician performs his public relations responsibility with enthusiasm and not with egotism.

In certain localities there is still a need to sell the board of education, teachers, parents, and community on the merits of speech therapy services. In other localities a predecessor may have been virtually ineffective in his public relations, or the predecessor may have been extremely effective in public relations. In either case, public relations responsibilities begin as soon as one begins work and before one begins working in the schools. For example, initial contact with the school administrators to discuss screening, diagnostic testing, scheduling, the therapy program, and other matters is necessary.

Public relations is an integral part of the total speech therapy program in the schools. Some of the most important purposes are to inform the public about certain aspects of the program, to educate the public with regard to speech and hearing problems, and to improve public understanding of the existing program. One could certainly add other purposes to this list. The quality of a clinician's public relations depends upon his ability to meet people, and talk and work with them. Clinicians must set a good example with their own speech and language as they strive to build relationships with others.

Before a new program is initiated or at the beginning of each year of an ongoing program, the clinician should give some thought to the development of primary and secondary public relations goals. The clinician should not set idealistic public relations goals. As the clinician is setting these goals, he should ask the questions, Are they appropriate? Can they be attained? How can they be attained? How well can they be attained? Will they be attained?

Personal Contact

There are various communication media which can and should be used for public relations. In many cases the most effective relations are built through personal contact with individuals or groups. The clinician performs public relations whenever he discusses any aspect of his program with others. The clinician should always remember that the manner in which he works and conducts himself, and the language he uses create an impression of himself, his profession, and his program.

It is surprising how much the clinician can accomplish by talking with others about various aspects of his program. One cannot assume that teachers, parents, and community groups know about the services which are provided by the clinician. One should utilize situations which provide for opportunities to talk with individuals or groups about the program and make it known to the appropriate personnel that he is available and willing to talk to groups about the board of education's clinical speech program.

Personal contact is one of the major means of public relations communications. The effectiveness of talking to others about the *program* cannot be underestimated, for it is through this daily personal contact that the clinician is able to build and bolster his public relations. In a sense, much of the clinician's communication deals with public relations even though the clinician may not talk directly about his program. Personal contact may also be achieved when the clinician talks to interested groups such as the Parent-Teachers Association. When a clinician has an opportunity to speak to a group, he should be organized and provide specific information about certain aspects of his program.

The Newspaper

One of the most effective ways of informing the public about the therapy program is through the newspapers. The clinician can accomplish a great deal by utilizing the public relations benefits of the newspapers. Newspaper editors have various policies of obtaining and printing news. Many newspapers have reporters who make daily rounds to gather news. School offices are often included on these rounds and the reporter may stop daily or weekly in search of news. The reporter should be informed whenever the clinician has some information which he desires to have printed. In some localities the newspaper office depends upon the school personnel to call the news office whenever there is news or information to share. It is important for the clinician to talk with his employer about any material he wishes to have printed.

The clinician should write out, in detail, any information which he desires to have printed in the newspapers. There are two reasons for this suggestion. The first and most important reason is that it is necessary to obtain all of the facts that one desires to have printed. Unless the material is written out it is easy to omit some of the details. The second reason for writing out any material which is submitted to a newspaper is that news articles are often written according to format and style of the newspaper, and the article may not contain all of the information the clinician submitted and new implications may appear. Whenever a clinician submits written articles that have been cleared with his administrator, he is in a much better position to defend the material than if he talked with the reporter without the knowledge of his administrator. Wise clinicians keep copies of all news releases on file for future reference and as a permanent record.

The clinician may use the community, city, county, state, and school newspapers to promote his program. Local neighborhood or community newspapers are usually read by many parents and other persons in the community; therefore, the clinician can reach a large percentage of the local population and inform them about various facets of his services in this manner. Public relations can be performed through routine articles or through feature stories. For example, a short article on speech screening dates, times, and places is considered to be routine information. One might provide additional information in such an article by indicating how the parents will be informed if their child's speech is considered to be satisfactory and the procedure which is followed when a child is discovered with a speech problem. Feature articles are excellent for informing the public about the speech program. In a feature article the clinician has an opportunity to be more specific than in a short news article. Of course, feature articles can be supported by pictures which attract attention to the story.

Radio and Television

Public relations can also be performed very effectively through the use of radio and television. There are at least three ways in which the public can be informed through this media. The clinician can prepare items for the news broadcast, make arrangements for a feature program, or in some instances have a regularly scheduled program. Closed circuit television is also becoming a reality in some school districts.

Local stations often want news items pertaining to public school services. The reporter may not use all of the material which is submitted as only the most important news is selected for each newscast. Many radio and television stations have a daily public interest program and it is relatively easy to make arrangements to appear on such a program. If the clinician has an opportunity to appear on such a program, he should prepare information of the best quality so as to create a good public impression. Many local stations have a daily feature program which is designed to interest housewives. When the clinician makes arrangements to appear on this type of program, he has an opportunity to talk to many parents. One suggestion for a feature program is to use the information contained in the annual report to the board of education. The major purposes of the program, the number of children served, and the way they were served can be effectively reported to the public through such a program.

A few clinicians have been very fortunate in arranging regularly scheduled radio or television programs. These clinicians are indeed fortunate, as this is an excellent way to give long-range support to the program. Consider the advantages of talking to many parents and families at length about the causes of specific types of speech problems and how these problems can be helped. The major arrangement to be completed for a regularly scheduled program is the financial agreement. Even though a clinician may sell the board of education on the need to have a regular program, he may be of little assistance in meeting the financial needs. With the backing of the board of education, one might be able to finance such a program through local interest groups or service clubs.

Preparing Releases

The following suggestions are offered for preparing press, radio, and television news releases. At the top of a news release put your name, title, employer, city, state, and date of release.

The first paragraph is called the lead and should contain all the important information concerning who, what, where, when, and how. The release should be typed and double or triple spaced. The most important information should be presented first. The rest of the story should give fuller details, based on the information in the lead.

Write a simple, direct copy. Avoid technical terms, opinions, flowery adjectives. Be accurate with all names, dates, figures, and locations. When you include pictures with the release, provide 5 x 7, or 8 x 10 glossy prints. Type the caption, identifying people and specifying event, and paste it under the picture.

Evaluating Effectiveness

Good public relations cannot be developed in a short period of time. Therefore, the clinician should plan long-range public relations objectives for school personnel, those in the home environment, professionals, lay organizations, and the general public. The clinician who develops good relationships with all of these groups will have much better acceptance and support of his program than if he only develops good relationships with only one or two of these groups.

Periodically it is good to evaluate the effectiveness of your public relations. You need to ask if your goals are being met and, if so, how effectively are they being met. Not only should the clinician evaluate his public relations, but this topic might be considered periodically at staff meetings. Sometimes the best improvements which can be made come about through suggestions of co-workers. When public relations is evaluated either personally or in a staff meeting, it is wise to reevaluate the present and long-range goals. When goals are attained, new goals need to be developed in an effort to create greater understanding and build more effective relationships for the future.

SUMMARY

Records and reports play a significant role in public school speech and hearing programs. The systematic recording of selected basic information facilitates the development of a meaningful sequence of services for speech impaired children in the schools.

The primary purpose for preparing reports is to inform, while the primary purpose for keeping records is to preserve an account of the clinician's services. Effective records and reports serve as the primary tool of continuity of service to the children.

A major study of records and reports was initiated in the Iowa public schools in 1961. After three years of study a state committee designed nineteen coordinated record and report forms. Many of these forms are illustrated in this chapter. A core of certain basic information is illustrated in the Cumulative Speech and Hearing Record which was designed by the Iowa committee.

Various types of records and reports are needed for administrators, teachers, parents, and the clinician. A method for identifying the purposes for specific records and reports is suggested. Records and reports should be coordinated as they are designed. The clinician should plan to spend at least one half day each week working on his records and reports. Secretarial help is essential to the preparation and maintenance of records and reports. Clinicians should strive to coordinate their records and reports with school cumulative records and they should take the initiative to transfer therapy records when a child moves.

All public school clinicians perform public relations directly and indirectly. The most important public relations asset is the clinician himself. Various communication media such as the press and radio should be utilized to inform the public of the clinical speech program.

DISCUSSION TOPICS

1. Discuss the major purposes for keeping records and reports as outlined in this chapter.
2. Read and discuss the manual *Basic Records and Reports for Public School Speech and Hearing Programs.*
3. Discuss the core of information contained in the Cumulative Speech and Hearing Record.
4. Study and discuss the various diagnostic articulation tests which are currently used.
5. Prepare an outline of a speech clinician's responsibilities in the schools with respect to records and reports.

6. Discuss the need to keep administrators, teachers, and parents informed through records and reports.
7. Prepare and discuss a list of things you might consider in each of the four main headings of the Progress Report illustrated in this chapter.
8. List and discuss the main reasons for having a secretary for assisting with record keeping and reporting.
9. Discuss the most important aspects of public relations.
10. Prepare and discuss an outline for a talk to the PTA.

BIBLIOGRAPHY

1. Committee for the Development of Speech and Hearing Record and Report Forms to be Recommended for Use in Public School Programs. *Basic Records and Reports for Public School Speech and Hearing Programs.* Des Moines, Iowa, Department of Public Instruction, 1963.
2. JOHNSON, W.; DARLEY, F. C., and SPRIESTERSBACH, D. C.: *Diagnostic Methods in Speech Pathology.* New York, Harper, 1963.
3. JOHNSON, W., *et al.*: *Speech Handicapped School Children,* rev. ed., New York, Harper, 1956.

AUTHOR INDEX

A

Ainsworth, S., 78, 95, 236, 239, 240, 241, 262
Andersland, P. B., 256
Anderson, M., 279
Auer, J., 140, 157

B

Barker, J. O., 283
Beitzel, B., 170
Bingham, D. S., 165, 166, 237, 245, 251, 252, 265, 281, 282, 289, 297, 298, 303
Black, M., 80
Brungard, M., 258
Bryngelson, B., 242
Buck, M., 255, 256, 324
Byrne, M., 250, 256, 313

C

Carter, E. T., 255, 256, 324
Cartwright, D., 291
Coates, N., 251, 266

D

Darley, F., 244, 245
Diehl, C., 235, 236, 237, 239
Drexler, H., 246, 255, 258

E

Egbert, J. H., 323
Eisenson, J., 164
Engnoth, G., 210
Ervin, J. E., 167

F

Farquhar, M., 210, 256
Fein, B. G., 171
Fletcher, S. G., 261
Freeman, G. G., 98
Freilinger, J. J., 203
Frick, J., 298, 299, 300, 303, 306

G

Garbee, F. E., 72, 79
Glaspey, E., 242
Gross, F. P., 168

H

Hahn, E., 196, 197, 201, 202
Hale, A. R., 258
Hejna, R., 242
Hoffman, L. W., 73
Hoffman, M. L., 73
Holderman, B., 170
Holliday, A. R., 324

I

Irwin, R. B., 163, 169, 236, 239, 240, 256, 262, 265

J

Johnson, K., 33, 34, 36, 40, 42
Johnson, W., 233, 240, 259, 343
Jordan, E. P., 283

K

Kaplan, L., 126
Katinsky, G., 257
Knight, H., 81, 82, 196, 197, 201, 202, 207

L

Lukens, J., 98

M

MacAshan, H. H., 155
MacLearie, E. C., 168
McDonald, E., 244, 258, 282, 293, 298, 299, 300, 303, 306
McWilliams, B. J., 256
Milisen, R., 242, 256
Montgomery, J., 242

SUBJECT INDEX